Extending Microsoft Business Central with Power Platform

Leverage Power Platform to create scalable Business Central solutions with high business value

Kim Congleton

Shawn Sissenwein

BIRMINGHAM—MUMBAI

Extending Microsoft Business Central with Power Platform

Associate Group Product Manager: Alok Dhuri

Publishing Product Manager: Uzma Sheerin

Senior Content Development Editor: Rosal Colaco

Technical Editor: Jubit Pincy

Copy Editor: Safis Editing

Project Manager: Prajakta Naik

Associate Project Manager: Manisha Singh

Proofreader: Safis Editing

Indexer: Hemangini Bari

Production Designer: Alishon Mendonca

Developer Relations Marketing Executives: Deepak Kumar and Mayank Singh

Business Development Executive: Puneet Kaur

First published: August 2023

Production reference: 1110823

Packt Publishing Ltd

Grosvenor House

11 St Paul's Square

Birmingham

B3 1RB

ISBN 978-1-80324-071-8

www.packtpub.com

To my mother, for teaching me to think creatively. To Cherie, for putting up with all the long hours working on this book on top of everything else and for always encouraging and supporting me. To Ms. Belinda Allen, for all of your support, encouragement, and mentorship. You are the true definition of a mentor, and we are so grateful to have you as ours!

– Kim Congleton

To my parents; thank you for always pushing me to be the best version of myself and standing by me through thick and thin. Your unwavering belief in my abilities has driven this book, and I am forever grateful for your love and encouragement.

To my husband, Derek; you have been my rock and biggest cheerleader throughout this journey. I couldn't have asked for a better life partner, and your presence makes every achievement more meaningful.

As I reflect on the completion of this book, my heart is filled with immense love and pride. I am humbled by the profound impact that being a mom has had on my life. To my incredible children, Ash and Alyssa; you are my greatest source of inspiration. Your presence has given me the strength and motivation to pursue my dreams.

And to you, Ms. Belinda Allen; I want to echo Kim's sentiments and express my heartfelt gratitude for your guidance and wisdom. Your belief in my potential kept me striving for excellence. Your mentorship has been invaluable, and I am deeply thankful for your impact on my journey.

– Shawn Sissenwein

Contributors

About the authors

Kim Congleton is a Microsoft Certified Professional and started her technology career over 25 years ago. She fell in love with technology at an early age when her mother gave her a book on programming with DOS 2.0. Ever since then, she has been learning technologies in order to build solutions for people and companies. She has been a system analyst, developer, solution architect, consultant, chief operations officer, and chief technology officer. She began her journey with Microsoft Navision on version 4.0 and quickly fell in love with ERP systems. Her passion is using technology to solve complex problems as simply as possible. She is a NAVUG All-Star and has presented at numerous Microsoft and user group conferences. The Power Platform has given her the opportunity to become a true citizen developer and do that.

Shawn Sissenwein is a Microsoft Certified Professional and works as a solution architect. With over 20 years of experience in the NAV and Business Central space, Shawn has developed a deep understanding of the platform and its capabilities. Her primary role revolves around architecting and developing solutions that enable organizations to optimize their operations and achieve their business goals. With over a decade of experience in international projects and organizations, Shawn has honed her ability to understand and adapt to different business environments and cultural nuances. Shawn's ability to navigate cultural differences has been vital in delivering successful implementations for multinational clients. Passionate about continuous learning, Shawn keeps up to date with the latest advancements and best practices in the NAV, Business Central, and Power Platform space. Shawn brings valuable insights through speaking engagements, fostering collaboration and networking among industry peers.

About the reviewers

Stefano Demiliani is a Microsoft MVP on Azure and business applications, an MCT, a CTO, an Azure solution architect, and a long-time expert on different Microsoft technologies. He's an official trainer for Microsoft IT and WE and has been a speaker at many international conferences.

He has worked with Packt Publishing on many IT books, and he's the author of some of the most successful books in the Microsoft Dynamics world.

Steven Renders is a trainer/consultant with skills spanning business and technical domains, with more than 20 years of experience. He provides training and consultancy focused on Microsoft Dynamics 365 Business Central and Power BI.

Steven is a partner at Plataan, Companial, based in Belgium. Plataan is a leading offline and online learning company. It helps organizations and individuals excel through learning and training programs.

On January 1, 2016, Steven received the Microsoft® MVP award. This award is given to exceptional technical community leaders who actively share their high-quality, real-world expertise with others.

Steven is the author of the following books:

- *Microsoft Dynamics NAV 2009: Professional Reporting*
- *Microsoft Dynamics NAV 2015: Professional Reporting*

His specialties include Microsoft Dynamics 365 Business Central and business intelligence and reporting.

Table of Contents

Preface   xiii

Part 1 – Part Fundamentals

1

Business Central and Power Platform – Better Together   3

Technical requirements	3	The Business Central and Power Platform ecosystem	14
How Business Central and Power Platform are better together	4	Power Pages	16
		Power Virtual Agents	17
Setting up your development environment	5	Power Automate	20
Business use case – the K&S Solutions Inc. company	13	Power Apps	22
		Summary	37

2

Getting to Know Business Central APIs   39

Technical requirements	40	Creating your first GET request in Postman	60
An introduction to Business Central APIs	40	Exercise 2.1 – using Postman to call an API in Business Central	66
How to connect to Business Central APIs	44	What are the limits of working with APIs?	68
Configuring Azure Active Directory for OAuth use with Postman and Business Central	46	Tips and tricks to work with APIs and Business Central	69
Adding API permissions	55	Summary	70

3

Connecting to Business Central in the Cloud and On-Premises   71

Key differences between connecting
to Business Central versus on-premises 71

Connecting to Business Central on-
premises   73

Connecting to Business Central in
the cloud   83

Building a Power Automate flow   92

Summary   108

4

Working with Virtual Tables and Dataverse   109

Technical requirements   110

Introduction to Microsoft Dataverse   112

Setting up a Power Platform environment 113

Creating a new table in Dataverse   116

Integration between Dataverse and Business
Central   117

Understanding virtual tables   123

Virtual tables – key benefits   123

Virtual table restrictions and limitations 124

Setting up virtual tables   125

Creating a model-driven app   137

Building the model-driven app   138

Summary   145

Further reading   145

Part 2 – Doing the Work of Designing, Building, and Implementing

5

Best Practices for Building Power Apps for Business Central   149

Technical requirements   149

Exercise for creating the Contact canvas app 150

Citizen developers versus pro
developers   151

Different types of Power Apps and

deciding which type of app to create   152

Data sources and their different types 154

Repeatable components   155

Reference apps   155

Fluent Theme Designer   157

How to import components   158

Creating a canvas app   161
Customizing fields, labels, and descriptions   168

Summary   178
Further reading   179

6

Building Flows for Business Central   181

Technical requirements   181

Well-documented business process
flows   181

Triggers and actions for Power
Automate   183
Exercise – creating a flow for a new vendor   185
Building a Power Automate flow from scratch   200

Using a Business Event in a Power Automate
flow   212
Inserting a record into BC using Power
Automate   222
Advanced Power Automate setups   232
Best practices   234
Summary   237

7

Delivering Solutions   239

ALM for admin, citizen, and pro
developers   239
Environment overview   241
Solutions   243
Types of solutions   244

Solution components   245
Creating solutions   245

Summary   259
Further reading   260

Part 3 – Common Business Cases in Business Central for the Power Platform

8

Automating Approvals and Reducing Manual Business Processes   263

Technical requirements   263

Setting up approvals in Business
Central   264
Configuring your environment for approvals   264

Importing users into Business Central   268
Configuring the approval process in Business
Central   270

Setting up Power Automate
integration   274
How to enable Power Automate in Business
Central by user   275
How to enable Power Automate permission in
Business Central by user(s)   276

Exercise for setting up purchase approvals
using a Power Automate template   277

Common troubleshooting tips for
approvals   286
Summary   287

9

Connecting Power BI for Business Central Data   289

Technical requirements   290
Exercise for creating a Power BI report and
dashboard   290

Enabling Power BI reports within
Business Central   291
Adding additional Power BI reports to the
Business Central home screen   294

Connecting to data in Power BI using
out-of-the-box APIs   295

Reviewing different visuals and
publishing reports   312
Power BI visuals   312
Power BI report editor   314
Publishing the report   324
Dashboard   327

Summary   332
Further reading   333

10

Extending Functionality by Using Several Power Platform Solutions 335

Extending functionality in Business
Central using several Power Platform
solutions   336
Case study – creating a Power Apps app from
Power BI Desktop   336

Case study – a new item setup   355
Creating a solution   355

Best practices to extend functionality
in BC using several Power Platform
solutions   389
Summary   390

Part 4 – Tips and Tricks for Common Issues

11

User Adoption and Licensing Mapping Guide 393

User adoption	393	Microsoft 365 plans and licensing	400
Envision	394	The Microsoft 365 admin center	400
Onboarding	395	Business Central license	401
Scale	396	Power Platform license	401
Adoption best practices	397	**Summary**	**402**
Power Platform Maturity Model	**399**	**Further reading**	**402**

12

Understanding the Center of Excellence and Why It Is a Valuable Tool 405

Technical requirements	406	Power BI dashboards	418
Center of Excellence	**406**	Production CoE dashboard	419
Creating a dedicated environment to run a CoE and import a CoE solution	408	**Governance and audit compliance processes**	**420**
Importing the Creator Kit and CoE solution	412	**Business Central plus Power Platform**	**421**
Additional admin tools and monitoring Power BI dashboards	**417**	**Summary**	**422**
		Further reading	**422**

Index 423

Other Books You May Enjoy 432

Preface

We have been in the technology field for a long time and we have seen a lot of changes in technology over the course of our careers. Some of the most exciting changes in technology have been in the last couple of years. The emergence of Business Central as a cloud-based application and the ability to extend it using the Power Platform has opened a lot of opportunities for people like us, who are a little technical and understand the database structure and functionality of Business Central. Over the last couple of years, we have been lucky enough to work with Belinda Allen, who taught us the definition of a citizen developer and mentored us as we explored the Power Platform.

In this book, we are going to show you what your journey can look like to become a citizen developer. We will get you started on your journey with the basics, and then it'll be up to you to build on top of that.

Power Platform is the next step to learning how to maximize your business's capabilities by seamlessly integrating it with Business Central on-premises and in the cloud. After that, you will learn how to set up virtual tables and create a simple model-driven application using Dataverse. Your objective is to develop apps based on Business Central processes through Power Apps, including both Canvas apps and model-driven apps. The book also discusses how Power Automate incorporates new processes and automation into business processes, as well as creating or modifying them. As you advance, you'll connect to Business Central APIs that can be implemented to connect with Business Central data, and finally integrate Power BI natively with Business Central to construct advanced reports and dashboards.

Throughout this book, you'll gain experience in customizing Business Central with Power Platform to deliver more scalable and maintainable solutions.

Who this book is for

The target audience of this book is Business Central Power Users and technical consultants who want to expand their capabilities using the Power Platform. Basic familiarity with Business Central is needed; however, you need not have any technical expertise in programming or software development.

What this book covers

Chapter 1, Business Central and Power Platform – Better Together, provides an overview of how Business Central and the Power Platform can be used to build solutions. This will be an introduction to some core concepts every user needs to know and understand to be able to start working. There has been a fundamental shift in designing solutions for Business Central since the platform moved to the cloud. With the release of Business Central in the cloud, and other low-code/no-code tools, Microsoft created a platform that is more than just an ERP. It is important to understand all the tools in the ecosystem that can be used to create solutions. We provide an overview of the different tools in the ecosystem, including Power Apps, Power Automate, Power Virtual Agents, Power BI, Dataverse, Teams, SharePoint, and Office 365.

Chapter 2, Getting to Know Business Central APIs, provides an introduction to Business Central APIs. We will also dive into how you access the APIs in Business Central. We'll explore what is available as an API, how to know what endpoint to use, and what the limits to using the APIs are. Lastly, we'll provide some tips on working with APIs.

Chapter 3, Connecting to Business Central in the Cloud and On-Premises, discusses how the first and most critical step of using Business Central with the Power Platform is to understand how to connect the two. In this chapter, we will explore all the ways to do that and what to do if you are running Business Central on-premises versus in the cloud.

Chapter 4, Working with Virtual Tables and Dataverse, provides an introduction to Dataverse and virtual tables. You will learn how to set up virtual tables and use Dataverse to enhance Business Central's functionality, as well as creating a simple model-driven app.

Chapter 5, Best Practices for Building Power Apps for Business Central, covers the concept of Power Apps, what different types there are, how the different types can be used, and when to use each type. You will learn best practices and examples of how Power Apps can extend Business Central's functionality.

Chapter 6, Building Flows for Business Central, teaches you about the concept of Power Automate, which uses well-documented business processes and turns them into instant flows. You will learn about flow triggers and actions and how they are used. Finally, key components will be discussed in creating, editing, and managing flows.

Chapter 7, Delivering Solutions, teaches you how to create a solution. After that, you will learn about the managed and unmanaged solution concepts. Lastly, the chapter will discuss application life cycle management for Power Platform.

Chapter 8, Automating Approvals and Reducing Manual Business Processes, teaches you how to connect Business Central and Power Automate and the advantage of combining Business Central workflows with the functionality of Power Automate. We will review what is needed to be set up in Business Central and how it is used with common business processes. Lastly, you will learn about common troubleshooting flow error messages and the Vendor portal.

Chapter 9, Connecting Power BI for Business Central Data, explains how to connect to Business Central and use out-of-the-box APIs. We will review setting up parameters in your BC report to connect to different databases and company portals, along with basic best practices in data modeling. In this chapter, we will use Power BI Desktop and publish it to a workspace and BC. We will review different visuals and give hints about which visuals to use for the story you are trying to tell.

Chapter 10, Extending Functionality by Using Several Power Platform Solutions, uses an example of using BC data, the power of Power BI, and use Power Apps to provide an organization with an easy way to make decisions and update Business Central data using Power Apps. Finally, you will learn how to create a custom API.

Chapter 11, User Adoption and Licensing Mapping Guides, gives the reader a better understanding of the importance of user adoption and licensing guides. The reader will learn what the dual license includes. After that, readers will gain an understanding of when a premium license is required and learn how to get up-to-date license requirements. Lastly, we will provide links to user adoption tools and resources.

Chapter 12, Understanding the Central of Excellence and Why It Is a Valuable Tool, teaches you the concepts and methodology around the Power Platform Center of Excellence. It will cover getting started with the Center of Excellence and how to take advantage of what the tool has to offer.

To get the most out of this book

To get the most out of this book, you will need access to the Microsoft developer environment. This is an environment that will allow you to use a free trial of the Power Platform, Outlook, Office, and other Microsoft services.

The second thing you will need is a Business Central environment. Microsoft enables you to set up a free trial for that as well. We have provided URLs for logging in to the various environments after you have created them. We will assume that you have a basic working knowledge of Business Central for this book and that you do not have a basic working knowledge of the Power Platform.

Software required	Links
Microsoft developer environment sign-up	`https://developer.microsoft.com/en-us/microsoft-365/dev-program`
Business Central free trial	`https://learn.microsoft.com/en-us/dynamics365/business-central/trial-signup`
Power Platform login	`https://admin.powerplatform.microsoft.com/`
Power Automate login	`https://powerautomate.microsoft.com`
Power BI login	`https://powerbi.microsoft.com`
Power App login	`https://powerapps.microsoft.com`
Business Central	`https://businesscentral.dynamics.com/`

We will cover signing up for a free trial of the developer environment and Business Central in the first chapter of the book.

If you are using the digital version of this book, we advise you to type the code yourself or access the code from the book's GitHub repository (a link is available in the next section). Doing so will help you avoid any potential errors related to the copying and pasting of code.

Download the example code files

You can download the example code files for this book from GitHub at `https://github.com/PacktPublishing/Extending-Business-Central-with-the-Power-Platform`. If there's an update to the code, it will be updated in the GitHub repository.

We also have other code bundles from our rich catalog of books and videos available at `https://github.com/PacktPublishing/`. Check them out!

Conventions used

There are a number of text conventions used throughout this book.

`Code in text`: Indicates code words in text, database table names, folder names, filenames, file extensions, pathnames, dummy URLs, user input, and Twitter handles. Here is an example: "Log in to Business Central and search for `Purchase`."

A block of code is set as follows:

```
SubmitForm(frmEditCustomer);
Navigate ('Home Screen');
'PowerApp->Refreshadataset-2'.Run()
```

Bold: Indicates a new term, an important word, or words that you see onscreen. For instance, words in menus or dialog boxes appear in **bold**. Here is an example: "Select **Licenses** and then **Dynamics 365 Business Central for IWs**."

> **Tips or important notes**
> Appear like this.

Get in touch

Feedback from our readers is always welcome.

General feedback: If you have questions about any aspect of this book, email us at customercare@ packtpub.com and mention the book title in the subject of your message.

Errata: Although we have taken every care to ensure the accuracy of our content, mistakes do happen. If you have found a mistake in this book, we would be grateful if you would report this to us. Please visit www.packtpub.com/support/errata and fill in the form.

Piracy: If you come across any illegal copies of our works in any form on the internet, we would be grateful if you would provide us with the location address or website name. Please contact us at copyright@packt.com with a link to the material.

If you are interested in becoming an author: If there is a topic that you have expertise in and you are interested in either writing or contributing to a book, please visit authors.packtpub.com.

Share Your Thoughts

Once you've read *Extending Microsoft Business Central with Power Platform*, we'd love to hear your thoughts! Scan the QR code below to go straight to the Amazon review page for this book and share your feedback.

https://packt.link/r/1-803-24071-7

Your review is important to us and the tech community and will help us make sure we're delivering excellent quality content.

Download a free PDF copy of this book

Thanks for purchasing this book!

Do you like to read on the go but are unable to carry your print books everywhere?

Is your eBook purchase not compatible with the device of your choice?

Don't worry, now with every Packt book you get a DRM-free PDF version of that book at no cost.

Read anywhere, any place, on any device. Search, copy, and paste code from your favorite technical books directly into your application.

The perks don't stop there, you can get exclusive access to discounts, newsletters, and great free content in your inbox daily

Follow these simple steps to get the benefits:

1. Scan the QR code or visit the link below

https://packt.link/free-ebook/9781803240718

2. Submit your proof of purchase
3. That's it! We'll send your free PDF and other benefits to your email directly

Part 1 – Part Fundamentals

Welcome to our comprehensive guide exploring the powerful collaboration between Business Central and Power Platform. In the following chapters, we will dive into the fundamentals that make these two tools work seamlessly together, optimizing your business processes and efficiency. From understanding the Business Central API and its capabilities to harnessing the potential of virtual tables and Dataverse, we will equip you with the knowledge needed to connect to Business Central in both the cloud and on-premise environments, unlocking the true potential of your organization's initiatives.

This part contains the following chapters:

- *Chapter 1, Business Central and Power Platform – Better Together*
- *Chapter 2, Get to Know Business Central APIs*
- *Chapter 3, Connecting to Business Central in the Cloud and On-Premises*
- *Chapter 4, Working with Virtual Tables and Dataverse*

1

Business Central and Power Platform – Better Together

This chapter will provide an overview of how Business Central and Power Platform can be used to build solutions. This will be an introduction to some core concepts each user needs to know and understand to be able to start working. There has been a fundamental shift in designing solutions for Business Central since the platform has moved to the cloud. With the release of Business Central in the cloud and other low-code no-code tools, Microsoft created a platform that is more than just an ERP. It is important to understand all the tools that are in the ecosystem that can be used to create solutions. We will provide an overview of the different tools in the ecosystem, including Power Apps, Power Automate, Power Virtual Agents, Power BI, Dataverse, Teams, SharePoint, and Office 365.

In this chapter, we're going to cover the following main topics:

- How Business Central and Power Platform are better together
- The Business Central and Power Platform ecosystem
- Power Virtual Agents
- Power Automate
- Power Apps

Technical requirements

Here is the link for the Microsoft 365 Developer Program for Power Platform: `https://developer.microsoft.com/en-us/microsoft-365/dev-program`.

Go to this link to get a free trial of Business Central: `https://learn.microsoft.com/en-us/dynamics365/business-central/trial-signup`.

How Business Central and Power Platform are better together

When Shawn and I started our careers in information technology over 25 years ago, Business Central was a little-known ERP that was starting to gain traction. Back then, there was a very limited toolset that we had to work with. We had to build all the customizations into the ERP code, and it was a crazy time. Often, these customizations would be built by different developers with very different approaches, and you would end up with what we would refer to as spaghetti code. The resulting code would often lead to people not being able to upgrade promptly or force people to re-implement it. With the move to Business Central and the cloud, the architecture and solution design has changed and provided us with a toolset that's unlike anything we have ever had before.

In this chapter, we will explore why Business Central and Power Platform are better together, and we will begin to learn more about the different components that comprise it. The latest releases of Business Central provide a robust set of technology that many businesses are using to run their day-to-day operations. On its own, there is a great deal of functionality that Business Central provides, such as financials, purchasing, sales, manufacturing, and warehousing. However, it is impossible to anticipate every business need, so there are gaps in the software that most companies will find while evaluating it. This is not unexpected, and this is where Power Platform is often used to extend the software.

On its own, Power Platform provides a tool for building apps, but its real power lies in that it can be used to integrate systems. Before, we had to build the functionality inside the ERP; now, we can connect to it. Building solutions this way makes upgrading and using a cloud model for an ERP more sustainable for a company.

As we mentioned earlier, Business Central is a solid ERP that allows a company to run its operations. However, there are always scenarios that create use cases for extending it to meet a business' needs. Microsoft's message has always been that it is meant to be extended. They will admit they did not build Business Central to provide expert-level manufacturing or warehouse functionality. What they did was build it to provide a base of manufacturing functionality; they expected ISVs or partners to extend it further to meet customer requirements. The requirements to manufacture food differ from the requirements to manufacture auto parts. The process may be the same but certain things are required by the FDA to be captured in the process. One of those is the quality measurements during the production process. This would be an example where a Power App extends Business Central and allows the functionality to capture the quality measurements and tie them back to the production order and to the item and lot that was produced. Before Power Platform, this would have been built inside the ERP and would have been something that only a developer or your partner could do. It may have also been part of a bigger solution from an ISV, and it may have required purchasing a lot of functionality you wouldn't need when you only needed one small part. Now, with Power Platform, we have the option to be minimalist and only build small pieces of functionality that are needed.

Power Platform was also designed to provide a set of tools that work better together. Each piece is designed to provide a certain set of tools that work well together. This toolset enables you to interact, create, and analyze your data in different ways.

In the next section, you will set up a development environment. You will use this environment in the exercises in the following chapters.

Setting up your development environment

As you get started on this journey, you should know that there are a couple of resources that will make it easier. Microsoft has a website dedicated to learning about these different productions. This is a resource that we use all the time and you can find it at `https://learn.microsoft.com/en-us/`.

Microsoft has provided an easy and free development environment that you can use to begin your learning journey with Business Central and Power Apps. By using the following link, `https://developer.microsoft.com/en-us/microsoft-365/dev-program`, you can set up a developer environment with an E5 license and have 25 users. The E5 license provides you with access to the following programs:

- Word
- Excel
- PowerPoint
- Outlook
- OneNote
- SharePoint
- OneDrive
- Microsoft Teams

This license provides you with the access you require to build solutions and test them with multiple users.

To set up a developer environment, follow these steps:

1. Go to `https://developer.microsoft.com/en-us/microsoft-365/dev-program` and click **Join now** to create your environment:

Figure 1.1 – The Microsoft Developer Program setup screen

2. Once you select **Join now**, you will be prompted to log in. Click **Create one!** to create a new account to be used for this environment and then click **Next**:

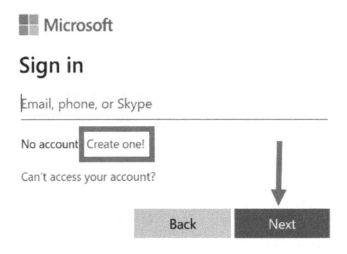

Figure 1.1a – Microsoft Developer Program – Sign in

3. The **Create account** screen will open. Click **Get a new email address** and then **Next**:

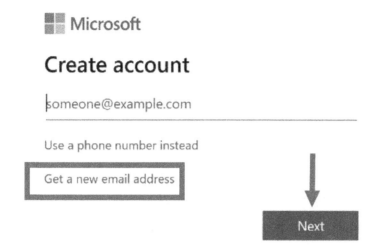

Figure 1.1b – Microsoft Developer Program – Create account

4. The **Create account** screen will open. Here, you can enter an email address to use for your environment. Enter a new email address and click **Next**:

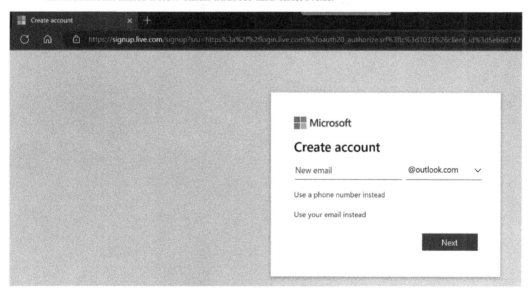

Figure 1.1c – Microsoft Developer Program – entering an email address

5. The next screen will prompt you to select your **Country/region** and enter your **Birthdate**. Once you've done this, click **Next**:

Figure 1.1d – Microsoft Developer Program – Country/region and Birthdate

6. The next screen will prompt you for your password. Enter the password you would like to use and click **Next**:

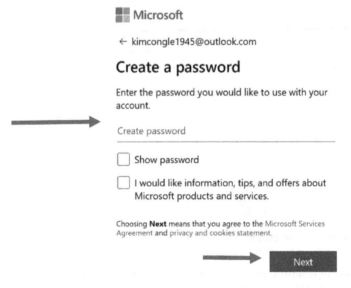

Figure 1.1e – Microsoft Developer Program – Create a password

7. The next screen will verify that you are not a robot. Click **Next**:

Figure 1.1f – Microsoft Developer Program – verification screen

8. Once you've done this, you will see the **Join the Microsoft 365 Developer Program!** screen:

Figure 1.2 – Join the Microsoft 365 Developer Program!

9. Fill in the required fields – that is, **Country/Region**, **Company**, and **Language preference**. Make sure you select a country region code; it should be the same one you picked when you created your email. Once you've done this, a screen will appear where you can choose how you would like to configure your sandbox. It will default to **Instant sandbox**; leave it as is and click **Next**. You will see the following screen when you're configuring the sandbox:

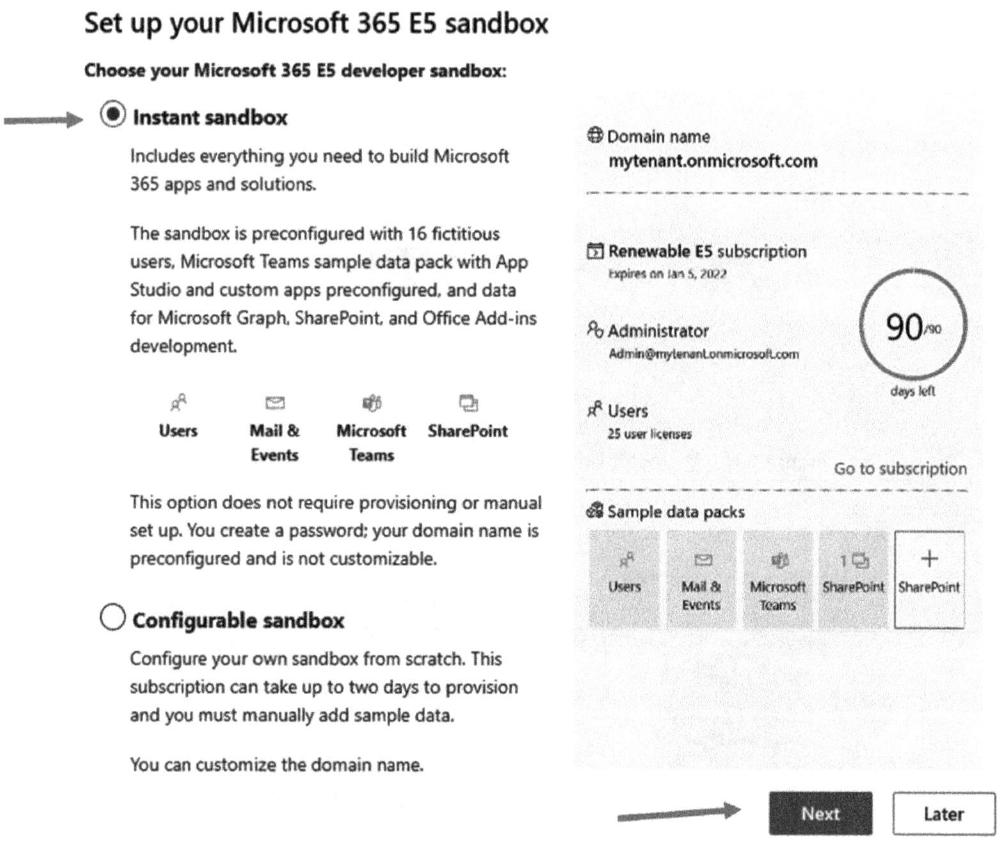

Set up your Microsoft 365 E5 sandbox

Choose your Microsoft 365 E5 developer sandbox:

⊙ **Instant sandbox**

Includes everything you need to build Microsoft 365 apps and solutions.

The sandbox is preconfigured with 16 fictitious users, Microsoft Teams sample data pack with App Studio and custom apps preconfigured, and data for Microsoft Graph, SharePoint, and Office Add-ins development.

Users	**Mail & Events**	**Microsoft Teams**	**SharePoint**

This option does not require provisioning or manual set up. You create a password; your domain name is preconfigured and is not customizable.

○ **Configurable sandbox**

Configure your own sandbox from scratch. This subscription can take up to two days to provision and you must manually add sample data.

You can customize the domain name.

⊕ Domain name
mytenant.onmicrosoft.com

🗓 Renewable E5 subscription
Expires on Jan 5, 2022

👤 Administrator
Admin@mytenant.onmicrosoft.com

90/90
days left

👥 Users
25 user licenses

Go to subscription

👥 Sample data packs

Users	Mail & Events	Microsoft Teams	1 SharePoint	+ SharePoint

Next   Later

Figure 1.3 – Set up your Microsoft 365 E5 sandbox

10. After clicking **Next**, a screen will open and prompt you to set up an admin username and password. At this point, you can also add an alternative password for the other 16 users that will be created in the environment. We recommend setting up two different passwords so that when you start testing, you can log in as different users with different permissions. The following screenshot shows where you can add the admin user and set up passwords for additional users:

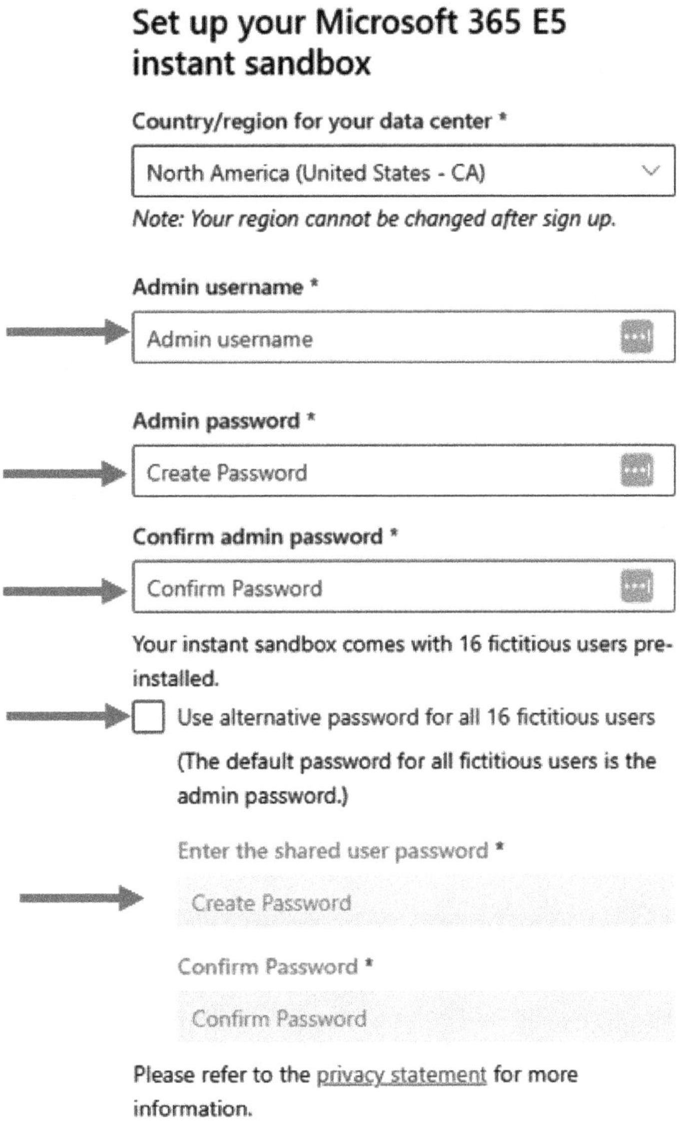

Set up your Microsoft 365 E5 instant sandbox

Country/region for your data center *

North America (United States - CA)

Note: Your region cannot be changed after sign up.

Admin username *

Admin username

Admin password *

Create Password

Confirm admin password *

Confirm Password

Your instant sandbox comes with 16 fictitious users pre-installed.

☐ Use alternative password for all 16 fictitious users

(The default password for all fictitious users is the admin password.)

Enter the shared user password *

Create Password

Confirm Password *

Confirm Password

Please refer to the privacy statement for more information.

Figure 1.4 – Setting up an admin username and password for
your Microsoft 365 development environment

Once you have set up these passwords, you will be prompted for your phone number to complete the setup process. Once the development environment has been created, check out everything under the **Home** menu to see what is available. The first exercise in this chapter will involve using **Image (preview)**. You'll also notice that each choice for building an app has an accompanying video that you can watch and learn about the functionality.

There are multiple ways to learn about Power Platform from the **Home** menu. Here, you will find announcements and links, but also a whole menu item devoted to learning about Power Platform. The **Learn** menu contains courses, articles, and communities where you can enhance your skills with Power Platform. This is where Shawn and I started, and it will help you with your journey as well.

The following screenshot shows the different options you have for learning about Power Platform. From the menu at the top where the first arrow is, you will see that there are **Overview**, **Courses**, **Articles**, **Community**, and **Support** options that you can access. The other arrows highlight different learning videos and modules you can use:

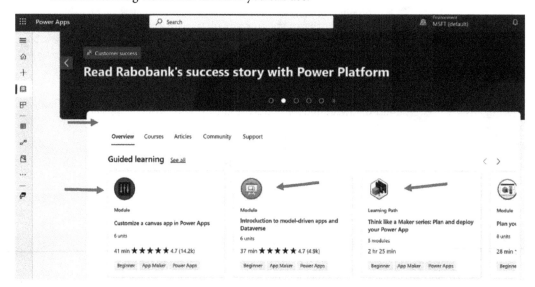

Figure 1.5 – Developer Program for Power Platform – Guided learning options

The other environment you'll need to sign up for is a free Business Central trial. Once you've signed up for it, you will need to link your Business Central environment to your Power Platform development environment by logging in to your Business Central environment with the same login you used to set up your Power Platform environment. This will provide you with a copy of the **CRONUS** database, as shown in *Figure 1.6*. Go to `https://learn.microsoft.com/en-us/dynamics365/business-central/trial-signup` to set up your Business Central environment:

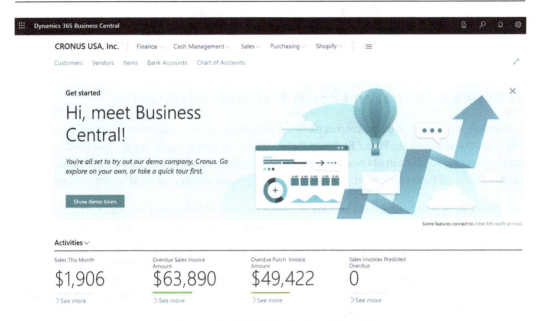

Figure 1.6 – CRONUS in Business Central

Now, let's take a look at a use case.

Business use case – the K&S Solutions Inc. company

For the examples in this book, we will use the following use case, which is a combination of all the different companies and solutions that Shawn and I have worked on over the last 25 years of our careers. This is a fictitious company; any similarities to another company are unintended.

K&S Solutions Inc. is a rapidly growing company that offers a couple of different services to its clients. They have outgrown their current solution of a homegrown warehouse management and manufacturing system and QuickBooks and need to switch to something else that can support their growth. They also do a lot of their financials and reporting in Excel, not in their current systems. Their goal of finding a new system such as Business Central is to move all their transactions and reporting to one system. They would like to use Business Central to manage their financials and inventory in one system. They are a 150-million-dollar company with 75 users, and they provide their customers with the following services:

- Division A provides 3PL services for 20 different customers out of a warehouse in Reno, NV. They also have a second location, which is a refrigerated storage unit that stores food-related items.

- Division B manufactures and sells packaging machines and distribution-related equipment.

- Division C provides fulfillment and kitting services for a large food manufacturer.

- Division D provides a call center for this large food manufacturer.

The company is experiencing 25% growth year over year through acquisitions and sales. They must find a new solution to replace the current system. They have a detailed outline of their requirements; we will show possible solutions as examples in this book.

The Business Central and Power Platform ecosystem

In this section, we will look at the pieces that make up the Business Central and Power Platform ecosystem. Power Apps, Power Automate, Power BI, Power Pages, and Power Virtual Agents are the four products that make up Power Platform. Each of these products provides a different option and tool for integrating with Business Central. All these apps can be accessed from the **App** menu within your development environment:

- **Power Apps** is one of the most exciting tools that can be used to extend Business Central. We have been using apps for years and now, we can use them at work as well. For a solution architect, this is an excellent tool that acts as a rapid low-code development environment where we can build a quick solution when needed. Power Apps enables us to utilize Business Central as the data source for applications that allow workflows and business logic to be extended. The advantage for the person developing the Power App is that you do not have to be a developer. This allows people who may understand the business process but are not necessarily a developer, before a tool is completed, to build a solution that they couldn't in the past. Here is a screenshot of the home screen of Power Apps:

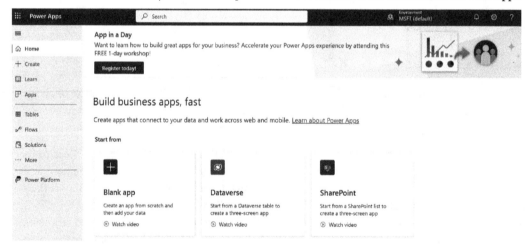

Figure 1.7 – The Power Apps home screen

- **Power Automate** is also an exciting tool because it allows us to create automated workflows inside Business Central and build flows from Business Central to other applications. This is one area that Business Central's predecessor, Microsoft Dynamics NAV, always struggled with. Power Automate is frequently used to extend Business Central with approval workflows, but there are many other things that it can be used for. We'll explore these options later in this book. The following screenshot shows the home page for Power Automate:

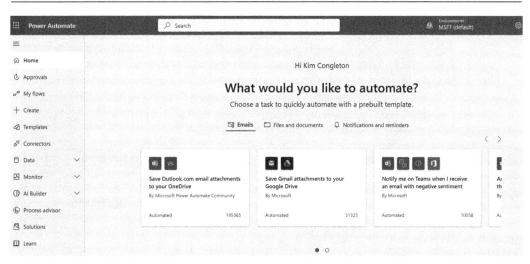

Figure 1.8 – The Power Automate home screen

- **Power Virtual Agents** are chatbots that utilize **artificial intelligence (AI)** to answer questions that are both internal and customer-facing. When it comes to Power Platform, Power Virtual Agents is probably the one that is used the least to extend Business Central. Later in this book, we will explore how we can use this feature. It is a powerful tool that can be used with many connectors and in tandem with Power Automate to build some powerful solutions. The following screenshot shows the home screen for Power Virtual Agents. It contains learning resources such as all the other pages you can use. We will look at these when we cover how Virtual Agents work:

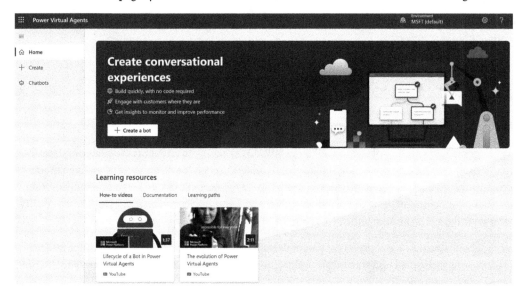

Figure 1.9 – The Power Virtual Agents home screen

- **Power BI** enables you to connect to data sources so that you can model data and create reports and dashboards that allow your users to analyze and interact with your companies' data. Power BI provides several tools for transforming and modeling data. This puts the power of building datasets into the hands of subject matter experts, not just in the hands of a developer. It allows a user to model a dataset from a data warehouse and refine it further, depending on the report they are trying to build. The following screenshot shows the home screen for Power BI online. You can see the different menu options on the left-hand side:

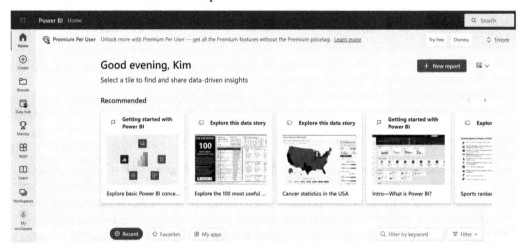

Figure 1.10 – The Power BI home screen

While this screenshot is of Power BI online, this is not the client you will use to build Power BI reports. We will talk more about using the desktop client to build Power BI reports later.

Now that we have a good overview of the different pieces of the Power Platform, let's look at each of these pieces in more detail. There is a lot to explore regarding the different Power Platform solutions.

Power Pages

Power Pages is the newest addition to the Power Suite. Microsoft Power Pages is a reliable and flexible low-code **Software-as-a-Service (SaaS)** platform. It allows users to create, host, and manage modern external-facing business websites effortlessly. With Power Pages, you can quickly design and configure websites that are compatible with various web browsers and devices. Its enterprise-grade security ensures your data is protected while providing the convenience of a user-friendly interface.

Power Pages replaced Power Apps and Dynamics 365 portals. This is a recent change and there is no migration or upgrade process you can use within the Power Pages design studio to edit your existing sites and create new ones.

> **What is Dataverse and what does it have to do with Power Platform?**
>
> **Dataverse** is a powerful and versatile data service provided by Microsoft. Formerly known as the **Common Data Service** (**CDS**), it serves as a secure and scalable storage platform for a wide range of business applications and data solutions. Dataverse allows users to securely store and manage data in a standardized format, making it easier to access, analyze, and share across different applications and services within the Microsoft ecosystem. It provides a rich set of capabilities, including data integration, data modeling, security, and business logic customization, empowering organizations to build robust and interconnected solutions tailored to their specific needs. Dataverse is frequently used in conjunction with Power Platform to build well-rounded solutions.

Power Virtual Agents

Power Virtual Agents allows you to build solutions with chatbots that can answer questions from users, but it can also automate activities in Business Central as part of the conversation. Power Virtual Agents is comprised of topics, entities, and actions. Let's look at each of these in more detail:

- **Topics**: Topics are the building blocks for how a conversation will go with a chatbot. Topics can be user topics or system topics. User topics are lessons to help you see how nodes can be used to create conversations. System topics are topics you are likely to need as you're building chatbot conversations:

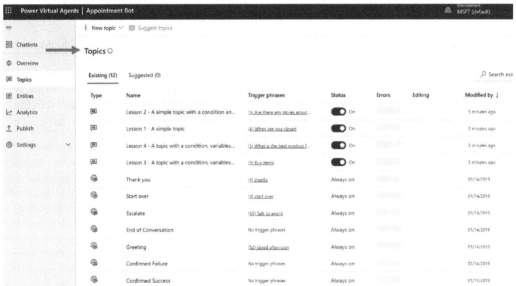

Figure 1.11 – Power Virtual Agents – Topics

The preceding screenshot shows examples of topics for a pre-built example in the system. These topics are examples of a conversation you might have naturally with someone.

- **Entities**: Entities are information units that represent real-world subjects. They could be a ZIP code, city, phone number, or a person's name. Some pre-built entities are used in everyday conversations. The following screenshot shows various pre-built entities, including **Age**, **Color**, and **Date and time**:

Figure 1.12 – Power Virtual Agents – Entities

While pre-built entities have been used in this example, keep in mind that you can build your own entities as needed.

- **Actions**: Actions allow you to utilize flows you have already built in your environment or use with a new flow that you build within the Power Virtual Agents authoring canvas. In the following screenshot, you can see that you can easily add an action to a solution that calls a flow that you have already created:

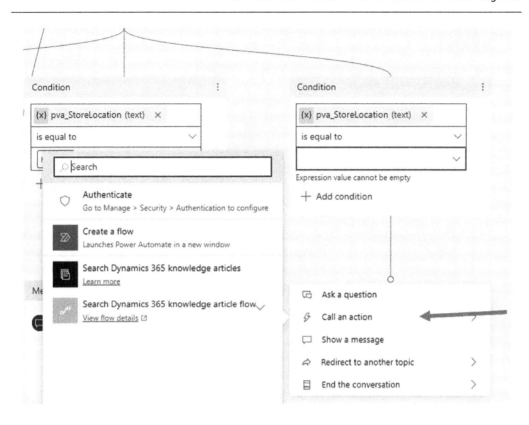

Figure 1.13 – Power Virtual Agents – actions

As you can see, actions allow you to combine chatbots with flows to create solutions that enable you to automate a response. For example, one solution you could build is a chatbot where you could enter a sales order and ask for the tracking number for it. Here, you could create a Power Automate solution that looks up the sales order, finds the tracking number, and returns the results. This is something that would save time for your customer service department.

In this section, we learned about Power Virtual Agents and looked at its different components. Here are some key things you should know about Virtual Agents:

- It can only call flows that are built in the same Microsoft Dataverse environment as the chatbot solution

- Chatbots can be published on Teams, Facebook, mobile apps, and live websites

- Authentication methods for chatbots include a Microsoft account, Facebook, and Azure Active Directory

- Analytics data is included so that you can analyze the performance of your chatbot

Power Automate

As its name suggests, Power Automate allows us to build solutions that automate business processes. The following tasks can be automated:

- Business process approvals

- Automatic reminders

- Tasks on your local computer

- Connecting to publicly available APIs and data sources and returning information or writing information

Power Apps includes many templates that provide a starting point for you to begin building your automation. If you search for `Business Central` after going to **Templates**, you'll see a selection of templates you can use. Most of them are for approvals but there are a couple that involve scenarios such as blocking a customer. The following screenshot shows the different available templates:

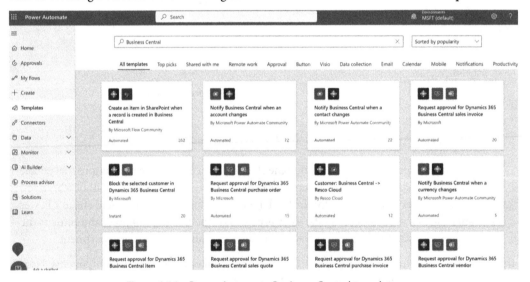

Figure 1.14 – Power Automate Business Central templates

If there is not a template in this list for the automation you would like to build, you can build a new one. These templates are helpful for you to see what is possible and how to do certain things. I always say let's not reinvent the wheel if we don't have to.

If you select the template for blocking a customer, you will see more information about that template, as shown in the following screenshot:

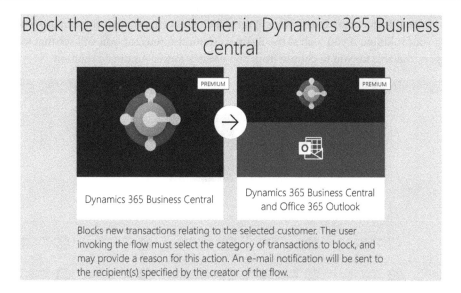

Figure 1.15 – Power Automate example of a Business Central template

If you cannot find a template, there are also several connectors you can use to build Power Automate solutions. There are connectors for Excel, Dataverse, Power BI, and others. As shown in the following screenshot, there are several programs you can connect to:

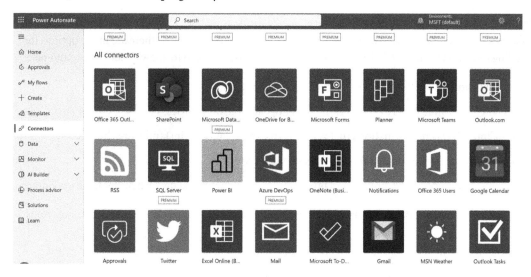

Figure 1.16 – Power Automate connector examples

If you look at the different connectors, you will see the different triggers that you can use when you are building your solution. If you look at the Business Central connector, you will see that there are several triggers available for you to choose from and use in a Power Automate solution:

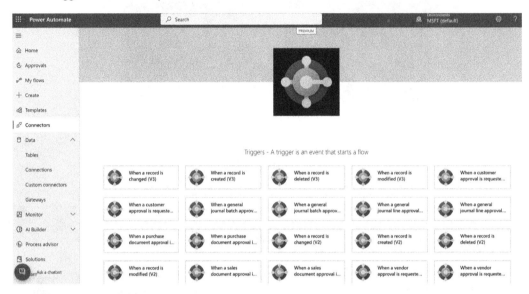

Figure 1.17 – Power Automate Business Central connector trigger examples

In this section, we explored the Power Automate home page and what we can use to start building solutions. Some of the available templates can be used as a starting point and there are many options for building a solution from scratch. Here are some key things that you need to know about Power Automate:

- You can create a flow from scratch, templates, or connectors
- There are three types of flows: cloud, desktop, and business process flows
- Cloud flows are automations that are triggered automatically, instantly, or scheduled
- Desktop flows automate tasks on the web via desktop
- Business process flows streamline a business process for users to allow them to get their work done

Now that we've looked at Power Virtual Agents and Power Automate, let's take a closer look at Power Apps.

Power Apps

Power Apps has a couple of building blocks that allow you to build solutions, and those are apps, services, connectors, and a data platform. These key pieces all work together to provide a platform that allows you to interact with Business Central so that you can affect data and metadata.

There are three different types of Power Apps – model-driven apps, canvas apps, and portals:

- Model-driven apps allow you to build forms and views for your data, but most of the layout is determined by the components you add to the app. Model-driven apps are responsive and will work with a tablet or mobile device without any extra design from you.

- Canvas apps allow you to build apps from a blank canvas. They provide flexibility and allow you to interact with data in your app by adding data sources. Canvas apps also use formulas that are similar to those used in Excel. This is the most flexible option to use when working with Power Apps.

- Portals allow you to build externally facing websites with no code. These portals will also interact with data held in the Dataverse.

Power Apps allows you to use AI with your apps with no code. There are four AI models in Power Apps:

- Text classification
- Object detector
- Form processor
- Prediction

There are multiple ways to start building solutions: **Blank app**, **Dataverse**, **SharePoint**, **Excel**, **SQL**, **Image (preview)**, and **Figma**. *Figure 1.18* shows the different starting places you can build your app from:

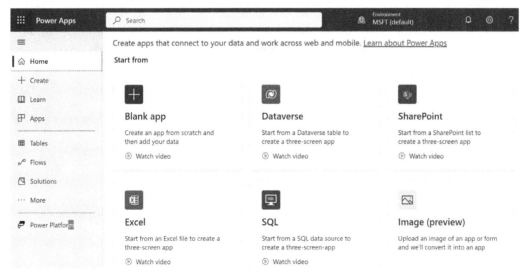

Figure 1.18 – The Power Apps home screen

Each of these choices will start a wizard for creating an app For example, if you select **Blank app**, you will be presented with the three options shown in the following screenshot:

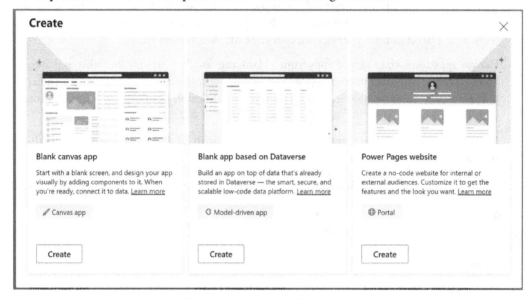

Figure 1.19 – Creating a Power App

As you can see, you can create a canvas app, a model-driven app, or a portal. We will talk about these in more detail later in this book. You also have the option to start with a template. There are no Business Central Power App templates you can use at the time of writing, but it is only a matter of time before there will be. The following screenshot shows the available templates:

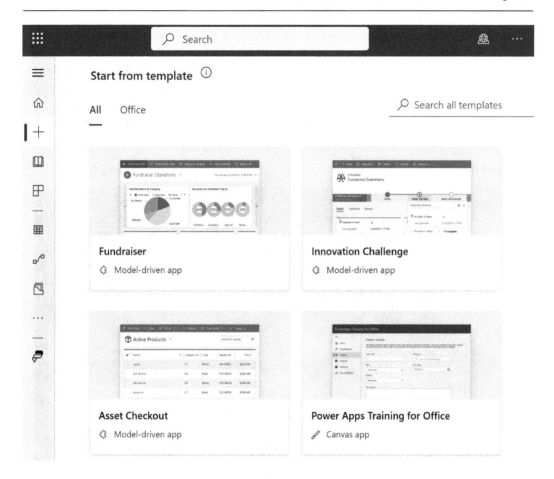

Figure 1.20 – Power Apps templates

Now that we've learned about Power Virtual Agents, Power Automate, and Power Apps, let's learn more about Power Apps and create our first Power App.

Exercise 1 – creating a truck check-in app

I often joke about designing things on the back of napkins and how I could draw an app on a piece of paper and then take a picture of it and create an app from the picture. This works as a starting point and allows the design process to be iterative between you and the end user. It gives you a solid foundation for you to build and refine an app. For this exercise, we will use an example from our case study to demonstrate how easy it is to do this.

K&S Solutions Inc. needs to perform equipment safety checks at the start and end of shifts. This is not a piece of functionality that currently exists in Business Central. However, it is an important piece of documentation the company needs to comply with for its audit requirements. Before, this was done on a piece of paper. The company needs to capture the equipment tag, brakes (checkbox), steering (checkbox), horn (checkbox), condition (good, OK, or bad), date of the inspection, and a section for comments. This is a perfect opportunity to do a quick design on a piece of paper and take a picture of it. Let's take a look:

1. Draw the app on a piece of paper:

Figure 1.21 – Power App drawn on a piece of paper

2. Take a picture of the paper with your phone.

3. Log in to the Power Apps home page in your development environment. To do this, go to `https://powerapps.microsoft.com/en-us/` and select **Sign In**. This will take you to the following screen:

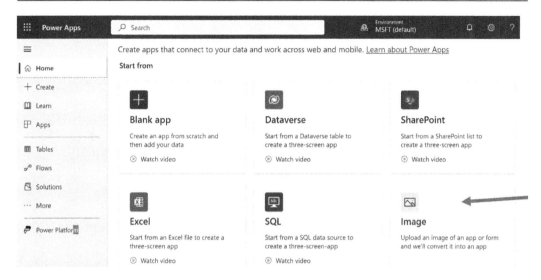

Figure 1.22 – The Power Apps home screen – Image

4. Click **Image**.

5. A wizard will open that will walk you through what you need to do to convert an image into an app. Click **Next** to continue:

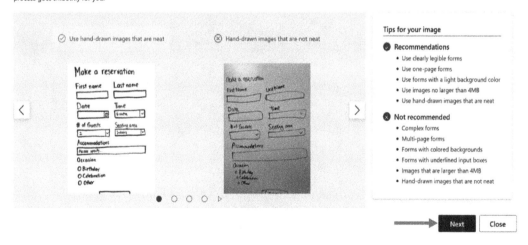

Figure 1.23 – Tips for your image

6. Enter a name for the app.

7. Choose the file you wish to upload.

8. Click **Next**:

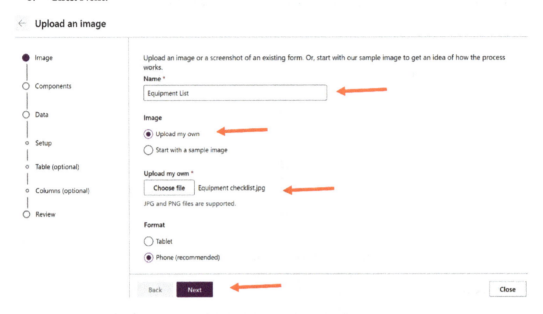

Figure 1.24 – Power Apps – Upload an image

9. The Power Apps **Draw tags and assign components** window will open:

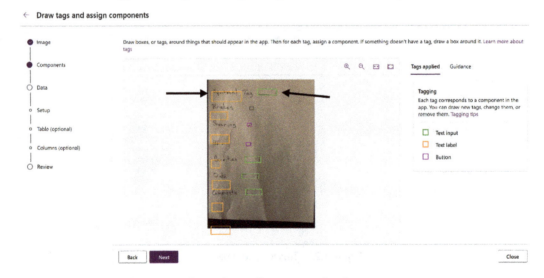

Figure 1.25 – Power Apps – Draw tags and assign components

> **Important note**
>
> The layout will not be perfectly aligned with the drawing. In the preceding screenshot, you'll notice that the green boxes and orange boxes are not perfectly aligned with the text in the drawing. This is okay; do not try to align them. It will capture the text the way it is. You also may not get the same controls as what my screenshot captured. This is okay as well. The point of this exercise is to help you create your first app. We'll learn more about how to create more complex apps later in this book.

10. Select the first box on the screen; you will see a menu that shows what the component has been set to. This is important because it allows you to change any components as needed:

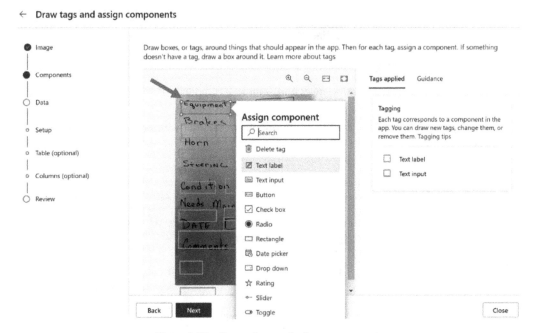

Figure 1.26 – Power Apps – Assign component

11. You can remove any of the components that are not correct. In the following screenshot, the wizard picked up the checkbox as a button. Click on the box to select it. Then, click **Delete tag** – the component will be removed:

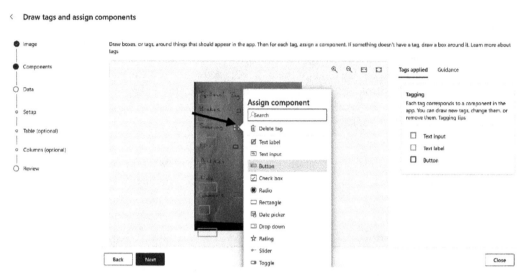

Figure 1.27 – Power Apps – remove components

12. You can also add any of the missing components. In the following screenshot, I have added three checkboxes:

Figure 1.28 – Power Apps – Check box

13. Click on the box next to **Condition** and select a drop-down component. Click on the box next to **Date** and then select **Date picker**. Click **Next**:

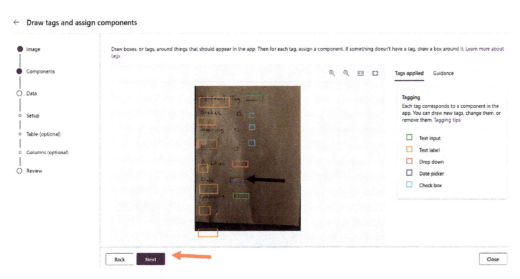

Figure 1.29 – Power Apps – Draw tags and assign components

14. Click **Skip this for now** regarding **Data**. We will cover connecting to Dataverse later in this book:

Figure 1.30 – Power Apps – Set up your data

15. With that, the Power App has been created. It's not perfect but it is a good start and it does 70% of the work for you. The next steps would be to clean up the fields, save your work, and publish your app:

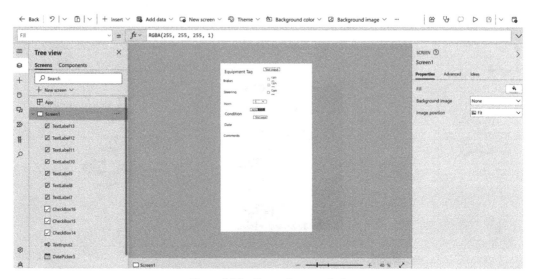

Figure 1.31 – Power App created

16. Click on the **Equipment Tag** text label and then look at the properties for it to the left. Here, you can modify **Font size**, as well as other settings. For all the text labels for the items in the left-hand column, make their font size 22 and bold, and align them to the left:

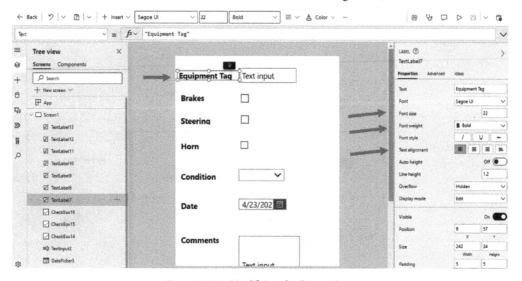

Figure 1.32 – Modifying the Power App

17. Click on the boxes for the checkboxes. Click on **Advanced** and, under **DATA**, change **Text** from **Option** to " ":

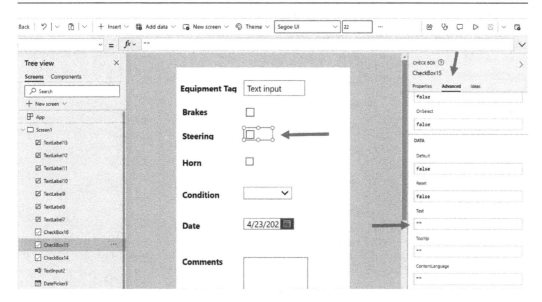

Figure 1.33 – Modifying the Power App

18. Click on the **DropDown4** component and update the options from **1,2,3** to " ", "Good", "Ok", "Bad" and set the default to " ", which is blank. Make the text input box bigger for the comments:

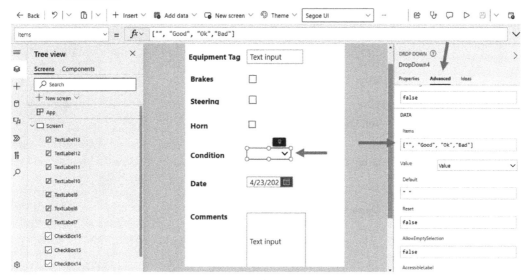

Figure 1.34 – Modifying the Power App

19. Click **Save** at the top right of the screen to save the app. Then, select **Preview** to preview it:

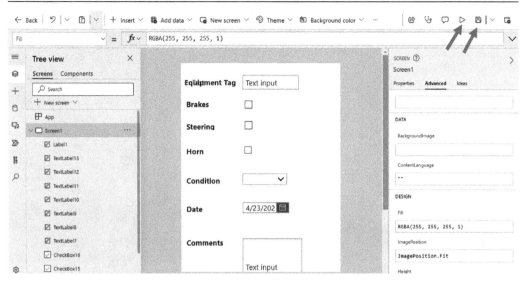

Figure 1.35 – Saving and previewing the Power App

20. The preview screen will open for the app:

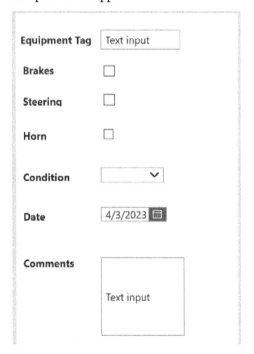

Figure 1.36 – Power Apps preview screen

21. From here, you can interact with the screen and fill it out:

Figure 1.37 – Power Apps preview screen with data

22. To publish the app, select **Publish** in the top-right corner of the screen:

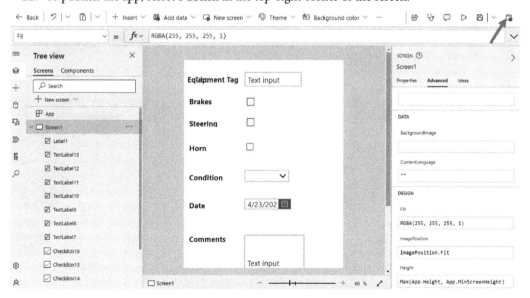

Figure 1.38 – Publishing the Power App

23. The **Publish** wizard will open; select **Publish this version**:

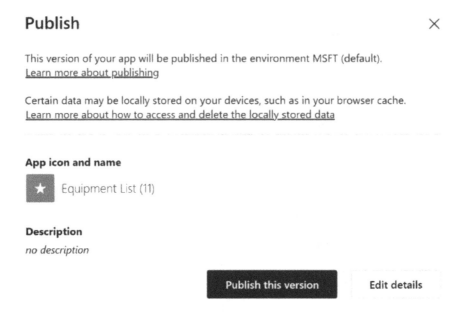

Figure 1.39 – Power Apps – Publish this version

24. Enter some text in the **Description** box for your app and click **OK**:

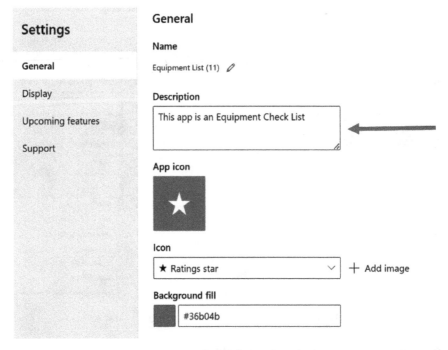

Figure 1.40 – Power Apps – Description

Congratulations! You have published your first app. Your new app will be listed under **Apps** on the Power Apps home page. This was a basic app, but it should have given you a feel for how quickly you can create a simple app that you can use to capture data. There are many different variations of this app you could build and make more complex if needed.

Summary

In this chapter, we learned about Business Central and Power Platform and how they are better together. Power Platform allows us to extend Business Central's functionality and build solutions that will fill in Business Central's gaps in terms of its functionality. We also learned about Power Platform's ecosystem and each of its components. We reviewed Power Virtual Agents, Power Automate, and Power Apps. Then, we created our developer environment and walked through our first example of creating a Power App from a drawing.

In the next chapter, we will learn about APIs and dive into how to connect to APIs and how to access them. We'll explore some of the limitations of working with APIs and some of the tips and tricks for working with them.

2

Getting to Know Business Central APIs

In this chapter, we will introduce Business Central **Application Programming Interfaces** (**APIs**). APIs are a core piece of integrating with any system, and Business Central is no different. It is common when discussing integrating solutions with Business Central to ask what APIs are available to connect to pull data from another system. It is important to understand this concept, as it relates to the Power Platform. You will use APIs in many of the examples we have in this book to build solutions.

In this chapter, we will cover the following main topics:

- An introduction to Business Central APIs
- How to access Business Central APIs
- What are the limits of working with APIs?
- Tips for working with APIs

Technical requirements

Here is the link for the Postman environment: `https://www.postman.com/downloads/`.

You can download the Power BI Desktop from here: `https://powerbi.microsoft.com/en-us/downloads/`.

An introduction to Business Central APIs

In this section, we will learn more about Business Central APIs and what they are. This knowledge is essential when we talk about building solutions that are low code or no code and connect to Business Central.

Microsoft provides APIs out of the box to extend Business Central, which allows you to interact with Business Central functionalities. These are built on ODATA web services that allow you to build solutions to call restful APIs. In Business Central, you can create new APIs that call a Query or Page object. We will explore how to do this in the next section.

APIs allow you to read, create and update data in the following ways:

- **To get data**: Send a `GET` request to the API URL

- **To create new records**: Use a `POST` method

- **To update a record**: Use a `PUT` method

- **To delete a record**: Use a `DELETE` method

The APIs out of the box cover several areas across Business Central, such as Finance, Sales, Customers, Items, and Purchasing. They do not cover everything in Business Central, but you will have a decent number of APIs to choose from to start. To view the APIs, do the following:

1. Open your Power BI Desktop app and select **Get data** from the menu. The **Get Data** menu will open. Select **Online Services**, **Dynamics 365 Business Central**, and then **Connect**:

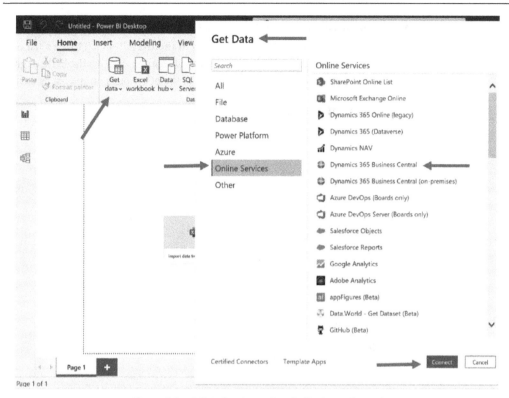

Figure 2.1 – A list of web services in Business Central

2. The **Navigator** window will open. Select the carrot icon next to **PRODUCTION**, **CRONUS USA, Inc**, and then **Advanced APIs**.

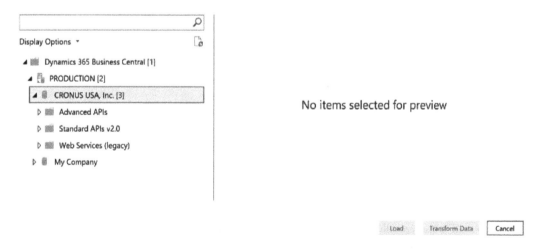

Figure 2.2 – A list of APIs in Business Central in Power BI

3. The **Advanced APIs** window will open and show you what is available for APIs. You will see that there are a lot of different APIs available to you. Select **Standard APIs v2.0** to see a list of those. Select one of the APIs, such as customers, and you will see the data available through the API. While you are here, make sure you explore some of the other ones on the list as well.

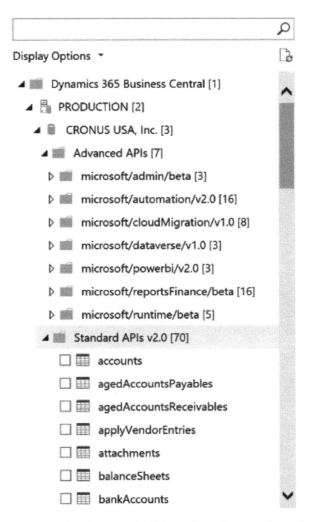

Figure 2.3 – A list of standard APIs in Business Central in Power BI

Advanced APIs versus standard APIs

Advanced APIs are typically used for ISV extensions, any custom APIs you develop, and some Microsoft APIs. Microsoft has the most frequently used APIs in the **Standard API v2.0** section.

4. Select **customers**, and you will be able to see the data in a window on the right of the screen. This will just give you a preview of the data. If you have a large amount of data in a table, not everything will be shown in this window.

Navigator

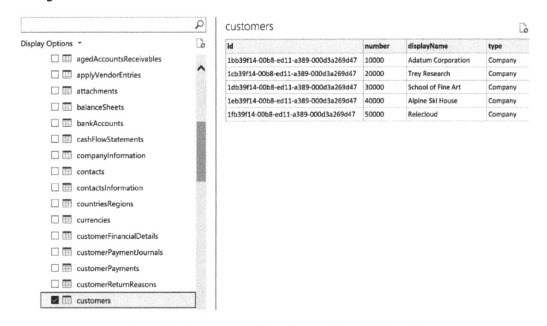

Figure 2.4 – A customer API from Business Central in Power BI

As you can see in the two preceding examples, these are two very simple ways to see what is available through the APIs. I do use Power BI to look at the API and to see what data is available a lot when I build a solution. It's a quick and easy way to see what data is there and what it looks like.

After you explore the list of APIs, it's very important to familiarize yourself with the API terms of use from Microsoft. This document contains essential information you need to know when using the APIs. It will cover the terms of use, which include the API guidelines related to your APIs. It also contains information for security and compliance with applicable privacy and data protection laws.

API additional resources

You can find the terms of use for APIs at `https://learn.microsoft.com/en-us/legal/microsoft-apis/terms-of-use`.

You can find more information about the API (v2.0) at the following URL: `https://learn.microsoft.com/en-us/dynamics365/business-central/dev-itpro/api-reference/v2.0/`.

How to connect to Business Central APIs

In the previous chapter, we explored one way of connecting to the APIs in Business Central. In this section, we will focus on Postman. **Postman** offers multiple advantages to access Business Central APIs. It provides a user-friendly interface that simplifies API testing, allowing you to easily set up and execute requests. With built-in authentication support, you can seamlessly authorize your requests using various methods. Postman's request-building capabilities and parameterization options make it easy to handle complex API requests, while its organization and history features help you effectively manage your requests. You can automate testing and generate documentation, making collaboration smoother. Additionally, Postman assists in monitoring, debugging, and sharing API collections, making it a valuable tool to work with Business Central APIs. The following is a high-level overview of the steps:

1. Install Postman.
2. Set up a new application in Azure Active Directory.
3. Setup an Azure Active Directory application in Business Central.
4. Create your first GET request from Postman for Business Central APIs.

While this book is low code and no code, Postman is an important tool to learn so that you can use it with APIs. It may feel a little bit technical when you use it, but it is easy to use once you have it set up and running.

To install Postman, do the following:

1. Download Postman from `https://www.postman.com/downloads/`.

Figure 2.5 – Download Postman

2.   After installing Postman, select **Create Account** to create your account.

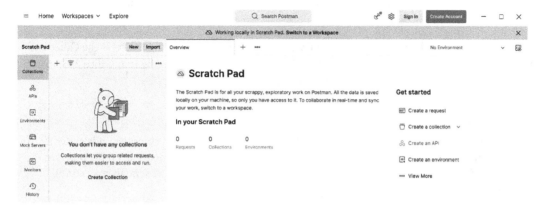

Figure 2.6 – Creating an account in Postman

3.   Postman will open, and you can begin working with it. You can close the welcome screen and begin working.

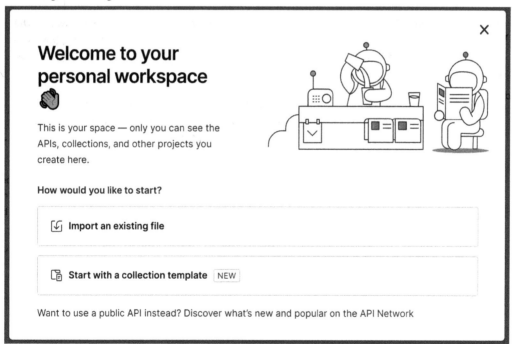

Figure 2.7 – The Postman welcome screen

Once Postman is installed, there is more work that must be done. The hardest part of using Postman is setting up all the security in Business Central and Azure Active Directory to allow Postman to return any data from the APIs.

Next, we will set up security in Azure Active Directory. For that, you will have to access the Office 365 admin center in your developer's environment. You can get to that by logging into Office 365, using the username and password for your developer's environment.

> **Logging into the developer environment**
>
> If you are using your developer environment on your work or personal computer, it is easier if you open a separate web browser that is either incognito or private, depending on the browser you use. This will help you avoid issues where your work or personal credentials may conflict with your developer's environment.

Configuring Azure Active Directory for OAuth use with Postman and Business Central

The most complicated part of getting Postman to work with Business Central is actually all the setup that has to be completed in Azure Active Directory, not in Business Central. We will cover all the steps over the next few pages. If and when you're finished and Postman gets an authentication issue and can't log in, chances are an issue will be found in this part of the process. To set up Azure Active Directory, follow the following steps:

1. Log in to your developer's environment using this URL: `https://www.microsoft365.com/?auth=2&home=1`. Once you log in to Office 365, the home screen will open. Select the button in the top-left corner to display apps. Select **Admin**.

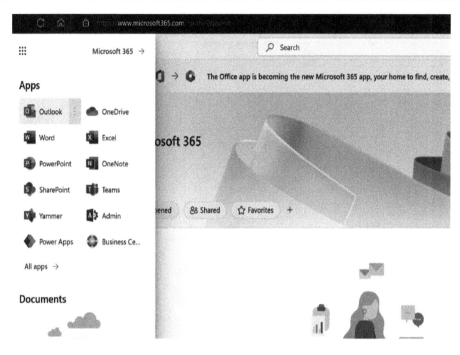

Figure 2.8 – The Office 365 welcome screen and menu

2. The admin screen will open. Select **Show all** from the menu on the left-hand side of the screen.

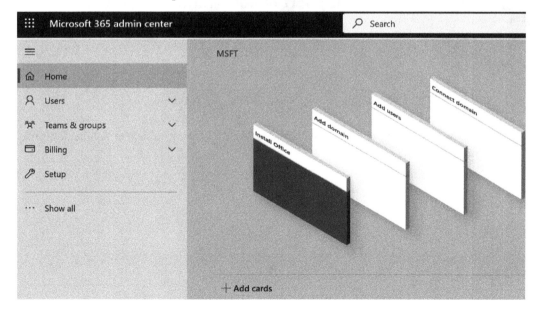

Figure 2.9 – The admin center screen

3. After the **Show all** menu expands, we can select **Azure Active Directory**.

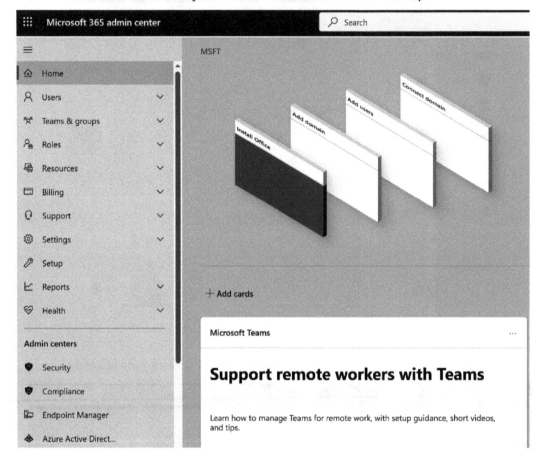

Figure 2.10 – The admin center screen and Azure Active Directory option

4. The **Azure Active Directory** menu will open. Select the carrot icon next to **Applications** to expand the **Applications** menu.

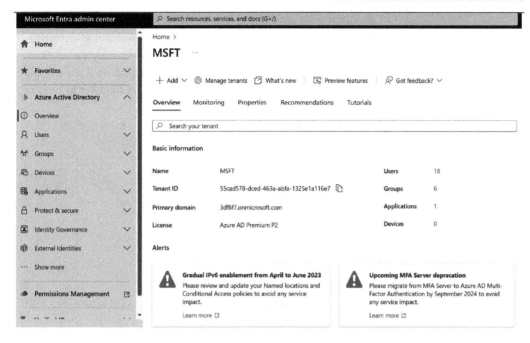

Figure 2.11 – The Azure Active Directory | Applications menu

5.   Select **App registrations** from the menu, and then select **+ New registration** when the window opens.

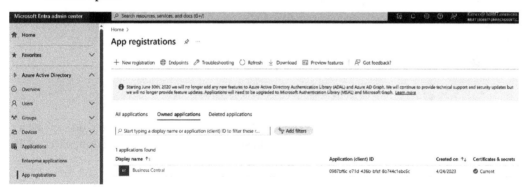

Figure 2.12 – A new app registration

6. Give your application a name and then leave all the other preset values alone. For this example, your developer's environment is a single tenant. In real life, when you start developing solutions, you may work with someone who has a multitenant environment. For this, we'll use a single tenant, so keep the default value under **Supported account types**. Select **Register** to register the application.

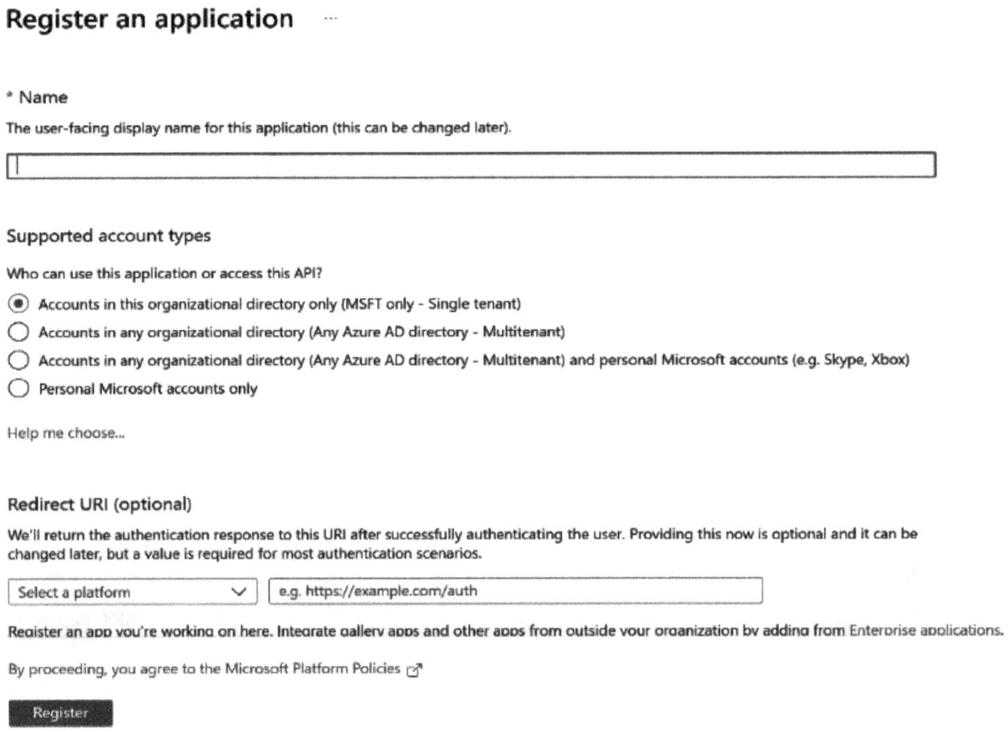

Register an application   ⋯

* Name

The user-facing display name for this application (this can be changed later).

| |

Supported account types

Who can use this application or access this API?

◉ Accounts in this organizational directory only (MSFT only - Single tenant)

◯ Accounts in any organizational directory (Any Azure AD directory - Multitenant)

◯ Accounts in any organizational directory (Any Azure AD directory - Multitenant) and personal Microsoft accounts (e.g. Skype, Xbox)

◯ Personal Microsoft accounts only

Help me choose...

Redirect URI (optional)

We'll return the authentication response to this URI after successfully authenticating the user. Providing this now is optional and it can be changed later, but a value is required for most authentication scenarios.

| Select a platform   ∨ | e.g. https://example.com/auth |

Register an app you're working on here. Integrate gallery apps and other apps from outside your organization by adding from Enterprise applications.

By proceeding, you agree to the Microsoft Platform Policies ☐

[Register]

Figure 2.13 – Registering a new app

7. A new app will be created. Once it is created, there are three things we need to do – create a secret, add a redirect URL, and set up API permissions. From the app home screen, select **Add a certificate or secret** under **Client credentials**.

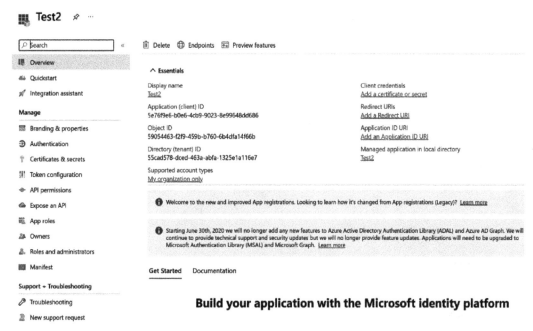

Figure 2.14 – Adding a client secret

> **What is a secret?**
>
> A **secret** in Azure Active Directory is a string of characters used to authenticate and authorize an application or service to access Azure Active Directory resources. Think of it as a more secure way to grant access and control for applications. In this case, we'll use it in Postman to authenticate to Azure AD.

8. The **Certificates & secret** screen will open. Select + **New client secret** to add a new secret.

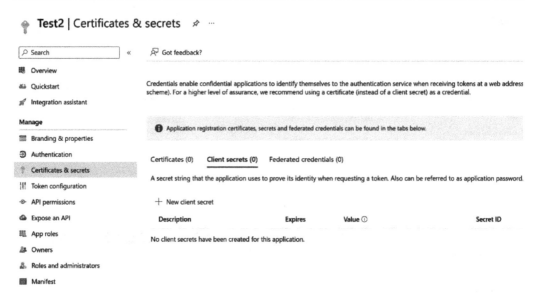

Figure 2.15 – Adding a new client secret

9. Fill in a description for the client's secret and select **Add**.

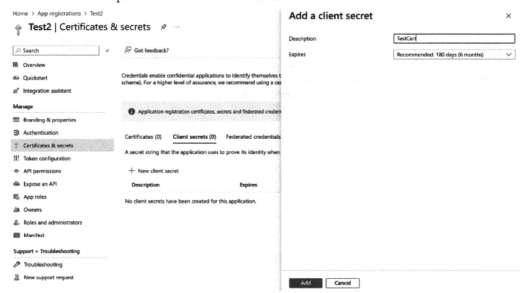

Figure 2.16 – Adding a new client secret

10. Once the secret is added, you'll want to copy the value and the secret ID to a notepad or similar so that you have them available for use in the Postman setup.

> **Important note**
>
> The **value** is extremely important to copy, as it is masked once you navigate away from the screen, and you will **not be able to copy it again**.

Figure 2.17 – After the new secret is added

11. The new thing we will want to add is the redirect URL. Select **Authentication** on the menu and then + **Add a platform**. When the **Configure platforms** window opens on the right, select **Web** under **Web applications**.

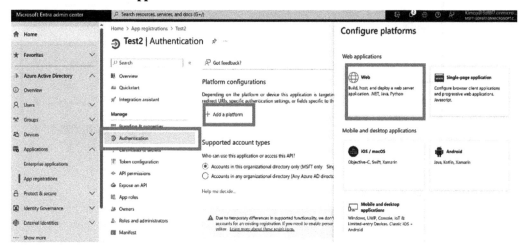

Figure 2.18 – The Authentication window to add the redirect URL

12. The **Configure Web** window will open. Enter the URL `https://businesscentral.dynamics.com/OAuthLanding.htm` in the **Redirect URIs** field. Then, select **Configure**.

Figure 2.19 – Adding the redirect URL

13. A new web platform will be added.

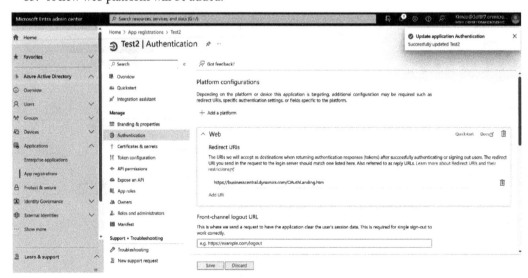

Figure 2.20 – The web platform redirect is added

The next step is to add API permissions.

Adding API permissions

This is a critical step, and it is an important one when you design your solution:

1. Select **API permissions** and then + **Add a permission**.

Figure 2.21 – Adding API permissions

2. When the **Request API permissions** screen opens, select **Dynamics 365 Business Central**.

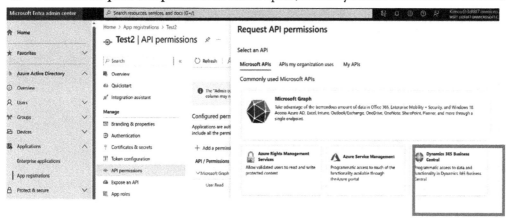

Figure 2.22 – Request API permissions for Business Central

Microsoft Graph

Note that **Microsoft Graph** is already set up with API permissions. We will touch on this in the next chapter, but as it's currently in its beta version, it's limited in what it can do to expose APIs for Business Central. Be sure to check out this URL to see what's new with Microsoft Graph: `https://learn.microsoft.com/en-us/graph/whats-new-overview`.

3. When the APIs open in Business Central, there are some permissions that will have to be set up – delegated and application permissions.

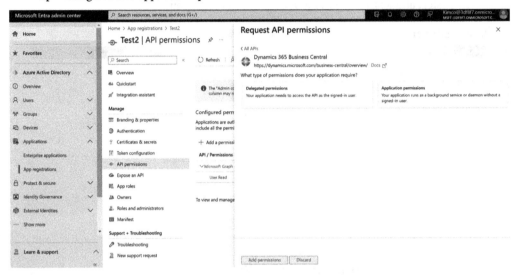

Figure 2.23 – Business Central – delegated versus application permissions

4. All of the permissions need to be set up as shown in the following screenshot. You can see the **Application** and **Delegated** permissions.

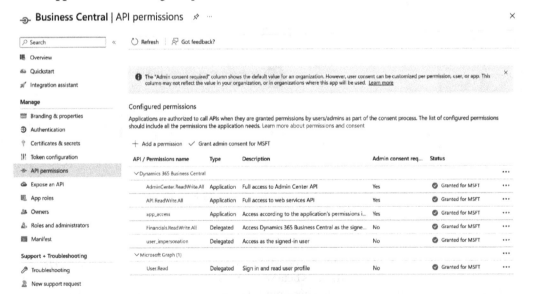

Figure 2.24 – Business Central – application permissions required

5. The next step is the configuration inside of Business Central. Log in to Business Central. Select **Tell me what you want to do**, type in `Azure`, and select **Azure Active Directory Applications** from the search results.

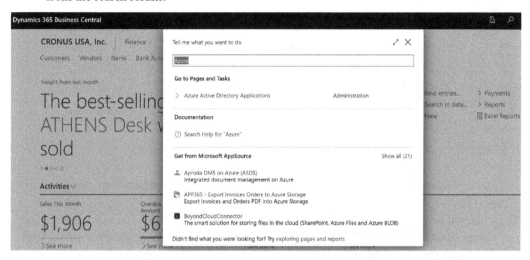

Figure 2.25 – Business Central – Azure Active Directory Applications

6. The **Azure Active Directory Applications** window will open. Select **+ New**.

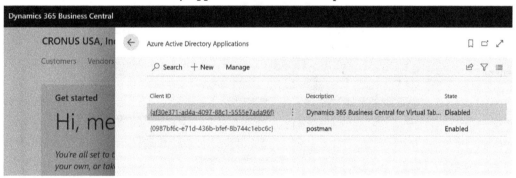

Figure 2.26 – Creating a new Azure AD application in Business Central

7. The window will open, and you can enter the necessary information. You can find the client ID you need to enter in the Azure AD overview of the application.

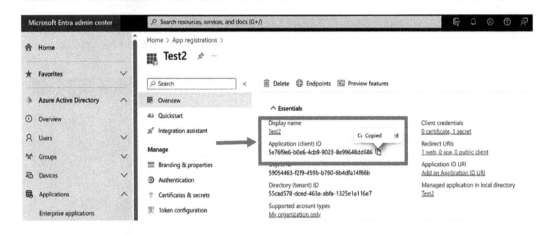

Figure 2.27 – Find the application ID in the Azure application registration

8. Once you have the application ID, enter it in the **Client ID** field, then enter a description, and change **State** to **Enabled**. Also, you must assign permissions for the application. Under **User Groups**, in the **Code** field, select **D365 BUS FULL ACCESS**. Select **Grant Consent** and follow the prompts to log in.

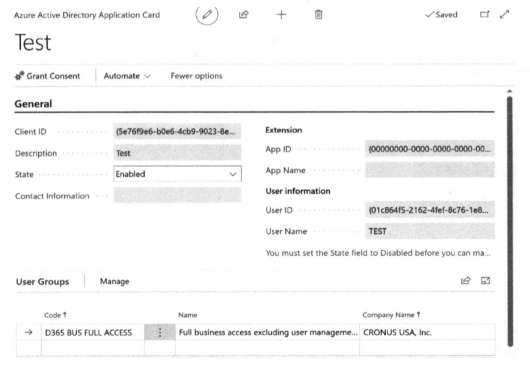

Figure 2.28 – Configuring the Azure AD application card

> **Permissions for applications**
>
> For the purposes of this exercise, we will use the permission set named **D365 BUS FULL ACCESS**. This does grant full access to Business Central functionality. We would highly recommend not using this in a real-world situation. Make sure you grant your application the least amount of access that you can get away with and still allow your application to run.

9.   Log in and select **Accept** for the app to receive permission.

 Microsoft

kimco@3df8f7.onmicrosoft.com

Permissions requested
Review for your organization

Test2
 App info

This application is not published by Microsoft.

This app would like to:

∨   Sign in and read user profile

If you accept, this app will get access to the specified resources for all users in your organization. No one else will be prompted to review these permissions.

Accepting these permissions means that you allow this app to use your data as specified in their terms of service and privacy statement. You can change these permissions at https://myapps.microsoft.com. Show details

Does this app look suspicious? Report it here

Figure 2.29 – Accepting the app permission

10.   Consent is granted for the app. Select **OK**.

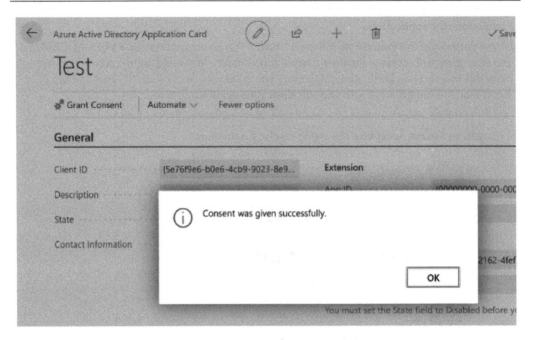

Figure 2.30 – Accepting the app permission

Next, we'll create our first GET request.

Creating your first GET request in Postman

The last thing that needs to be done now is to create a GET request in Postman and add all of the access information:

1. In Postman, select **NEW** for a new request.

Figure 2.31 – Creating a new request in Postman

2. To build your URL for the `GET` request, you have two options to construct it, and there are two pieces of information you will need. The URL will always start with `https://api.businesscentral.dynamics.com/v2.0/`, and then you need either your tenant ID or primary domain from Azure AD. This is found in Azure AD by selecting **Overview**. Then, the URL will look like either of the following:

- `https://api.businesscentral.dynamics.com/v2.0/55cad578-dced-463a-abfa-1325e1a116e7`

- `https://api.businesscentral.dynamics.com/v2.0/3df8f7.onmicrosoft.com`

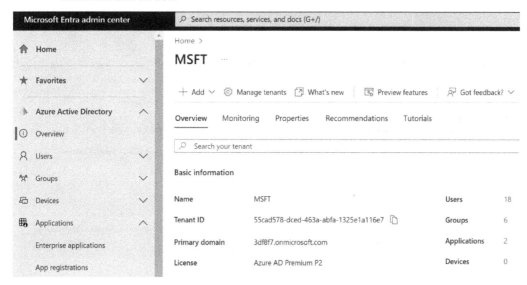

Figure 2.32 – Finding the tenant ID or primary domain in Azure AD

The next piece of information you need is the Business Central environment that you want to point to, which is either `Production` or your Sandbox. In my example, I point to my production environment, so my URL looks like either of the following:

- `https://api.businesscentral.dynamics.com/v2.0/55cad578-dced-463a-abfa-1325e1a116e7/Production`

- `https://api.businesscentral.dynamics.com/v2.0/3df8f7.onmicrosoft.com/Production`

Finally, we need to add `/api/v2.0/` to the URLs to see all the APIs available. The finished URL will look like either of the following:

- `https://api.businesscentral.dynamics.com/v2.0/55cad578-dced-463a-abfa-1325e1a116e7/Production/api/v2.0/`

- `https://api.businesscentral.dynamics.com/v2.0/3df8f7.`
  `onmicrosoft.com/Production/api/v2.0/`

3. Enter the URL we just created in the **GET** request box.

Figure 2.33 – Adding the URL in the Get Request Field

4. Select **Authorization**, and then select the type, which is **OAuth 2.0**:

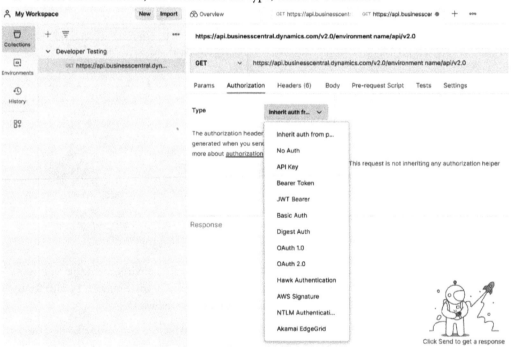

Figure 2.34 – Selecting the OAuth 2.0 authorization method

5. Select **Client Credentials** for **Grant Type**, and enter your application ID in the **Client ID** field and the value from your client secret in the **Client Secret** field. Enter the URL `https://api.businesscentral.dynamics.com/.default` in the **Scope** field. Enter the URL `https://login.microsoftonline.com/{yourenvironmentid}/oauth2/v2.0/token` in the **Access Token URL** field.

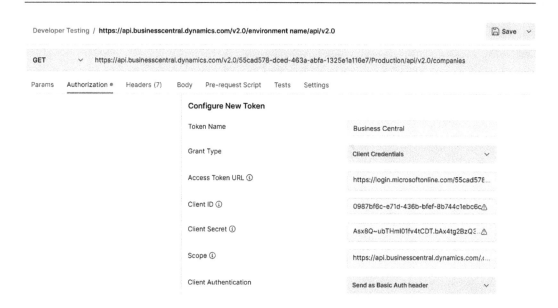

Figure 2.35 – Filling in the Authorization method

6. To build the access token URL, you will need your tenant ID from Azure AD, as shown in the following screenshot. You will then use it as your environment name at `https://login.microsoftonline.com/{yourenvironmentid}/oauth2/v2.0/token` and enter it in the **Access Token URL** field in Postman.

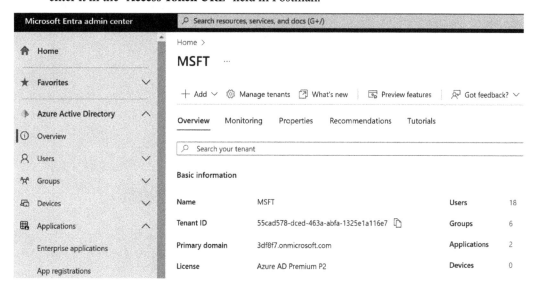

Figure 2.36 – The Azure tenant ID and environment ID

7.   Select **Get New Access Token.**

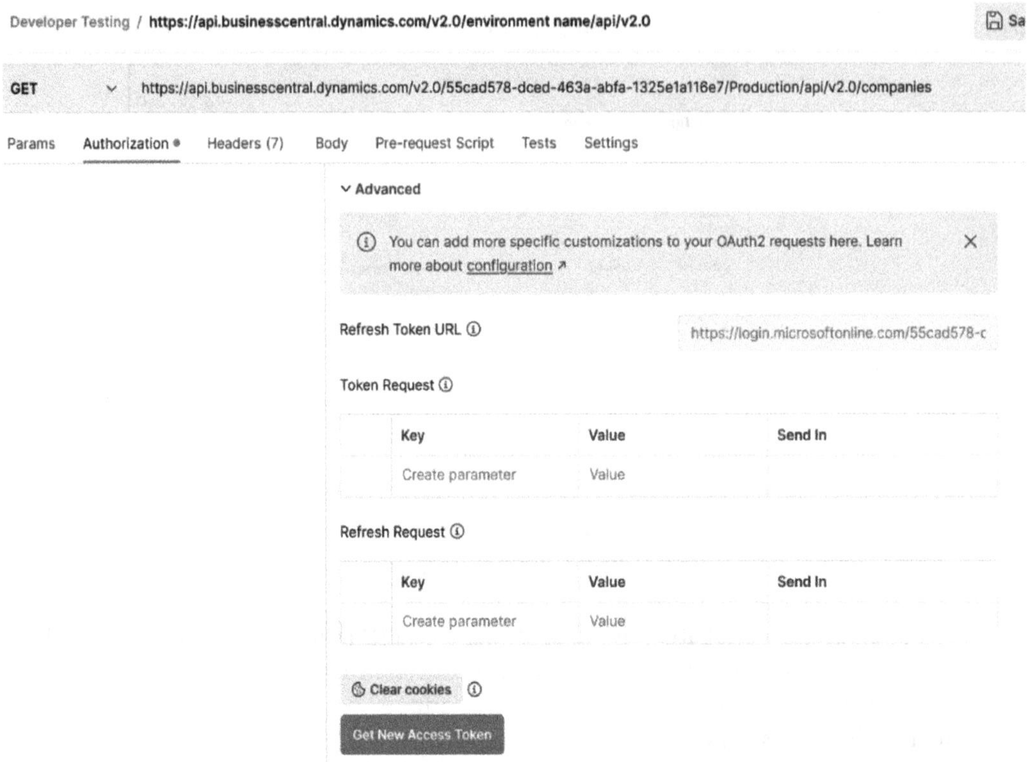

Developer Testing / **https://api.businesscentral.dynamics.com/v2.0/environment name/api/v2.0**   💾 Sa

| GET | ⌄ | https://api.businesscentral.dynamics.com/v2.0/55cad578-dced-463a-abfa-1325e1a116e7/Production/api/v2.0/companies |

Params   Authorization •   Headers (7)   Body   Pre-request Script   Tests   Settings

⌄ Advanced

ⓘ   You can add more specific customizations to your OAuth2 requests here. Learn   ✕
more about configuration ↗

Refresh Token URL ⓘ   https://login.microsoftonline.com/55cad578-c

Token Request ⓘ

	Key	Value	Send In
	Create parameter	Value	

Refresh Request ⓘ

	Key	Value	Send In
	Create parameter	Value	

🔄 Clear cookies   ⓘ

Get New Access Token

Figure 2.37 – Getting a new access token in Postman

8.   Select **Proceed.**

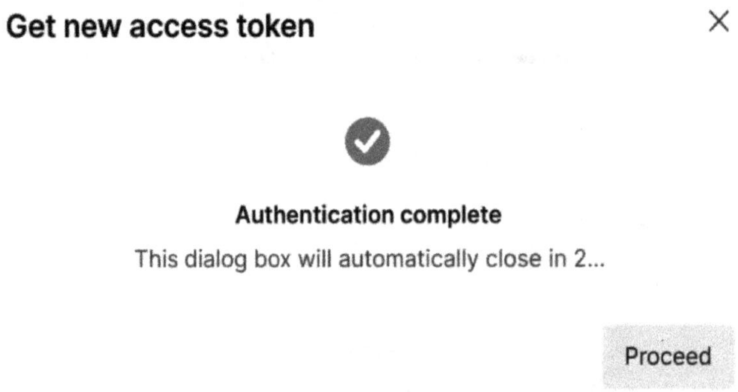

Get new access token   ✕

Authentication complete

This dialog box will automatically close in 2...

Proceed

Figure 2.38 – Getting a new access token in Postman

9. A new token will be returned. Select **Use Token**.

Figure 2.39 – A new token is returned

10. Select **Send**, and you will see the results in the bottom window. The GET request we entered will return us a list of all the available APIs.

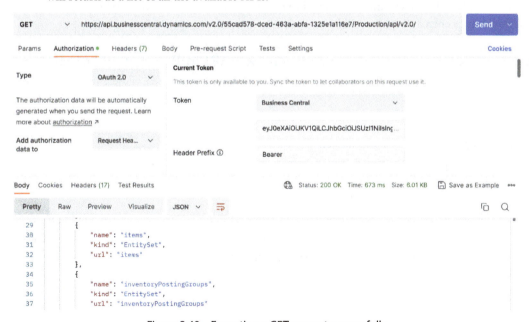

Figure 2.40 – Executing a GET request successfully

The hardest part of connecting Postman to Business Central is configuring your security in Azure for the App. While Microsoft provides instructions, they are high-level and do not show examples of what should be in them. For some people, this is enough, but for anyone who is not familiar with Azure AD, it can be confusing. There are several good blogs and videos that can fill in the blanks. I have not had a ton of experience with Azure AD, and I am lucky enough to have a friend who is good with security and figuring out Azure. I would say that this is probably the one place where it is difficult setting things up and probably one of the more technical aspects of using Postman.

> **Blogs and resources on APIs**
>
> Here are a few of the aforementioned blogs and videos that you can use to fill in any blanks. One of my favorite resources on Business Central and all things related to development for Business Central is Erik Hougaard's blog and YouTube videos. If you want to see what APIs for Business Central have to do with a theme park, check out this YouTube video: `https://www.hougaard.com/eli5-how-to-access-bc-web-services-api-with-oauth/` Another link that is very helpful is this one: `https://businesscentralgeek.com/how-to-use-postman-to-connect-with-business-central-apis`.
>
> *Full disclosure – we found the previous URL after we had figured it out. If we had found this one first, it would have saved us about two hours of banging our heads against the wall.*

Now that we have Postman configured, let's do a couple of exercises to use what we just learned. Let's use Postman to open a couple of APIs.

Exercise 2.1 – using Postman to call an API in Business Central

In this exercise, we will do the following:

- View all the APIs available under v2.0 of the APIs
- Create a GET request for customers
- Create a GET request for items
- Create a GET request for vendors

To view all the available APIs, use the URL `https://api.businesscentral.dynamics.com/v2.0/{yourenvironmentid}/Production/api/v2.0/` in the **GET** request to view all APIs. Select **Send** to have the GET request returned to the list. In the **Body** window, you can see the list of APIs.

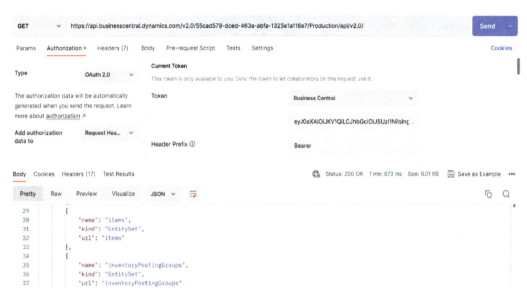

Figure 2.41 – Executing a GET request for all APIs

To view all the customers, add the word `customers` to the end of the URL you used previously so that it looks like this: `https://api.businesscentral.dynamics.com/v2.0/{yourenvironmentid}/Production/api/v2.0/customers`. All of the customers will be returned in the body of the request.

Figure 2.42 – Executing a GET request for all customers

> **Do it yourself**
>
> Do the same for vendors and items as you just did for customers. You should receive a list of data in the **Body** window.

What are the limits of working with APIs?

We've talked a lot about connecting to APIs, and we've even done it using a couple of different tools. What we haven't really discussed is what the limits of APIs are. The benefits of using an API to connect our solutions to Business Central are very exciting, and you will be tempted to use it for everything. However, with great power comes great responsibility.

There are limits to working with APIs and Business Central that we must consider. These are spelled out in detail in the terms of use for APIs, but we'll talk about a couple of the critical ones to keep in mind when creating solutions to use APIs.

The first one to keep in mind is API availability and limits. Microsoft sets limits on the amount of data and the number of requests you can send and receive through an API. Business Central is a cloud environment, and as such, Microsoft must ensure that no one client uses too many resources. When you build solutions, think through how frequently you will request data from Business Central and how much you will write back to Business Central.

> **More information on Business Central API**
>
> Here is a URL to learn more about the rate limits in Business Central: `https://learn.microsoft.com/en-us/dynamics365/business-central/dev-itpro/api-reference/v2.0/dynamics-rate-limits`.

If you pass too many requests and the system throttles the API, you will receive a `429` **HTTP status code** (too many requests). There are retry strategies and other things you can do to address this, and we'll talk more about these in the upcoming section.

It is important to understand that there are OData request limits through APIs. You can learn more about them here: `https://learn.microsoft.com/en-us/dynamics365/business-central/dev-itpro/administration/operational-limits-online`. These limitations can and will affect the performance of API requests.

Some of the other limitations and issues you can encounter using APIs include the following:

- **Authentication and authorization**: As you have seen, configuring access for Postman to access Business Central using OAuth 2.0 is not as easy and straightforward as you would expect. It is common to run into issues when you set up access to an API for the first time.

- **Data validation and error handling**: Business Central APIs enforce the same business logic for an object, including required fields or values. If your solution includes one of the limitations of the API and related issues, and you do not pass the value, you can run into an issue when data is validated through the API. This is usually caught during the initial testing and setup of the APIs.

- **API versioning**: Microsoft has done a lot in the last couple of API releases and versions, sunsetting some of the legacy web services. Make sure you use the latest API versions, and put a plan in place to verify the versions you will use after the major releases in April and October.

- **Customization and configuration**: In Business Central, you cannot customize existing APIs. If you have a customization in Business Central and you create a custom API, make sure you fully test those specifically. Some of the customizations may run into issues if a new release causes a conflict with the API.

- **Security**: This is also a big concern. As we saw earlier, setting up security needs to be considered when granting access to an application through the API. You need to make sure that sensitive data is not exposed inadvertently through an app that someone might not have access to. While we granted full access to the APIs through Business Central, that may not be what you want to do going forward.

Tips and tricks to work with APIs and Business Central

There are several things you can do to make your life easier when you work with APIs in Business Central, and they are the things to be careful with. Performance is the biggest concern you will have when you work with APIs. Since this is a low-code and no-code book, I won't list the ones that have to do with programming and building an API from scratch. However, you can read about them in the same URL provided in the previous *More information on Business Central* note box.

> **Resources to create APIs**
>
> There are limitations to what you can do with existing APIs and a low-code or no-code approach to creating solutions. There will be times when you need a custom API. To learn more about that, I recommend *Mastering Dynamics 355 Business Central*, a book by Stefano Demiliani.

To improve the performance of your solutions when working with APIs, do some of the following:

- Make sure you monitor your Power Platform solutions and verify that your solutions run properly. You can do this by visiting `https://admin.powerplatform.microsoft.com/` and then selecting **Analytics** and what you would like to monitor.

- Use filters. Be smart and evaluate whether you need to return all the data in a table from an API. Maybe your users only need to see the last year's worth of data.

- When you create your API, only return the fields you need. The Item Ledger entry table has many fields. If you only need 10 fields, only return those 10 fields.

- Limit your number of requests to the database through APIs.

- Make sure you test your APIs in the sandbox first before connecting your solution to the production environment.

- Use error handling as part of your solutions. Ensure your solution is thoroughly tested and that errors have been found as part of UAT.

- Understand the Business Central data model when working with APIs.

- Use a third-party tool to create new APIs as needed. This is way easier than learning how to write code to create a new one when needed. Do your research when selecting one of these, and make sure it is written by someone who understands APIs and Business Central.

> **Additional performance resources**
>
> One of the other things you can use is telemetry to monitor the performance of your solutions. This can be set up and used to analyze and find issues. For information on setting up telemetry for the Power Platform, go to `https://learn.microsoft.com/en-us/power-platform/admin/analyze-telemetry`.

Summary

In this chapter, we learned about APIs and Business Central. We learned how to access APIs using different tools available to us, such as Postman and Power BI. We also created an Azure AD application, a Business Central Azure AD application, and Postman to successfully execute `GET` requests to return information from APIs. We also looked at some of the limitations of APIs and what you need to know when working with them. Performance is one of the biggest concerns you will have to take into account when working with APIs. In the next chapter, we will explore connecting to Business Central APIs as part of different solutions.

3

Connecting to Business Central in the Cloud and On-Premises

In this chapter, we will introduce you to connecting to **Business Central** (**BC**) in the cloud and discuss what the differences are when connecting to an on-premises version of BC. We will explore how to connect to them, as well as how we can use connectors to integrate with BC.

We're going to cover the following main topics:

- Key differences between connecting to Business Central versus on-premises
- Connecting to Business Central on-premises
- Connecting to Business Central in the cloud

Key differences between connecting to Business Central versus on-premises

In this section, we will look at the key differences between connecting to BC in the cloud and your versions of BC on-premises. While we are going to discuss BC on-premises in the next couple of sections, one thing to note is that it is still available. However, it has limitations and is still an option for some specific examples, but BC in the cloud is where the software is going.

Most people running BC on-premises are doing so because they have an add-on or customization that requires them to for now. There are differences in some of the available add-ons and ISVs for BC in the cloud versus BC on-premises. Some add-ons and ISV solutions are only being developed for BC in the cloud. But that is a topic for a whole different book. Just be aware that even though we are talking about it, our preference and most of our solutions are designed around using BC in the cloud.

There are a couple of things that are different when you are connecting to BC on-premises versus in the cloud. Some of the key differences are as follows:

- **Location and infrastructure**: BC on-premises is installed and hosted locally in a company's infrastructure and APIs can be accessed through the local network. BC in the cloud is hosted on Microsoft Azure and APIs are accessed over the internet. If you need to access an on-premises API externally, things can get complicated and require additional gateways to be set up to allow traffic to it.

- **Authentication**: BC on-premises is usually done through a local Active Directory account, while BC in the cloud is through an Azure Active Directory account for authentication.

- **Connectivity**: BC on-premises requires an on-premises data gateway to be installed to allow data transfer between on-premises data and Power Platform.

- **Scalability and maintenance**: BC on-premises requires the local network administrators to maintain the local infrastructure for performance, security, and updates. In the cloud, Microsoft maintains all this infrastructure for you.

- **Licensing**: We'll discuss licensing later but there are different licensing requirements for on-premises versus cloud environments.

We have had clients that have built Power Platform solutions for BC on-premises and the hardest part of the project was being able to connect through their network and infrastructure to access their BC. Once that was up and running, the rest of the project went smoothly. It's always getting that initial connection going. Most of the time, the thing that makes it difficult is that the user doesn't have the proper permissions they need to create the connection or do what they need to do. This can cause delays in projects.

In the previous chapter, we learned about connecting to BC in the cloud using APIs and the BC Connector for Power Platform. APIs and the BC Connector are built into Power Platform and a lot of Microsoft tools to enable you to access your data. This is the advantage of BC in the cloud – the ability to integrate it with other tools is just easier because everything is in the cloud. There is no requirement to have a data gateway like there is regarding on-premises. Microsoft continues to build this into its newer tools as they are released. For example, when Microsoft released OneLake, it included the ability to connect to BC. Microsoft OneLake is a part of Microsoft Fabric. Microsoft Fabric is one source for all your data that provides an all-in-one analytics solution for enterprises. OneLake, also known as Microsoft Fabric Lake, is the data lake foundation that Microsoft Fabric services are built on.

> **More about Microsoft Fabric**
>
> You can learn more about Microsoft Fabric at `https://learn.microsoft.com/en-us/fabric/get-started/microsoft-fabric-overview`.

Connecting to Business Central on-premises

BC on-premises is still being used by some clients. There are several reasons for this, and it includes a solution that most likely is unable to move to the cloud because of an existing ISV or customizations. Some companies will move to this version and then figure out their strategy for moving to the cloud, while other companies may choose to run BC on-premises for as long as they can. There are differences between on-premises and BC in the cloud functionality, but that is a whole other book.

> **BC on-premises**
>
> To learn more about Microsoft's policy on the on-premises version of BC, go to `https://learn.microsoft.com/en-us/dynamics365/business-central/dev-itpro/terms/lifecycle-policy-on-premises`.

There are different things you must do to connect to BC on-premises because of the issue we talked about previously relating to infrastructure. To connect an on-premises version of BC with Power Platform, you must install an on-premises data gateway to be able to get access to your data.

This **on-premises data gateway** serves as a crucial connection bridge, enabling efficient and secure data transfer between local data sources (not stored in the cloud) and various Microsoft cloud services. These services include Power BI, Power Apps, Power Automate, Azure Analysis Services, and Azure Logic Apps. By utilizing this gateway, organizations can securely retain their databases and other data sources within their on-premises networks while effectively harnessing that on-premises data within cloud-based services. This enables businesses to leverage the power and flexibility of cloud services while maintaining the security and control of their on-premises data. *Figure 3.1* shows how this works:

On-premises data gateway

One gateway for multiple cloud services and experiences

Cloud services

Azure Analysis Services	Azure Logic Apps	Power BI	Power Apps	Power Automate

Gateway Cloud Service

- Encrypts and stores data sources credentials and on-premises data gateway details

- Routes queries and results between cloud services, on-premises data gateway, and data source

Azure Relay

On-premises data gateway

- Decrypts data source credentials and connects to data source

- Sends queries to data source and returns the results to gateway cloud service

On-premises data sources

SQL Server	SQL Server Analysis Services	Other data sources	Files, SharePoint	Business Central On-Premises

Figure 3.1 – On-premises data gateway

There is a lot to do regarding setting up and configuring this, as well as maintaining it. Microsoft has lengthy documentation around this part and it is typically something where you will need to enlist the help of your company's system administrator to help configure it. This is not something that an end user or even a systems analyst has access to, nor the permissions to configure and set up. This is also something that is not easy to set up in a developer's environment. If you are running BC on-premises and using Power BI already, then this may be running at your company. If this is new to your company, then you can find the directions and a lot more by reading the documentation at `https://learn.microsoft.com/en-us/data-integration/gateway/service-gateway-install`.

However, at a high level, you must do the following to utilize a gateway:

1. Check the requirements for what needs to be loaded on your servers before you start the installation. One of these requirements is that the person installing the gateway must be the admin of the gateway. A couple of other things to keep in mind are that gateways aren't supported on Server Core installations and Windows containers. They also should not be installed on a domain controller.

2. Download and install the gateway on a local server on the network. During installation, use the accepted installation path and accept the terms of use. The gateway will prompt you to enter an email address for your Office 365 organization account, after which it will prompt you to register your gateway. The following screenshot shows what it looks like to register a gateway:

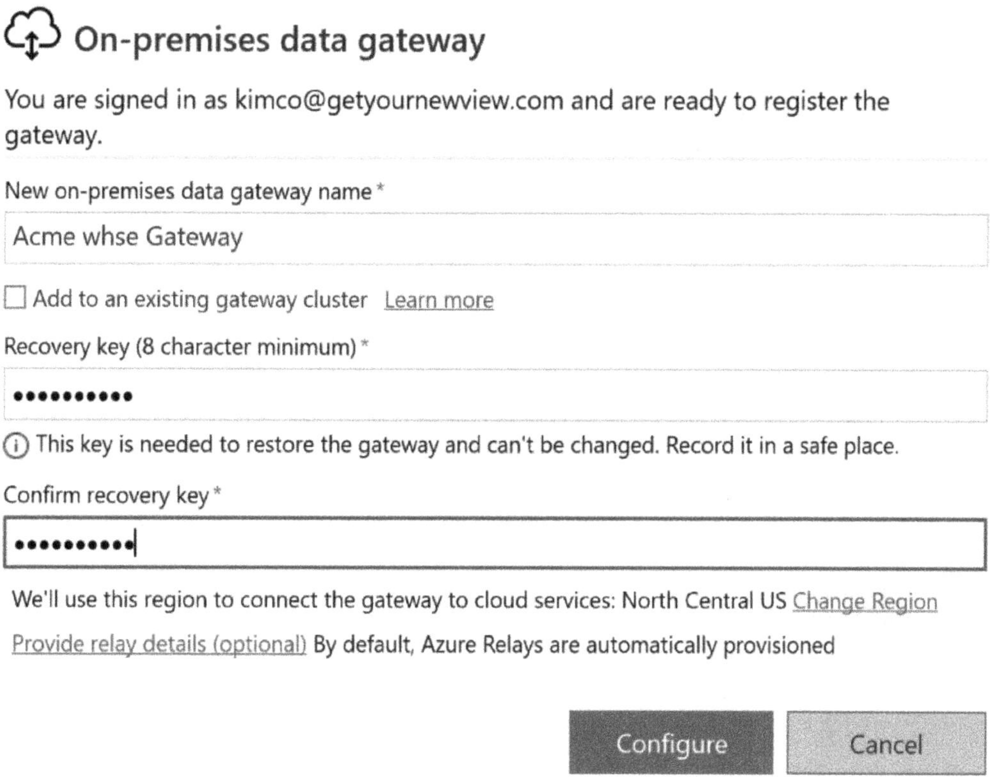

☁ On-premises data gateway

You are signed in as kimco@getyournewview.com and are ready to register the gateway.

New on-premises data gateway name *

    Acme whse Gateway

☐ Add to an existing gateway cluster Learn more

Recovery key (8 character minimum) *

    ●●●●●●●●●●

ⓘ This key is needed to restore the gateway and can't be changed. Record it in a safe place.

Confirm recovery key *

    ●●●●●●●●●●|

We'll use this region to connect the gateway to cloud services: North Central US Change Region

Provide relay details (optional) By default, Azure Relays are automatically provisioned

                                    Configure   Cancel

Figure 3.1a – Registering an on-premises data gateway

3. Once the data gateway has been registered, you'll see the final window of the setup, which will show you the details for all three services that are not available. These are the ones that will be used by Power Platform, Logic Apps, and Azure Analysis Services to connect to BC on-premises. The following screenshot shows the final window you'll see when the installation is complete:

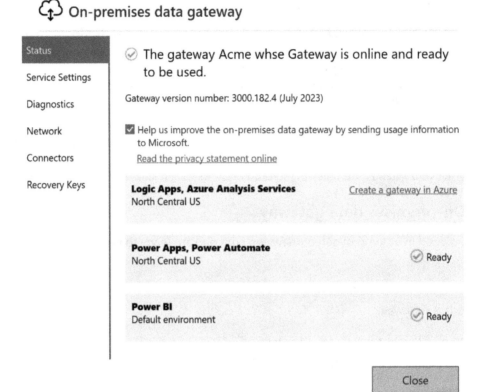

Figure 3.1b – The installation is complete for the on-premises data gateway

4. Depending on your company's network configuration and policies, you may or may not need to configure proxy settings to be able to access the internet. You may or may not need to do that, but this is something you'll want to check with your IT team. If you do need to configure proxy settings, this can't be done through the on-premises data gateway app and must be done within the .NET configuration file. There are three different files you will have to find on the server and modify. You can find specific directions on how to configure proxy settings at `https://learn.microsoft.com/en-us/data-integration/gateway/service-gateway-proxy`.

5. Once the on-premises data gateway has been installed, there is an app that you can use to manage the gateway. This app will allow you to view the status of the gateway, restart the gateway, run diagnostics, and manage other settings. This can be seen in *Figure 3.1b*.

6. There are a couple of things you must consider when working with gateways:

   • The gateway imposes a 2 MB payload limit for write operations

   • Read operations through the gateway have a 2 MB request limit and an 8 MB limit for compressed data responses

- The URL that's used in a GET request has a character limit of 2,048

- When employing the gateway in Direct Query Mode with Power BI, the uncompressed data response limit is 16 MB

For a more detailed list of considerations, refer to `https://learn.microsoft.com/en-us/data-integration/gateway/service-gateway-install#related-considerations`.

While setting up an on-premises data gateway, you will need to troubleshoot the issues that will arise. You can find the documentation for this at `https://learn.microsoft.com/en-us/data-integration/gateway/service-gateway-tshoot`.

Once you have an on-premises version of BC set up and an on-premises gateway configured, we can use these to connect to Power Platform. To use this gateway with Power Platform, you must do some setup in the application itself. You can find the detailed instructions at `https://learn.microsoft.com/en-us/power-bi/connect-data/service-gateway-data-sources`. However, at a high level, you must perform the following steps:

1. First, you need to log into Power BI online. You can do so by going to `https://app.powerbi.com/`. Once you have logged in, you'll want to set up a new connection. This can be done under **Settings | Manage connections and gateways**:

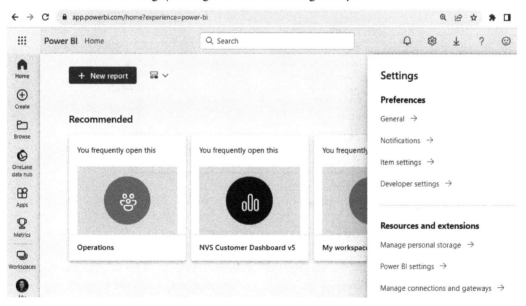

Figure 3.1c – Adding a new connection for Power BI

2. Select **New connection** and then provide details for **Gateway cluster name**, **Connection name**, **Connection type**, **Server**, and **Database**. The following screenshot shows the setup for my connection. Depending on the name of your server and gateway, your information will be different. See the detailed instructions for more information about the requirements around the different settings for the gateway:

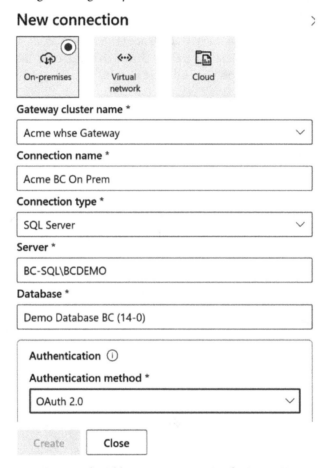

Figure 3.1d – Adding a new connection for Power BI

Once you've set this up, you can use the on-premises connection in Power BI for BC. The way this will work is that when you connect Power BI Desktop to BC (on-premises), a call will be made to Power BI through the new connection to the on-premises data gateway we have created and it will return data from the on-premises BC. There is one thing that you are now able to do with an on-premises database versus a cloud database. Since the on-premises BC still runs on a SQL database, you can create custom views that you can use in a Power BI report. I have an on-premises copy of BC that I've created to show my inventory on hand by location regarding the item and its description. The following screenshot shows the view I've added to my BC database:

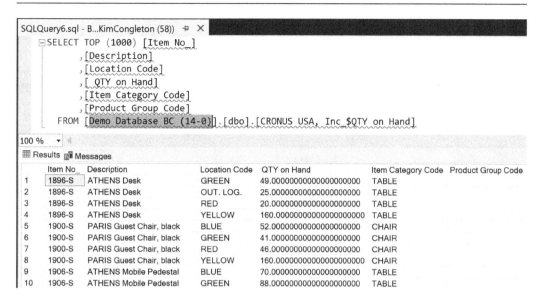

Figure 3.1e – Custom quantity on hand SQL view

To view this inside of Power BI and use it in a report, we have to take the following steps:

1. Open Power BI Desktop and click **Get data**:

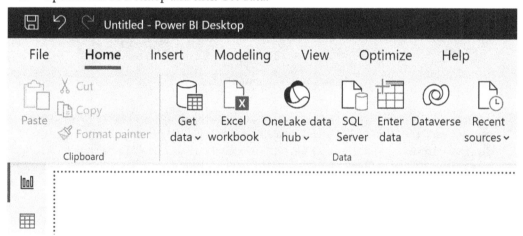

Figure 3.1f– Power BI – Get data

2. Select **Online Services | Dynamics 365 Business Central (on-premises)** and click **Connect**:

Figure 3.1g – Power BI – Get Data

3. The next window will prompt you to enter your information so that you can connect. For this, you will need the OData URL. The is typically in `http[s]://[computer]:[port]/[serverinstance]/ODataV4` format. An example is `https://localhost:7048/BC190/ODataV4`. Enter yours and click **OK**:

Dynamics 365 Business Central (on-premises)

OData URL

Company (optional)

Example: Microsoft

OK   Cancel

Figure 3.1h – Connection for Business Central (on-premises)

4. The next screen will prompt you for your login information so that you can connect to BC. There is one special thing you need to know about this login. The screen will prompt you for the username and password. Instead of your password, you'll want to use the web service access key instead. This can be found in BC under **User Card | Web Service Access**:

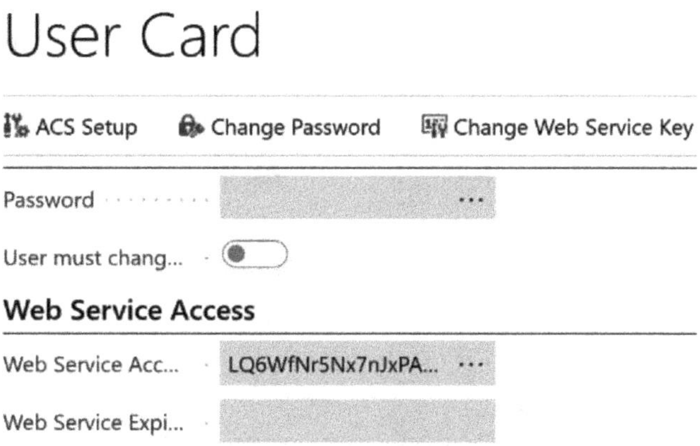

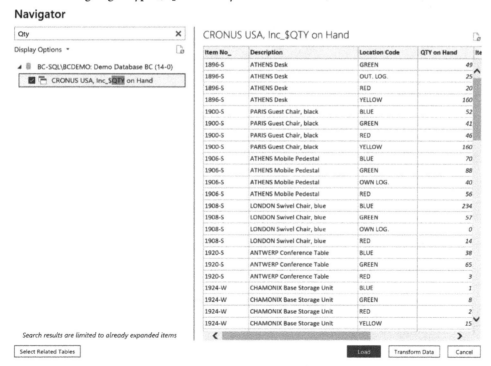

Figure 3.1i – Web access key in Business Central for a user

5. Next, the **Navigator** window will open and show you the data that's available that you can access. I'm going to type Qty to find my view and select it, and then click **Load**:

Figure 3.1j – Selecting a custom view to load

6. Once the data has been loaded, select the necessary matrix, as well as the necessary rows, columns, and values, as shown here:

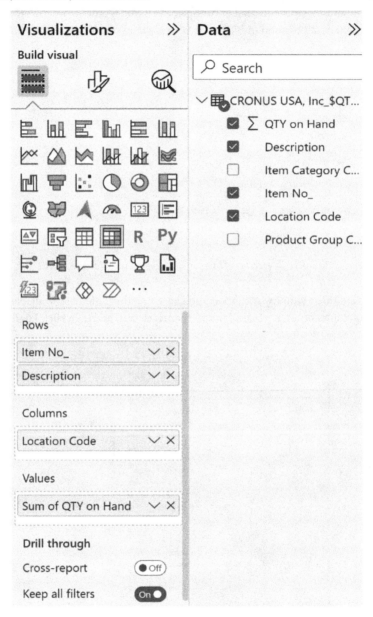

Figure 3.1k – Creating a Power BI report with custom data

The report will look as follows:

| File | Home | Insert | Modeling | View | Optimize | Help | Format | Data / Drill |

Paste | Cut | Copy | Format painter | Get data | Excel workbook | OneLake data hub | SQL Server | Enter data | Dataverse | Recent sources | Transform data | Refresh | New visual | Text box | More visuals | New measure | Quick measure | Sensiti

Clipboard | Data | Queries | Insert | Calculations | Sensiti

Item No_	BLUE	GREEN	OUT. LOG.	OWN LOG.	RED	WHITE	YELLOW	**Total**
⊞ 1896-S		49.00	25.00		20.00		160.00	**254.00**
⊞ 1900-S	52.00	41.00			46.00		160.00	**299.00**
⊞ 1906-S	70.00	88.00		40.00	56.00			**254.00**
⊞ 1908-S	234.00	57.00		0.00	14.00			**305.00**
⊞ 1920-S	38.00	65.00			3.00			**106.00**
⊞ 1924-W	1.00	8.00			2.00		15.00	**26.00**
⊞ 1928-S	149.00	-19.00			55.00		97.00	**282.00**
⊞ 1928-W	4.00	23.00			-1.00		41.00	**67.00**
⊞ 1936-S	36.00	46.00	4.00	0.00	50.00			**136.00**
⊞ 1952-W	9.00	-1.00			7.00			**15.00**
⊞ 1960-S	153.00				24.00			**177.00**
⊞ 1964-S	59.00	60.00		25.00	29.00			**173.00**
⊞ 1964-W	21.00	27.00			-2.00		8.00	**54.00**

Figure 3.1l – Power BI report

From this example, you can see how to connect to custom SQL views through Power BI using the on-premises data gateway to access the BC on-premises database. This is an advantage if there are some SQL views you may have already created for reporting purposes.

> **More information**
>
> To learn more about on-premises data gateways and Power Automate and Power Apps, go to
> https://learn.microsoft.com/en-us/power-apps/maker/canvas-apps/
> gateway-management and https://learn.microsoft.com/en-us/power-
> automate/gateway-manage.

Connecting to Business Central in the cloud

In the previous chapter, we talked about connecting to BC using APIs and Postman. There is also another option for connecting to BC in the cloud. When we were doing the previous exercise, you may have noticed that, when we were in Azure Active Directory and setting up permissions for the application, there was an enterprise application called Graph Explorer. This is another way to connect to BC in the cloud. See *Figure 3.2*:

Figure 3.2 – Microsoft Azure Active Directory – the Enterprise applications screen

Microsoft Graph is a powerful tool that allows developers to create custom applications that integrate with different Microsoft services, such as Microsoft 365, Azure Active Directory, and more. It serves as a central hub or *endpoint* that gives us access to a wide range of data and functionality across these services.

With Microsoft Graph, we can tap into user data, such as emails, calendars, contacts, and files, as well as organizational data such as users, groups, and permissions. This means we can build applications that work seamlessly with popular Microsoft services such as Outlook, OneDrive, SharePoint, Teams, and Azure Active Directory. This also includes BC data.

The great thing about Microsoft Graph is that it provides a consistent and secure way to interact with all this data. Instead of having to deal with separate APIs for each service, we can use Microsoft Graph as a unified API, simplifying our development process. This saves us time and effort as we don't have to learn about and integrate with multiple interfaces.

The Microsoft Graph API presents a unified endpoint (`https://graph.microsoft.com`) that grants access to comprehensive, people-focused data and insights within the Microsoft cloud ecosystem. This encompasses Microsoft 365, Windows, and Enterprise Mobility + Security. By utilizing REST APIs or SDKs, you can connect to this endpoint and develop applications that support various Microsoft 365 scenarios that cover productivity, collaboration, education, people, workplace intelligence, and more. Microsoft Graph also incorporates robust services for managing user and device identity, access, compliance, and security, thereby safeguarding organizations against data leakage or loss.

In the realm of Microsoft Graph, connectors facilitate the inbound flow of external data into Microsoft Graph services and applications, enhancing the Microsoft 365 experience, including Microsoft Search. These connectors are available for a wide range of commonly used data sources, such as Box, Google Drive, Jira, and Salesforce.

To facilitate the secure and scalable delivery of Microsoft Graph data to popular Azure data stores, Microsoft Graph Data Connect provides a suite of tools. The cached data serves as a valuable resource for Azure development tools, empowering you to construct intelligent applications.

You can set up Postman to use Microsoft Graph to access BC data. The setup for this is very similar to what we covered when we set up a connection for Postman in the previous chapter. We will not cover this in detail in this chapter but if you want to attempt this yourself, you can do so by following the instructions at `https://learn.microsoft.com/en-us/graph/use-postman`.

If you want to take a more detailed look at Graph Explorer, go to `https://developer.microsoft.com/en-us/graph/graph-explorer` and then select the person icon in the top-right corner to log in. See *Figure 3.3*:

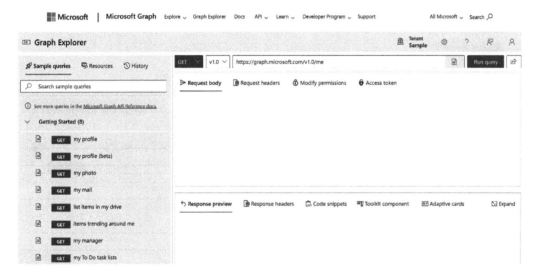

Figure 3.3 – Microsoft Graph – where to log in

The login screen will open. As shown in *Figure 3.4*, enter the **Username** and **Password** details for your development environment:

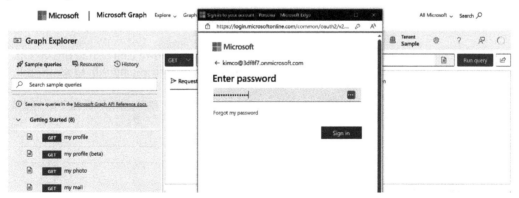

Figure 3.4 – Microsoft Graph screen and Office login

Once you have logged into Microsoft Graph, you will see the following screen. Select **Resources** from the menu on the left:

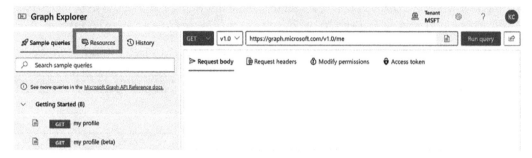

Figure 3.5 – Selecting Resources

The **Resources** menu will open, and you will see a list of available resources. Select the toggle next to **Switch to beta** (see *Figure 3.6*) to see the available BC resources:

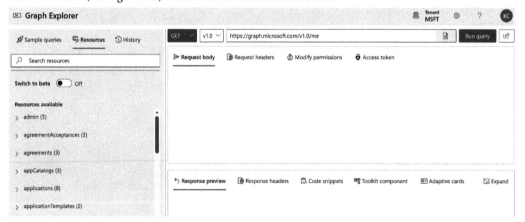

Figure 3.6 – Switch to beta

As shown in *Figure 3.7*, scroll down to find **financials**; select the drop-down icon next to this option to expand the list. Then, select the dropdown next to **companies**, then {**company-id**}, to see the full list of what's available:

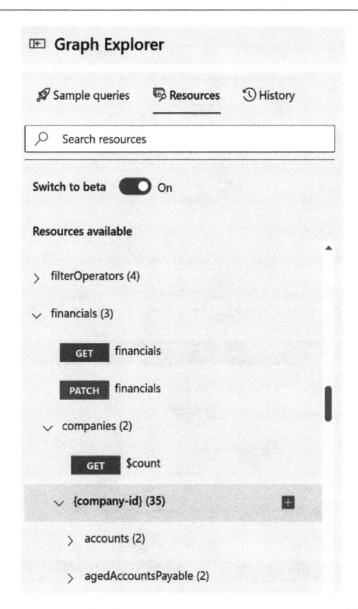

Figure 3.7 – Expanding the various menus to see what information is available

Scroll down and find **customers**, then click the drop-down icon to expand the commands available to you. Select **GET** (see *Figure 3.8*) and notice how it populates the **GET** query in the address bar. Notice how {company-id} is in { } and does not have a value. If you run the query as-is, you will receive an error because you do not have the value for the company ID you want to see the data from:

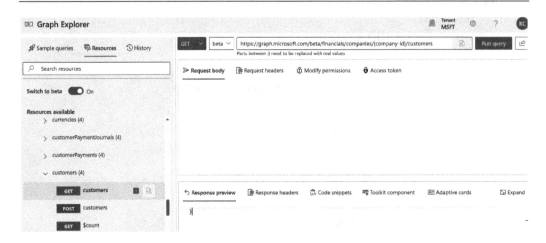

Figure 3.8 – Expanding the various menus to see what information is available

The company ID that is expected is the company ID from BC. You'll have to log into your BC account and get the company ID. To do this, log into BC and search for `companies`. Then, select **Companies** from the list. See *Figure 3.9*:

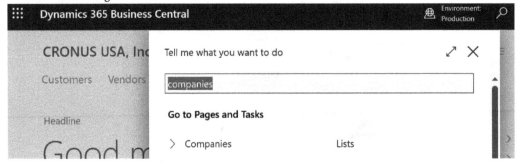

Figure 3.9 – Searching for companies in Business Central

The **Companies** page will open. Select the **help** button at the top of the screen. See *Figure 3.10*:

Figure 3.10 – The help button in Business Central

Select **Help & Support** from the **Other resources** menu:

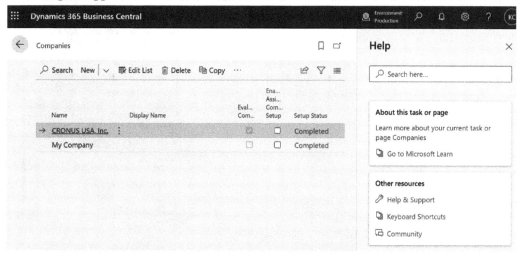

Figure 3.11 Selecting Help & Support under Other resources

Scroll down to the **Troubleshooting** section and select **Inspect pages and data**:

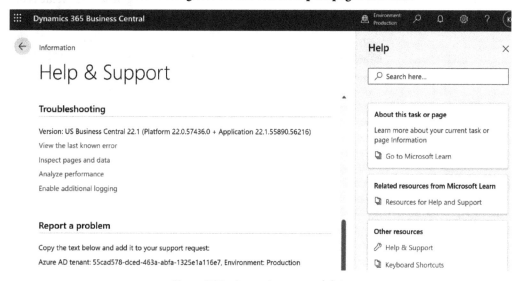

Figure 3.12 – Inspect pages and data

The **Page Inspection** window will open. Scroll down to find the ID, highlight it, and copy it:

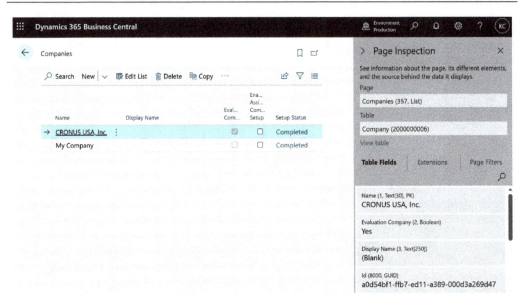

Figure 3.13 – Finding the ID in the Page Inspection window

Go back to your Microsoft Graph Explorer and paste the ID where the {company-id} value is in the query. Then, select **Run query**. You will see the values it returns in the **Response preview** window:

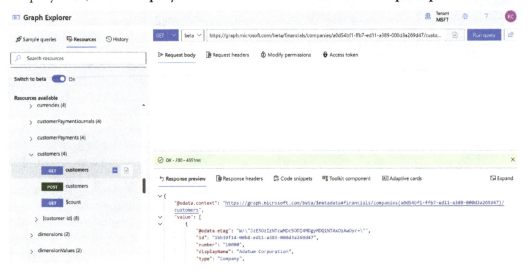

Figure 3.14 – Run Query results

There is a way to create custom connectors for BC as well, although some of the places where that used to be available no longer exist. You can create custom connectors in Power Automate but no longer in Power Apps. This may signal that Microsoft is trying to include more in its own BC Connector.

Creating a custom connector to BC is a technical and expert-level process and since this book is geared more toward you, the citizen developer, we are not going to show you how to create one. If you need one, then you are more likely to need someone with more expertise in building those, such as a developer. There are so many connectors available for BC now and more tend to get added each day. The following screenshot shows the extensive list of connectors available through Power Automate:

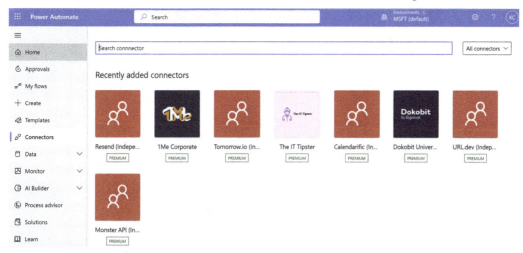

Figure 3.15 – Recently added connectors in Power Automate

Under **All connectors**, you can see that there a wide variety of connectors is available. This is the first page of many more connectors:

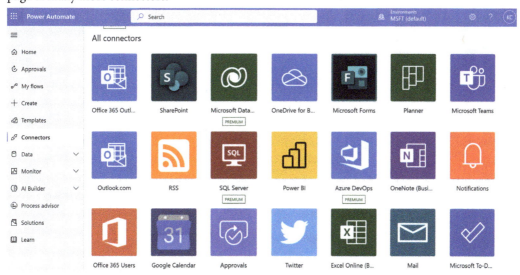

Figure 3.16 – All connectors available in Power Automate

> **Creating a custom connector**
>
> If you want to learn more about creating a custom connector from scratch, go to `https://learn.microsoft.com/en-us/connectors/custom-connectors/define-blank`. Keep in mind that this is expert-level stuff. So, don't get frustrated if it doesn't work the first time.

Building a Power Automate flow

Let's put using the BC Connector in the cloud into practice with Power Automate. In this exercise, K&S Company needs to know when a new customer is created in the system. They have a small team and the accounting manager must get notified when a new customer is created so that they can complete all the financial setup needed to ensure the posting groups, dimensions, and terms are set up properly. You determine that the solution that makes the most sense is a Power Automate flow that has been set up to send an email when a new customer record is created in BC.

To do this, you will need to perform the following steps:

1. Open Power Automate and select **My flows**, then **New flow**:

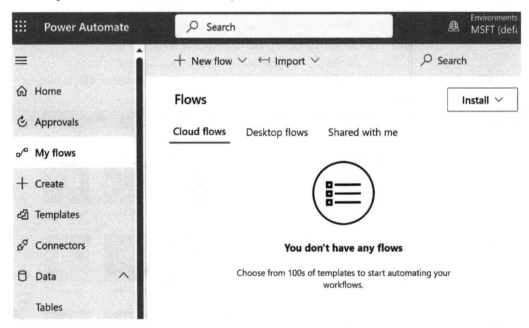

Figure 3.17 – Creating a new flow

2. Upon expanding this menu, you will see options for creating the new flow. Select **Instant cloud flow**:

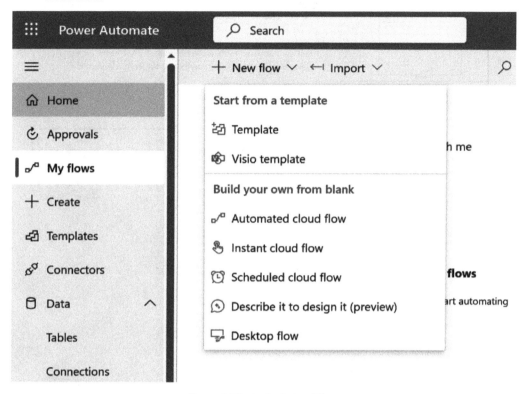

Figure 3.18 – Instant cloud flow

3. The **Build an instant cloud flow** window will open. Enter a name for the flow and select **Skip**:

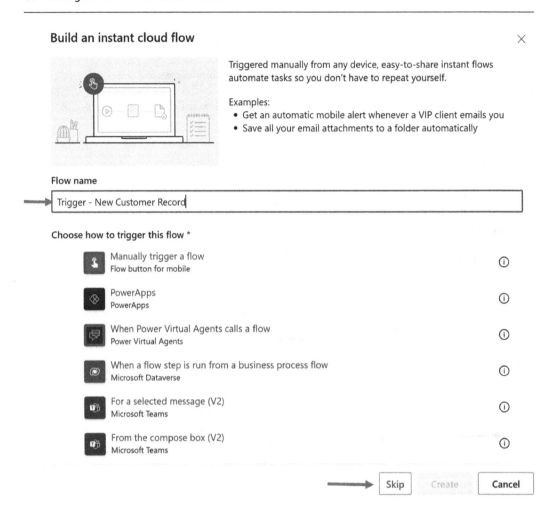

Figure 3.19 – Naming your flow

4. This will bring you to a screen where you can start building your Power Automate solution. We'll start by searching for Business Central and then selecting the respective connector. Make sure you select the one that is for the cloud and not on-premises:

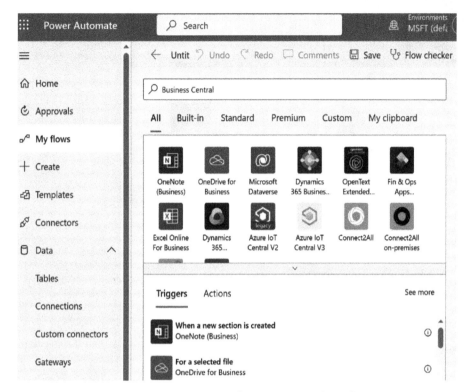

Figure 3.20 – Power Automate selecting Business Central triggers

5. When you select the **Business Central** connector, a screen will open where you can select what action you want to trigger the flow. Select **When a record is created (V3)**:

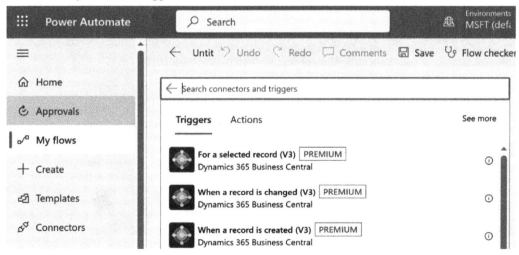

Figure 3.21 – Selecting When a record is created (V3)

6. A screen will open. Enter the fields shown in the following screenshot and select **+ New step**:

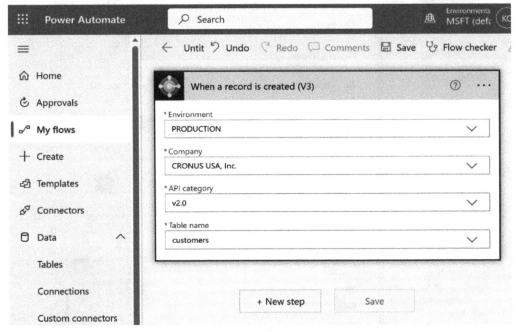

Figure 3.22 – Entering values for the trigger

7. In the new window, select **Business Central** again:

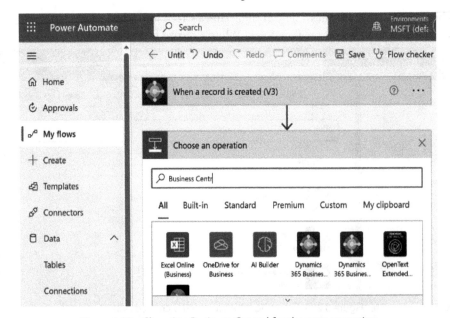

Figure 3.23 – Choosing Business Central for the next operation

8. Under **Actions**, select **Get record (V3)**:

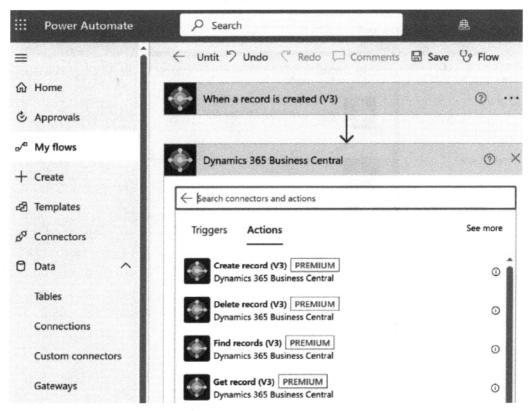

Figure 3.24 – Selecting Get record (V3)

9. Fill in the information shown in the following screenshot and select **Row id** for the **Row id** value. Select **+ New Step**:

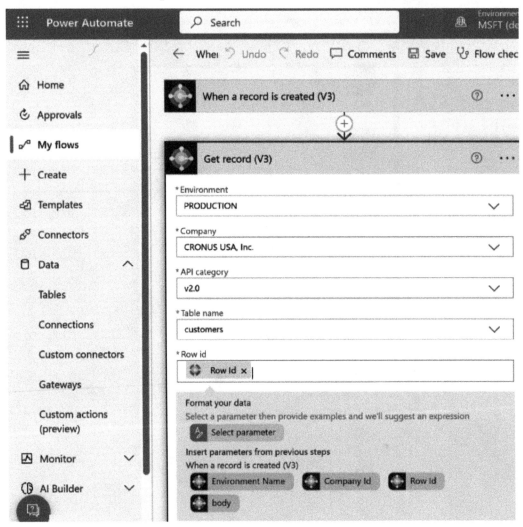

Figure 3.25 – Filling in values for the Get record (V3) action

10. Our last operation will be for Outlook to send an email. Search for `Outlook` and select **Office 365 Outlook**:

Figure 3.26 – Selecting Outlook for the next action

11. Next, select **Actions** and then **Send an email (V2)**:

Figure 3.27 – Selecting the Send an email (V2) action for Outlook

12. Enter your email in the **To** field. Enter something in the **Subject** line; then, in the body, select the fields you wish to populate in your email:

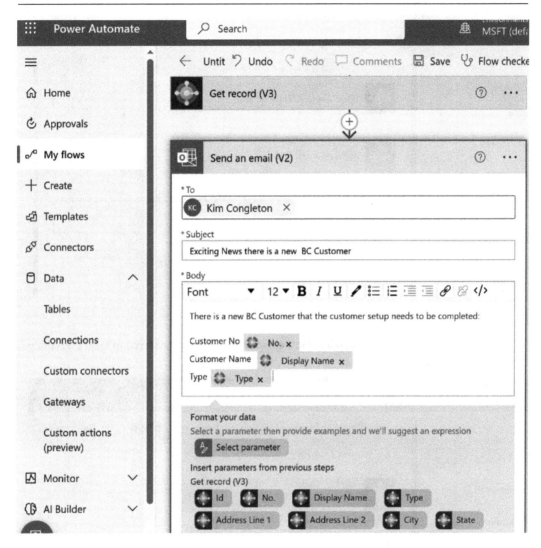

Figure 3.28 – Filling in the values for the Send an email (V2) action for Outlook

13. The next step is to save your flow. Select **Save** at the top of the screen:

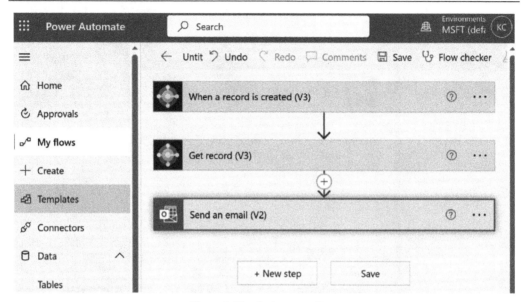

Figure 3.29 – Saving your flow

14. Once your flow has been saved, select **Flow checker** at the top of the screen to see if everything is fine with your flow:

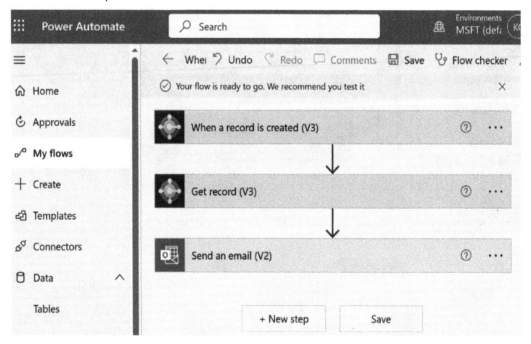

Figure 3.30 – Flow checker

15. After **Flow checker** has run, it will show you if you have any errors or warnings:

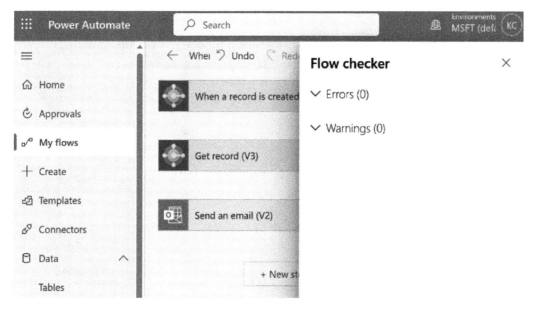

Figure 3.31 – Power Automate results after Flow checker has run

16. The last thing we must do is test the Power Automate flow. Select **Test** at the top of the screen:

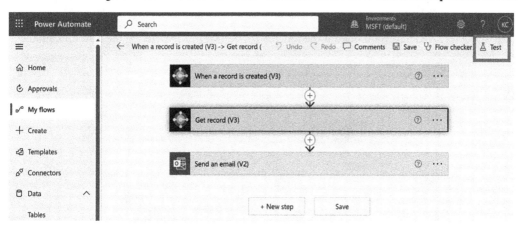

Figure 3.32 – Testing the new flow

17. Select **Manually** to run it the first time automatically and then select **Test**:

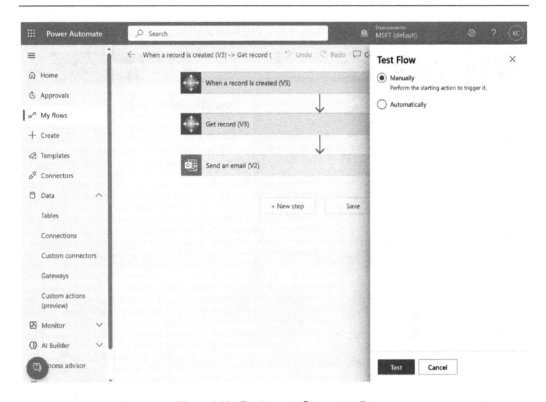

Figure 3.33 – Testing your flow manually

18. The screen will have a message at the top, instructing you to go perform the action manually:

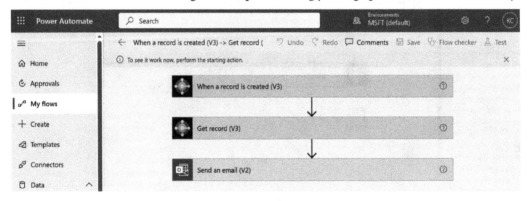

Figure 3.34 – Testing your flow manually

19. Open BC and select **Customers** from your home screen or search for it:

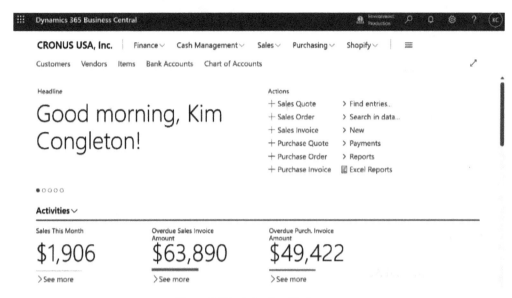

Figure 3.35 – Selecting Customers

20. The customer list will open. Select + **New**:

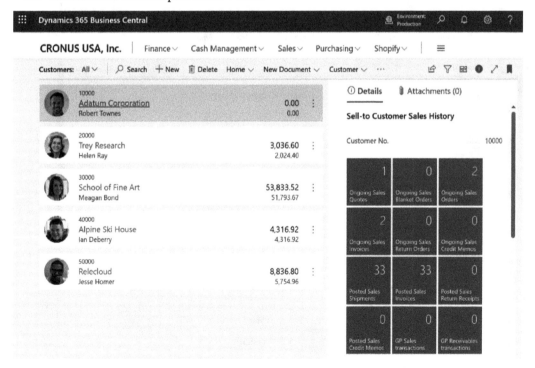

Figure 3.36 – Creating a new customer from the customer list

21. You will be prompted to select a template for your new customer. Select **CUSTOMER COMPANY** and click **OK**:

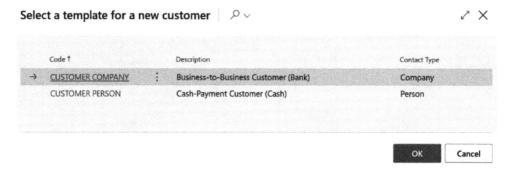

Figure 3.37 – Selecting the CUSTOMER COMPANY template for the new customer

22. Enter the **Name** and **Address** details of the new customer:

Figure 3.38 – Entering the Name and Address details of the new customer

23. Open Outlook and verify that you received an email notification for the new customer:

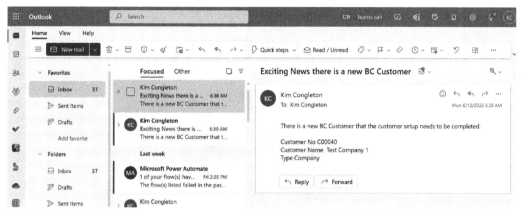

Figure 3.39 – Example of the email notification for the new customer

24. If you go back to Power Automate, you will see a confirmation message stating that Power Automate ran successfully:

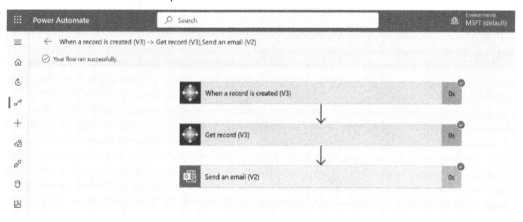

Figure 3.40 – Confirmation that Power Automate ran successfully

Congratulations! You have created your first Power Automate flow. While this one was simple and we did not drill into a lot of detail around Power Automate, this is a good example of how the BC Connector works with Power Platform. In future chapters, we will begin to explore Power Automate in more detail.

Summary

In this chapter, our primary focus was on establishing connections with Microsoft BC, both in the cloud and on-premises. We analyzed the key differentiators between these two connection methods, such as connectivity options, infrastructure management, and scalability potential. To connect on-premises, VPNs or secure web services are essential, whereas cloud connections offer a range of authentication options.

We also examined Microsoft's collection of connectors, which are specifically designed for integrating with BC, including Common Data Service, BC, and Power Automate connectors. Additionally, we explored the practical application of Microsoft Graph Explorer, which empowers us to access and manipulate BC data. Lastly, we successfully crafted our initial Power Automate flow. This chapter served as an invaluable guide to effectively connect and integrate with BC, irrespective of the deployment environment.

In the next chapter, we're going to explore Dataverse and virtual tables and how they can improve Business Central's functionality. Specifically, we'll set up virtual tables in Business Central to centralize data related to the safety procedures for employee processes. We'll show how this data can be stored in Dataverse, making it readily available for business users. We'll showcase how using Dataverse and virtual tables can help us move away from information scattered across paper documents or Excel sheets and instead maintain it in a centralized, efficient manner. You'll also learn about the limitations of using virtual tables, how to set them up, and how to use them to create a model-driven app.

4

Working with Virtual Tables and Dataverse

In this chapter, we'll introduce you to Dataverse and virtual tables. You will learn to set up virtual tables in Business Central to enhance Business Central's functionality and create a simple model-driven app. We will use Dataverse to store information related to employee process management safety. This allows us to centralize the data so that business users can access it. I will walk you through all the steps and explain the functionality.

We'll see how virtual tables work and how, with Dataverse, we can extend Business Central's functionality; this can be accomplished without a developer. Leveraging virtual tables and Dataverse eliminates the need for scattered information stored in paper documents or Excel spreadsheets. It provides a centralized location for efficient information sharing and maintenance.

By the end of this chapter, you will understand some of the limits and restrictions when using virtual tables. You will also understand how to set up and use virtual tables, tie them all together, and create a model-driven app for business users to view Business Central data, assign additional data, and store it in Dataverse.

In this chapter, we're going to cover the following main topics:

- Introduction to Dataverse
- Integration between Dataverse and Business Central
- Understanding virtual tables
- Creating a model-driven app

Technical requirements

Despite the added value of most paid tools, we have decided to use only free tools to make the content of this book available to you without any limitation; using the link in *Chapter 1*, make sure you have created a free development environment in Microsoft.

The following is required:

- Requires **Business Central version 17.0** and above; this should be included in the development environment; if you choose to use your own, confirm your Business Central version is 17 and above by logging in to Business Central, selecting the question mark (**?**) icon in the top-right corner, and going to **Help & Support** – alternatively, select *Ctrl + F1* and your help screen will pop up.
- The Business Central Virtual Table app is available on AppSource.
- This chapter's code examples can be found on GitHub at: `https://github.com/PacktPublishing/Extending-Business-Central-with-the-Power-Platform`.

This chapter will demand the following requirements for the model-driven app exercise.

K&S Solutions Inc., Division C needs the ability to track employee safety checklists and training sessions. This will let management know which employees are certified and their certification dates. This functionality doesn't currently exist in Business Central. It is, however, an essential piece of documentation the company needs to comply with audit requirements. We will also create a requisition request form for staff to request cleaning supplies. Here is a design I commonly use to lay out what data and tables are required:

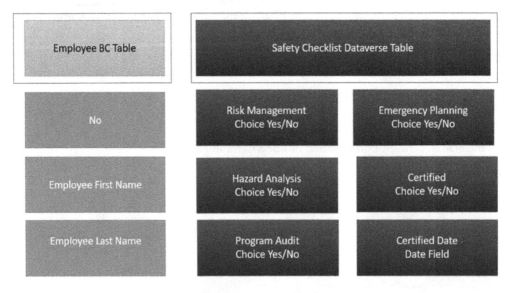

Figure 4.1 – Business Central and Dataverse table design – employee safety checklist

As you design and build your app, it is always a good idea to lay it out so that the business user can be involved in setting up the form; this is also helpful when creating the app. Then, you have a straightforward design.

Submit	Employee Process Management Safety Checklist App						✕
First Name	Last Name	Risk Management	Hazard Analysis	Program Auditing	Emergency Planning	Certified	Certified Date
Terry	Dodds	Yes	Yes	Yes	Yes	Yes	4/1/23

Figure 4.2 – Employee process management safety checklist app

Figure 4.3 is the design for the requisition request form for staff to request cleaning supplies using Dataverse and Business Central vendor virtual tables:

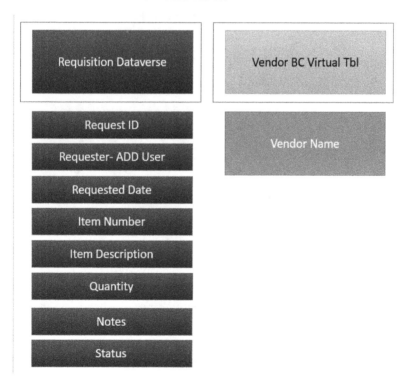

Figure 4.3 – Dataverse and Business Central virtual table – requisition request form

Figure 4.4 is the design layout for the requisition request form:

New Requisition Form	
Requester ID	Requester ID- Auto Generated
Requester	Requester- Auto Generated
Requested Date	Requested Date- Input
Vendor Name	Vendor Name- Select List
Item Number	Item Number- Input
Item Description	Item Description- Input
Quantity	Quantity- Input
Notes	Notes- Input
Status	Status- Select

Figure 4.4 – Requisition request form

Now that we have the design and layout, it is time to review what we need on the software side and the key components you will need to understand before we step through creating the employee process management safety app and requisition request form.

Introduction to Microsoft Dataverse

The definition of Dataverse is a vast collection of data. Microsoft Dataverse, formerly known as Microsoft **Common Data Service** (**CDS**) until November 2020, is a data storage and management layer that can be used with Dynamic 365 products and Power Platform. Now let's talk about how to use Dataverse to extend Business Central's functionality. Years ago, when I started in Navision in 1999, and yes, I am dating myself, if we wanted to add tables, fields, and functionality, we needed to write up the specs and have a developer create the functionality for us. Business analyst consultants or superusers that are not traditional developers can use Dataverse to store and manage data that can be combined with Business Central tables and data.

Dataverse allows you to store and manage the data used by apps securely. A standard table is a set of rows and columns. Each column within the table is designed to keep specific data types, such as first names, last names, job titles, and so on. Dataverse is how Power Apps, Office, and the Dynamics suite of products integrate with a single system of record for business data. This is today's version of Microsoft Access on steroids. I spent many years using Microsoft Access to store additional data that I couldn't add to Navision and used Microsoft Access for many reporting needs. Now, Dataverse keeps data in standard or custom tables, and you can build Power Apps and automate workflows against the data stored in Dataverse. In addition, it adds business rules and validation-defined role-based security. Using Dataverse instead of creating a structure from scratch has many advantages; it is easy to manage and secure, and you can integrate it with other Dynamics 365 data, built-in logic, and validation, to name a few things.

Microsoft Dataverse has a Teams component. We will not dive deep into this functionality, but I encourage you to read up on the topic. Like the entire Power Platform stack, it supports low-code and no-code apps, flows, and chatbots, all within Teams.

Setting up a Power Platform environment

It is essential to set up the environment properly now, as we will use it for the rest of the chapter and throughout the rest of the book. Doing so will help you understand the different types of environments and some tips and tricks. You don't want to develop in the default environment; everyone in your organization has access by default. So, let's go through the whole process, starting from the beginning:

> **Tip**
> Dataverse and Business Central environments must be in the same currency. Suppose you have multiple companies in Business Central with different currencies when integrating Business Central with Dataverse. In that case, the currency information will be synchronized, allowing you to store and access data in the respective currencies.

1. Sign in to Power Platform and select **Admin Center** (the gear in the top-right corner of the page).

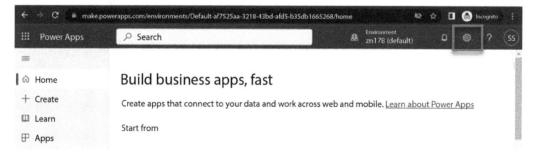

Figure 4.5 – Gear setting to navigate to Admin Center

2. In the navigation pane, select **Environments**, and then select **+ New**:

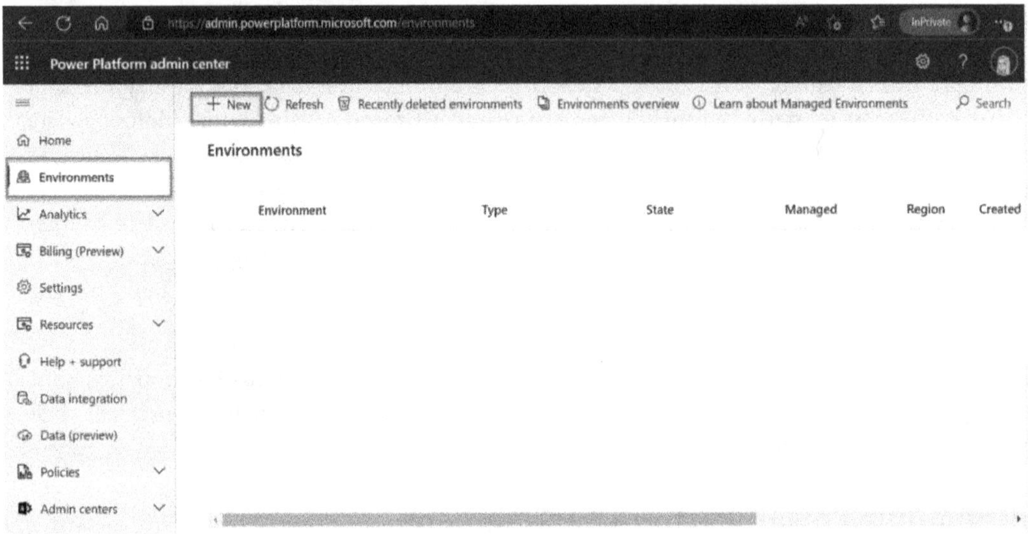

Figure 4.6 – Creating a new environment

3. If you are using a free development environment, we will create a sandbox. Enter these details for the respective fields:

    - **Name**: Extending BC with PA

    - **Region**: United States-Default

    - **Type | Sandbox Purpose | Optional**

    - Select **Yes** to create a database for this environment

4. On the next screen, you will enter information to create a new database for your environment:

    - Enter ExtendingBCwithPA into the **URL** field.

    - Set **Currency** to **USD** ($) – all the exercises for this environment will be in US dollars.

    - **Security Group** – you can edit and set security groups for this environment or select open access and everyone will have access to this new environment.

- Enable Dynamics 365 apps by sliding the respective button to the right, and then select **Save**.

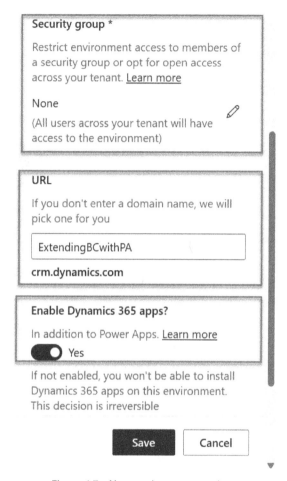

Figure 4.7 – New environment settings

5. This process will take a few minutes; once the environment is completed, the status will be ready, and you can start using it. You can switch to the new environment by going to the top-right section and selecting **Environment | ExtendingBCwithPA**.

Congratulations, you have created your first new environment to start playing in.

Creating a new table in Dataverse

Dataverse has many standard tables to pick from, and when possible, it is best to use an existing one since the structure and work are already done for you. However, this section will create a new Dataverse table to track the process management safety checklist and certification date. These will be fields that don't exist in Business Central, but we want to report on them down the road:

1. Open Power Apps and select **Tables**.

2. Select + **New table**:

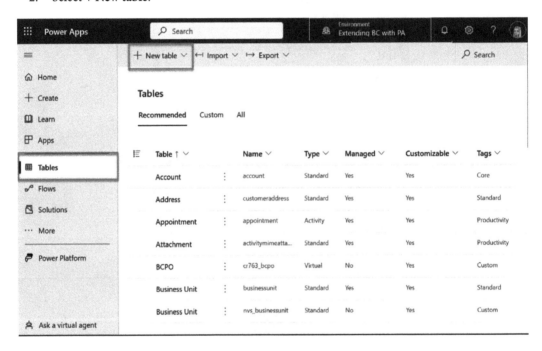

Figure 4.8 – Creating a new Dataverse table

3. The name of the table will be **Safety Checklist**. Enter `Safety Checklist` under **Display Name** and then click **Save**.

4. Add the following six new columns:

    A. **Risk Management**: **Data Type** will be a **Choice** field (Yes/No).

    B. **Hazard Analysis**: **Data Type** will be a **Choice** field (Yes/No).

    C. **Program Audit**: **Data Type** will be a **Choice** field (Yes/No).

    D. **Emergency Planning**: **Data Type** will be a **Choice** field (Yes/No).

E. **Certified**: **Data Type** will be a **Choice** field (Yes/No).

F. **Certified Date**: **Data Type** will be **Date and Time**, but we only need **Date**. To remove the **Time** option, select **Date** only for the format option.

5. To view the table in edit mode, open the table and select **Edit**. In the list of fields, you will also notice that the system created standards out of the box: **Created By**, **Created On**, **Modified By**, and **Modified On**, to name a few. These system-created fields can be used for auditing purposes.

Integration between Dataverse and Business Central

Now, we will discuss the integration of Business Central tables and allowing them to be available in Dataverse and other Power Platforms applications. This allows the tables to be replicated or exposed on Power Platform. Here are the steps to integrate Dataverse and Business Central:

1. Open Power Apps and select **Tables | + New table**:

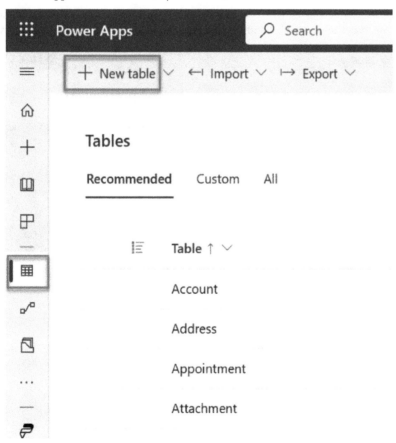

Figure 4.9 – Creating a new table

2. Add the table name and then select **Save**.

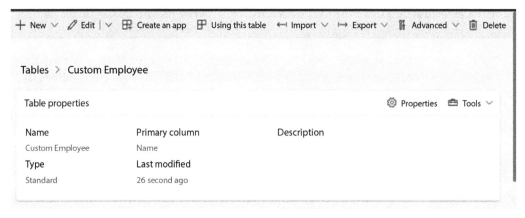

Figure 4.10 – Custom Employee table

3. The system creates some default columns automatically. To see the list of columns, select **Columns**:

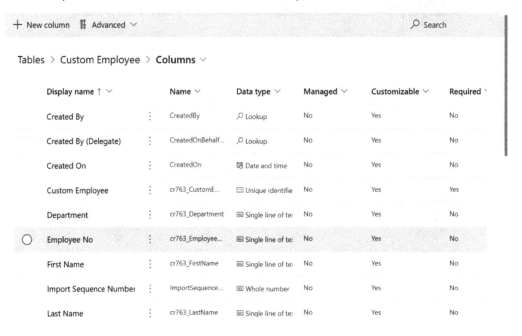

Figure 4.11 – List of columns

4. Select **+ New column** to add a column: enter `First Name` in **Display name** and then select **Save**.

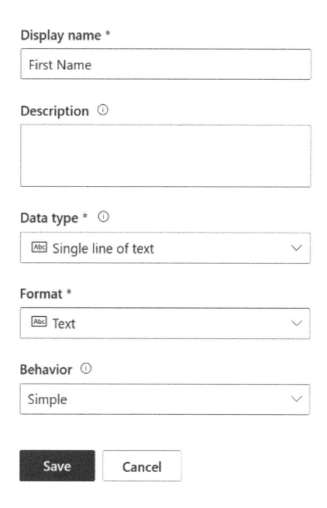

New column

Previously called fields. Learn more

Display name *

First Name

Description ⓘ

Data type * ⓘ

Abc Single line of text   ⌄

Format *

Abc Text   ⌄

Behavior ⓘ

Simple   ⌄

Save   Cancel

Figure 4.12 – Custom column

5. Add the following additional columns in the same way as you did in *step 4*: in the **Display name** column, add **Employee No**, **Last Name**, and **Department**.

We need to create a few keys, so go back to the **Table properties** screen and select **Keys**.

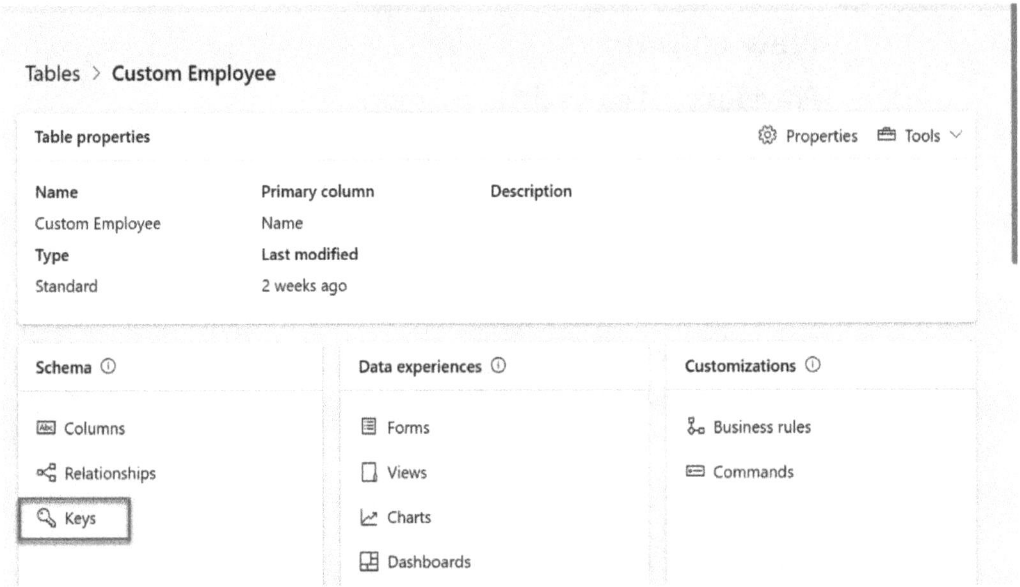

Tables > **Custom Employee**

Table properties   ⚙ Properties   💼 Tools ∨

Name	Primary column	Description
Custom Employee	Name	
Type	Last modified	
Standard	2 weeks ago	

Schema ⓘ

| 🔤 Columns |
| ⚬⟨ Relationships |
| 🔍 Keys |

Data experiences ⓘ

| 📋 Forms |
| ▢ Views |
| 📈 Charts |
| 🎛 Dashboards |

Customizations ⓘ

| ⚙。 Business rules |
| ▭ Commands |

Figure 4.13 – Table properties screen

6. To create a new key, select **+ New key**, and under **Display name**, enter Employee No. Then, select **Employee No** from the column field section and click **Save**.

7. The next step is to make sure we have an API for Business Central to connect to and import the Employee table data. Select **Business Central**, go to **Web Services**, and search for Employees. If one doesn't exist, create a new one and use the **Object Type** option **Page** and **Object ID** 5201. If you create a new one, make sure you publish it. Highlight the OData V4 URL so you have it for the next step. For example, https://api.businesscentral.dynamics. com/v2.0/af7525aa-3218-43bd-afd5-b35db1665268/Sandbox/ODataV4/ Company('CRONUS%20USA%2C%20Inc.')/Employee.

8. Go back to **Table properties** and then select **Import | Import data**:

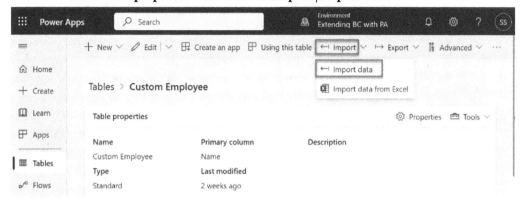

Figure 4.14 – Import data

9. Select **OData** and then connect to the data source. Then, copy and paste the URL from before, sign in with your account, and select **Next**:

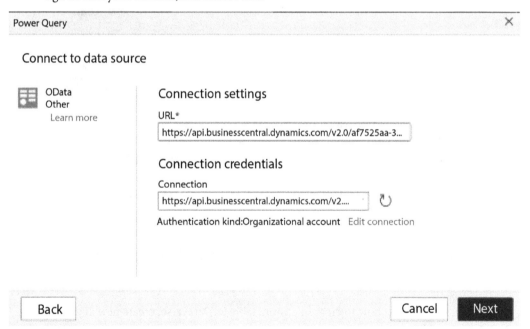

Figure 4.15 – Connect to data source

10. Once you are connected, Power Query will open and you can select **Next**. On the next screen, you'll see the map table screen and can select **Load to existing table**. In each of the columns, select **Destination table** and map to **Source column**.

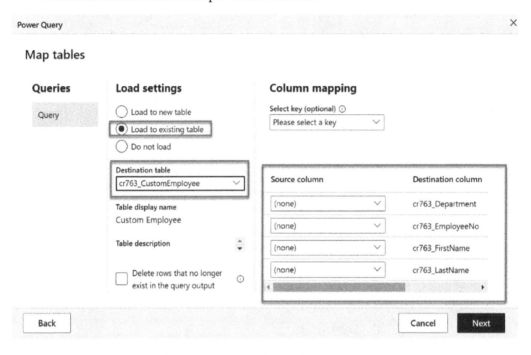

Figure 4.16 – Power Query table mapping

11. There are several options when refreshing data and setting how often to refresh it. Under **Refresh settings**, select **Refresh automatically**. Employees don't change often, so refreshing once a day is plenty. Set **Frequency based refresh** to every 1 day and select **Publish**.

> **Important note**
> This way of integrating Business Central tables into Dataverse will consume Dataverse storage space, and you will want to be aware of your capacity.

In this section, we reviewed how to create a custom table in Dataverse, create new keys, import a Business Central table, and review the options for refreshing the data and the frequency. Later in the chapter, we will use this table to create our model-driven app. The next section will discuss using virtual tables and how that differs from importing data into Dataverse.

Understanding virtual tables

In this section, we will review virtual tables and how they can be used to integrate with Power Platform.

First, we must understand what a virtual table is, as well as its key benefits, and any restrictions. The virtual table is a concept that allows you to create a custom table-like structure without requiring traditional database tables or physical data storage. Unlike the previous section, when we did a sync between a Business Central table and a Dataverse table, virtual tables do not use database capacity.

Virtual tables are commonly used to integrate with additional external systems and provide a way to enhance the capabilities of applications and build custom solutions tailored to specific business requirements. Virtual tables in Business Central serve as a crucial integration point for connecting with external systems and data sources. They enable seamless data exchange and consistency between Business Central and other applications. By utilizing virtual tables, you can integrate Business Central systems to exchange data bidirectionally, ensuring that information remains up to date and consistent across all connected systems.

The virtual tables act as a bridge, allowing you to map data. This integration capability is especially valuable when consolidating information from different sources. For instance, you can connect the **Customer** table in Business Central and the **Accounts** table in Dataverse. This link allows you to enhance the functionality of tables in both Business Central and Dataverse. One practical application of virtual tables is the ability to create a model-driven app and display sale order information directly on the Account card. This integration enables a seamless user experience by providing consolidated data in a single location, and the sales order information can be edited in one spot. You could expand the sales order app to include action from Business Central and allow the user to call the Ship and Invoice command in the model-driven app. The Ship and Invoice command could be used in an environment that doesn't require advanced warehouse functionality or has one or two staff members creating orders, shipping, and invoicing them. In this solution, you would use database storage for the Business Central customer information and Dataverse accounts information; only the sales order information would be your virtual table. This empowers you to create seamless connections and enhance both capabilities, enabling a unified view of data across your entire business ecosystem.

Virtual tables – key benefits

Virtual tables have several key benefits, including improving data processing, reduced data duplication, and integration with other systems. The data isn't stored in a table, which allows for less database storage, even though hard disk space is cheap, the cloud is better; it also reduces data replication and makes it easier to manage. I spent the first five years of my career as the data master managing data, particularly inventory data. This was a big task, so having a more straightforward system, not having to collect data in two or three places, and keeping it replicated is a big plus for me. I managed our inventory in Navision and had 80 medical labs running Access databases. Replication was a nightmare, and I spent many nights and weekends keeping everything in sync. I also spent three years running

POS systems; some of my stores had fantastic internet, and others didn't, and once the data is out of sync, it is a big job to update it. I would have loved to have had Virtual Table's functionality. I am so excited to have this feature and the opportunity to help you see the potential of using it.

Virtual table restrictions and limitations

Virtual tables have restrictions, and here are a few to consider before you create and use virtual tables. A complete list of limitations can be found on the Learn Microsoft website under *Create and Edit Virtual Tables*, but I will list a few main ones.

One of the big ones to consider is, "Does the data need to be part of an audit?" Since the data is not stored in the tables, the virtual tables don't support auditing. Existing tables can't be converted into virtual tables; in this case, you must manually create and transform the virtual table. Finally, virtual tables contain only the name and ID of the column, not other system-managed columns; if you need **Status**, **Created On**, and **Modified On**, it is not a good idea for data and tables that need to be audited to be virtualized. It is important to consider the amount of data and your volume of data if you are considering it for high-transactional scenarios; a virtual table might not be the best solution.

There are known limitations with Business Central virtual tables, including the following:

- Virtual tables can't be used in Charts. Microsoft Dataverse doesn't support virtual tables being used in Charts.

- Virtual tables can't be customized in Microsoft Dataverse, for example, by adding new columns. All modifications to virtual tables must happen in the API exposed on Business Central. However, custom APIs can be developed and consumed as virtual tables. I learned this limitation the hard way; this is going in the "what not to do" category, like "what not to wear."

- Attachments and Images/Pictures aren't supported for virtual tables.

- Advanced search has some limitations. Each query designed translates to an OData query in Business Central.

- The following predicates aren't supported: **Does Not Equal**, **Does Not Contain**, **Does Not Begin With**, **Does Not End With**, **Does Not Contain Data**, and **Contains Data**.

- You can't combine And/Or groups across columns.

- You can't filter on related tables.

- Power Apps portals can't be supported with virtual tables in the current preview.

Now that you have limitations and restrictions let's walk through how to set up virtual tables in Business Central.

Setting up virtual tables

If you didn't download the Business Central Virtual Table app from AppSource and install it in your Business Central environment, you will want to do that before moving on to the next steps of setting up your virtual table connection from Business Central to Dataverse:

1. You can manually do the Virtual Table setup from the setup screen inside of Business Central or use the assisted setup available on the **Dataverse Connection Setup** page; either way, before starting the setup, you will want to know the environment to which you want to connect and the admin username and password. Once you complete the setup, testing your connection is a good idea.

2. After running the assisted setup, which I recommend, open **Dataverse Connection Setup**, and your screen should be populated similarly to the following screenshot:

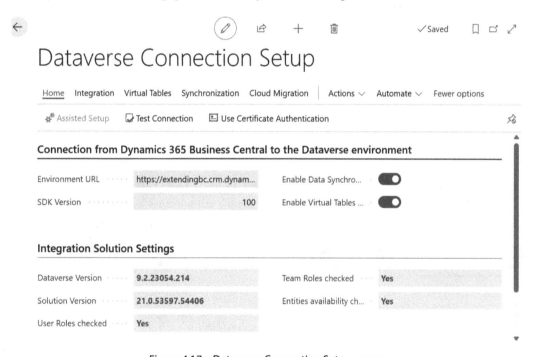

Figure 4.17 – Dataverse Connection Setup screen

3. To view all the available virtual tables, select **Virtual Tables | Available Virtual Tables**. This will take you to Power Apps. By default, most of the tables are not visible. We will want to make the **Purchase Order**, **Purchase Line**, and **Item** tables visible.

A few tips – when you open this screen in Power Apps, you will only see some of the available tables on one screen. To make this easier to find, set the filter on **API Route** to **v2.0**, scroll to find **Item**, open the **Name** column, check **Visible**, and save and close. Once you have this set to **Visible**, you can use this virtual table in Power Platform.

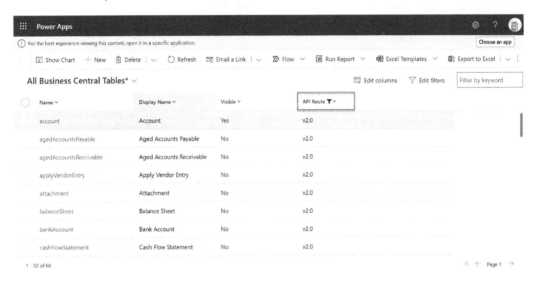

Figure 4.18 – All Business Central tables

4. Find the **Vendor** table by either scrolling through the list of **v2.0** tables or using the **Filter by Name** option.

5. Open the **Item** table and check the **Visible** checkbox; this will allow you to use the **Vendor** table:

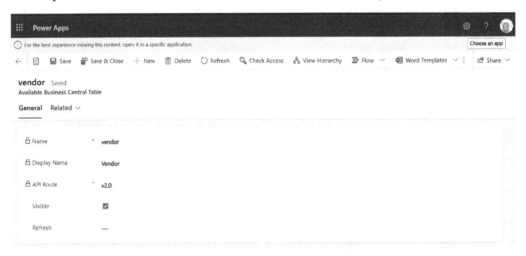

Figure 4.19 – Vendor table properties

> **Tip**
> If you want to add fields to a virtual table, this must be done in the Business Central API. Once you add the fields, they will be available to consume in other applications.

Now, let's look at an exercise on the requisition request form using a Business Central vendor virtual table.

Requisition request form exercise using a Business Central vendor virtual table

In this section, we will create a new Dataverse table to store employee requests for purchased items required for the warehouse:

1. Open **Power Apps** | select **Tables**. To create a new table, select + **New table**:

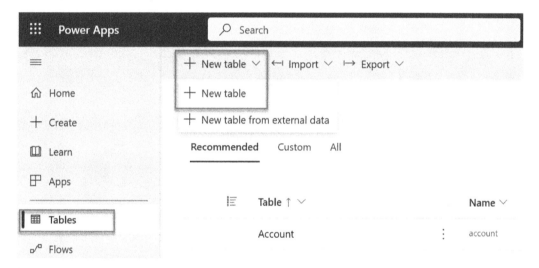

Figure 4.20 – New table

2. Enter Requisition under **Display name**, and Requisitions will be populated by default under **Plural name**.

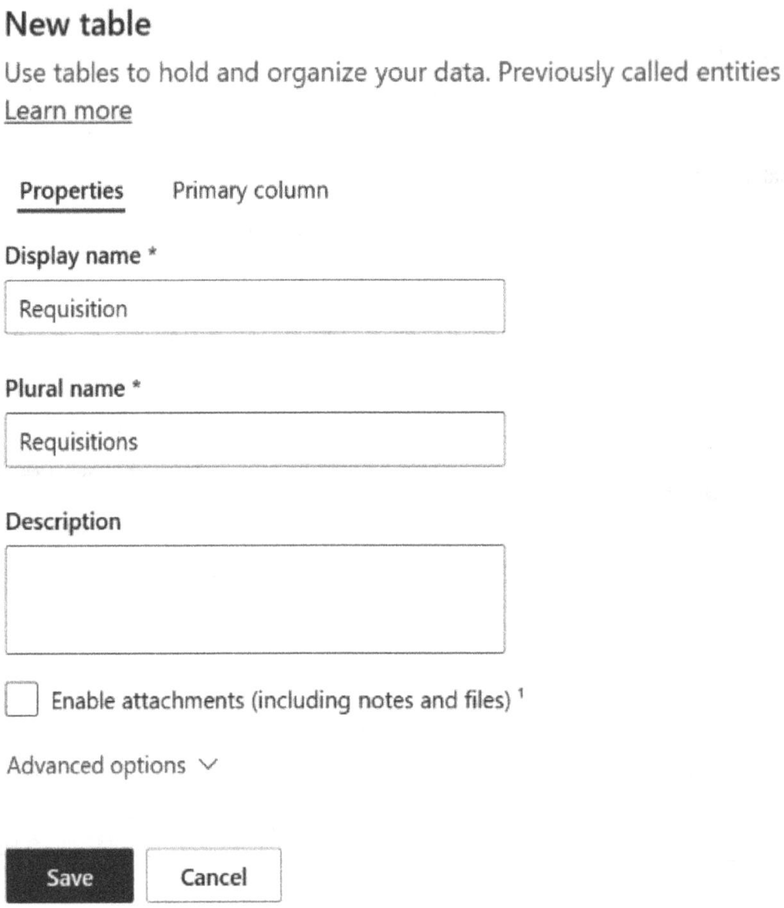

New table

Use tables to hold and organize your data. Previously called entities
Learn more

Properties   Primary column

Display name *

Requisition

Plural name *

Requisitions

Description

☐ Enable attachments (including notes and files) [1]

Advanced options ∨

Save   Cancel

Figure 4.21 – New requisition table

3. We need to add the following fields to the **Requisition** table: **Requester ID, Requested Date, Item Number, Item Description, Quantity**, and **Notes**. The first field to create is **Requester ID**, and we want this field to be the primary key and have the system auto-generate using a set number of series that we will define in the field setup properties. The system set up a few standard fields when we created the custom table. We will rename the default **Name** field `Requestor ID`, allowing this field to be the primary field.

4. Select **Columns**.

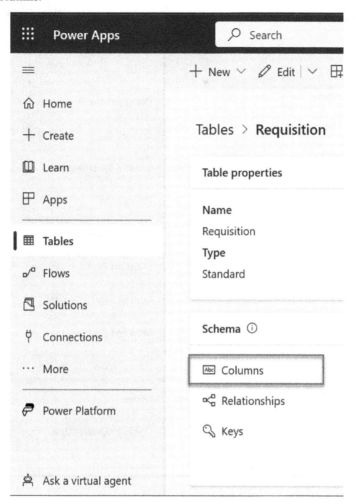

Figure 4.22 – Columns

5. Select the **Name** column and notice that **Name** is the **Primary name column** option.

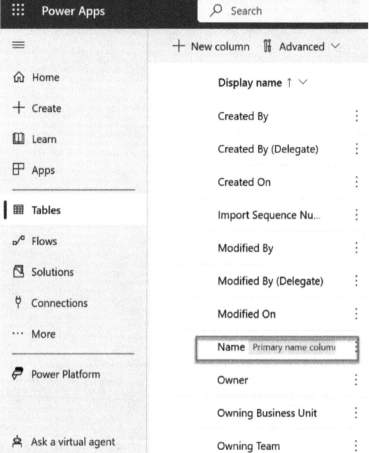

Figure 4.23 – Name

6. Rename **Display name** to Requestor ID in the **Data type** field, select **# Autonumber**, and in the **Prefix** field, enter RI. This will allow the number to start with RI. **Minimum number of digits** defaults to **4**; in most cases, you will want to increase the number of digits to allow for the number of requests. Set this to at least 6, and change **Seed value** from 1000 to 100000. In the **Preview** section, this will give you an idea of how the number will look; see *Figure 4.23*. This is like Business Central number series.

Figure 4.24 – Requester ID auto number series

7. Select + **New column** to add a column: enter `Requested Date` in **Display name**; under **Data type**, select **Date and time**, and you will want **Date only** for this field under **Format**. Then, select **Save**.

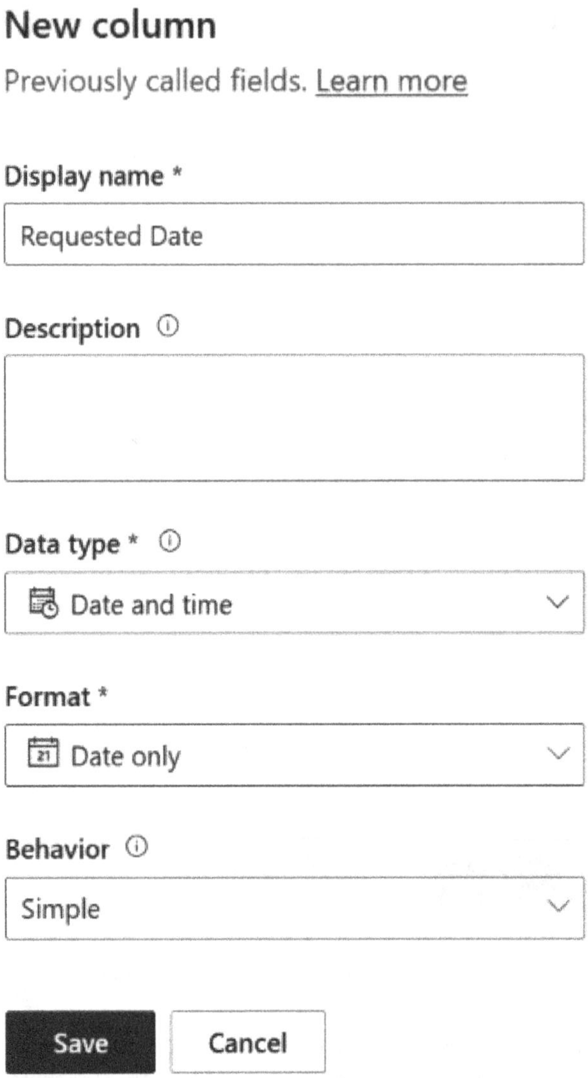

New column

Previously called fields. <u>Learn more</u>

Display name *

Requested Date

Description ⓘ

Data type * ⓘ

🗒 Date and time ⌄

Format *

📅 Date only ⌄

Behavior ⓘ

Simple ⌄

Save   Cancel

Figure 4.25 – Requested Date

8. Select **+ New column** to add a column: enter `Item Number` under **Display name** and then select **Save**.

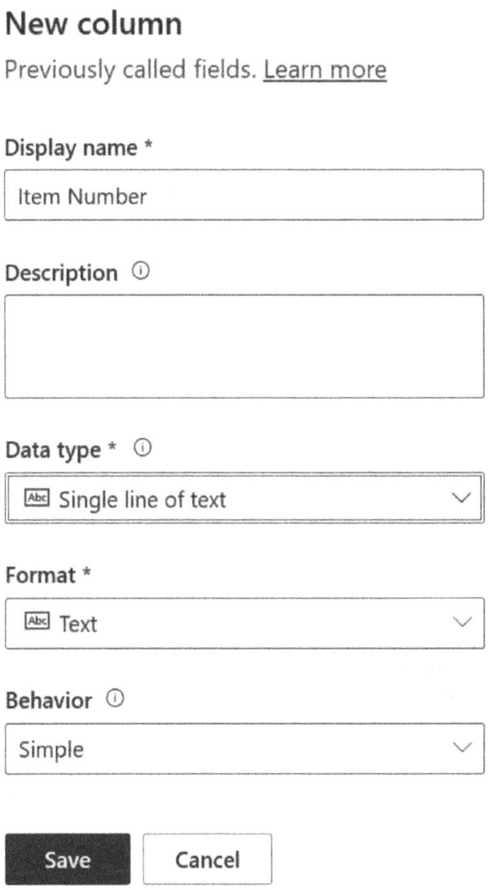

New column

Previously called fields. Learn more

Display name *

Item Number

Description ⓘ

Data type * ⓘ

| [Abc] Single line of text | ⌄ |

Format *

| [Abc] Text | ⌄ |

Behavior ⓘ

| Simple | ⌄ |

Save   Cancel

Figure 4.26 – Item Number

9. Add the following additional columns using *step 8*: in the **Display name** column, add Item Description and Notes.

10. Select **+ New column** to add a column: enter Quantity in **Display name**, and under **Data Type**, select **Whole Number**. Then, select **Save**.

    Next, we will add a column to connect to **Vendor Name** using the Business Central virtual table that we made visible.

11. Select **+ New column** to add a column: enter Vendor Name in **Display name**; in the **Description** field, enter Business Central Vendor Virtual Table. This field is informational, and it will be nice to know that it is linked to a vendor virtual table; in the **Data Type** field, select **Lookup,** and **Lookup** will allow us to select **Vendor** in the **Related table** field. Then, select **Save**.

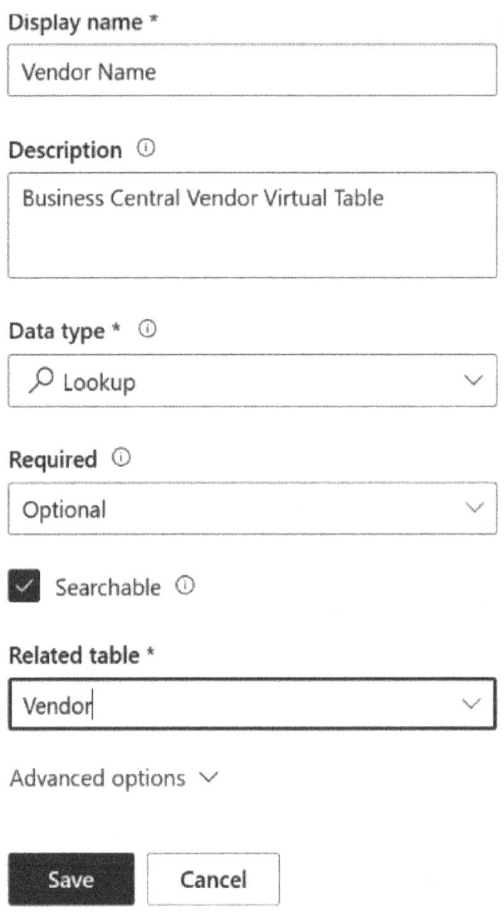

Display name *

Vendor Name

Description ⓘ

Business Central Vendor Virtual Table

Data type * ⓘ

🔎 Lookup   ⌄

Required ⓘ

Optional   ⌄

☑ Searchable ⓘ

Related table *

Vendor| ⌄

Advanced options ⌄

Save   Cancel

Figure 4.27 – Vendor Name

Three basic forms were created when we created the **Requisition** Dataverse table. These forms help define the user interface when working with the data in the table. The three types are **Quick View Form**, **Main Form**, and **Card Form** (see *Figure 4.28*). The main form is primarily used to view and edit data in the table and allows you to arrange the fields, and it is the default form that opens when the user opens a record. A quick-view form is a read-only form used as a summarized view of the fields, and it provides users with a quick glance at important details without the need to scroll or navigate to all the fields available in the table. This form is great for displaying key details of a record without allowing editing. The card form allows the user to create a new record or edit the data in an existing record. Each form provides different functionality and customization options based on the business requirements and can cater to specific user needs. We will wrap up this section by updating the main form created by default:

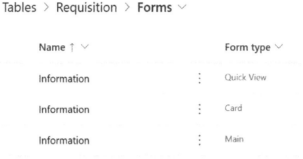

Figure 4.28 – Default forms

12. Select the **Requisition** table, and under **Data experiences**, select **Forms**:

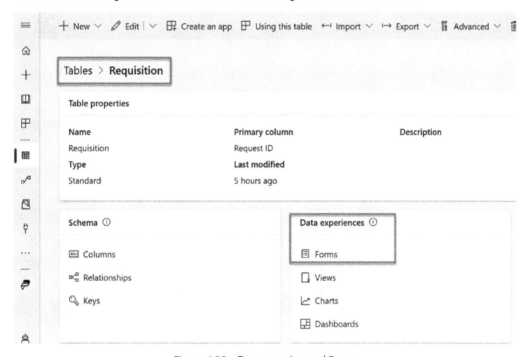

Figure 4.29 – Data experiences | Forms

13. In this section, you will see three forms called **Information**; select the one with the form type set to **Main**. This is the **Main** form for the **Requisition** table.

14. In this step, we will add the following fields: **Requested Date**, **Vendor Name**, **Item Number**, **Item Description**, **Quantity**, and **Notes**. On the left pane, you will see **Table columns**; you can either use the search bar or scroll down to find each field.

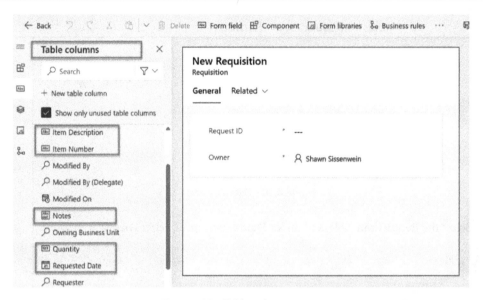

Figure 4.30 – Table columns pane

15. Drag and drop each field from the **Table columns** pane into the **New Requisition** section. Rename **Owner** to Requester by double-clicking on the field – the **Label** box will become available on the right side of the screen. The screen should look like *Figure 4.31*:

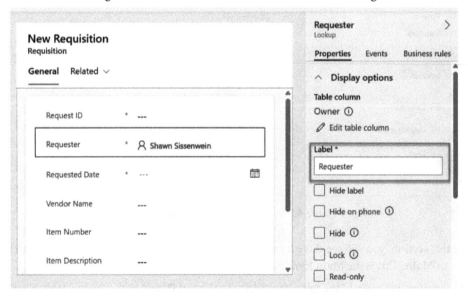

Figure 4.31 – Label property

16. Once all the fields are added and you have renamed the label for **Owner**, select **Save** and **Publish**.

Virtual tables empower you to establish connections, enrich data, and create seamless experiences between Business Central, Dataverse, or other systems. Combining virtual tables and Power Automate opens many possibilities for automating processes and enhancing functionality. In the final section of this chapter, we will create a model-driven app.

Creating a model-driven app

In this section, we will create a model-driven app that will allow employees to have a checklist of lessons that must be completed before becoming certified in management safety. In *Chapter 5*, we will break out the different types of apps; in this case, we will build a model-driven app since we want to offer a standardized approach and we have the flexibility to add business rules and workflows within the app later. This will also let management report on progress and find out which employees have completed the certification program.

Before we create the employee safety management checklist, we need to add a **Lookup** field in the **Safety Checklist** table connected to the **Custom Employees** table; this will provide us with the ability to select an employee's name:

1. Select **Tables** | **Custom** (this will narrow down the list of active tables) | **Safety Checklist**:

Figure 4.32 – Custom Dataverse table

2. Select **New Column** and add these details to the respective fields:

    - **Display Name**: `Employee No`

    - **Data type**: **Lookup**

    - **Related table**: **Custom Employees**, and then select **Save**

3. Enter a few records in your **Safety Checklist** table:

🔲 Safety Checklist columns and data

🔢 Employee No ⌄	⬭ Certified ⌄	🗓 Certified Date ⌄	⬭ Risk M... ⌄	⬭ Hazard +
Lina Townsend	Yes	4/10/2023	Yes	Yes
Jim Olive	No		Yes	Yes
Robin Bettencourt	No		No	No
Select lookup		*Enter or pick date*		

Figure 4.33 – Safety Checklist

Now that we have **Lookup** fields in our table, we can move on to the sections and start the model-driven app creation process.

Building the model-driven app

To build a model-driven app, you must perform the following steps:

1. To create a model-driven app, select **+ New App| Model-driven**, and then in the **Name** field, enter `Employee Safety Management Checklist`.

2. Select **+ Add Page** | Confirm that the Dataverse table option will be selected | **Next**.

3. Select the existing tables, **Custom Employees** and **Safety Checklist** | **Add**.

4. On the next screen, you will see **Custom Employees** and **Safety Checklists**:

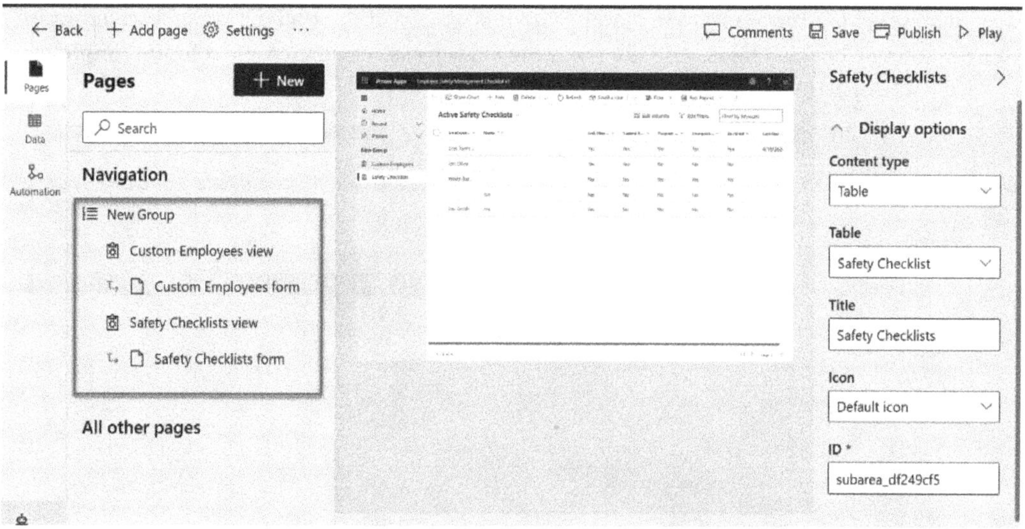

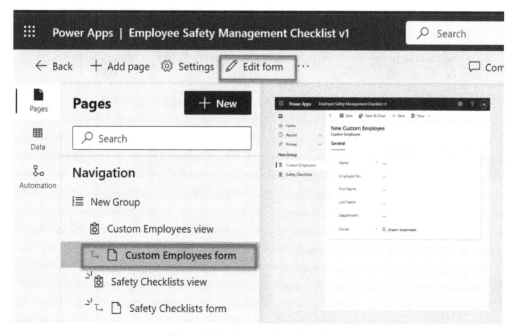

Figure 4.34 – Custom Employees and Safety Checklist

5. Select **Custom Employees view** | **Custom Employees form** | **Edit form**. Add the following fields to the form by dragging and dropping columns from the left – **Employee No**, **First Name**, **Last Name**, **Department**, and so on:

Figure 4.35 – Custom Employee form

6. Select **Back**.

7. Then, select **Custom Employee view** | **Edit view** – this will show all the available columns in the **Safety Checklist** table. Add the following fields by selecting the view column: **Employee No** and **Department**.

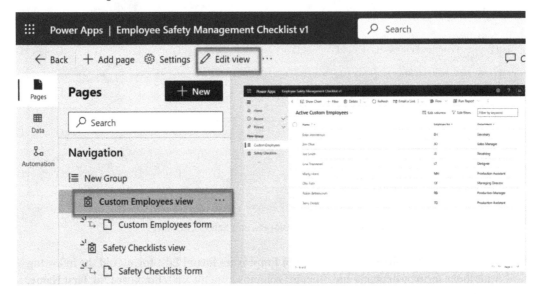

Figure 4.36 – Custom Employee view

8. Remove **Created On** by right-clicking on **Remove**.

9. Select **Validate** in the right corner; this will confirm that no performance impacts were detected for these column/filter combinations.

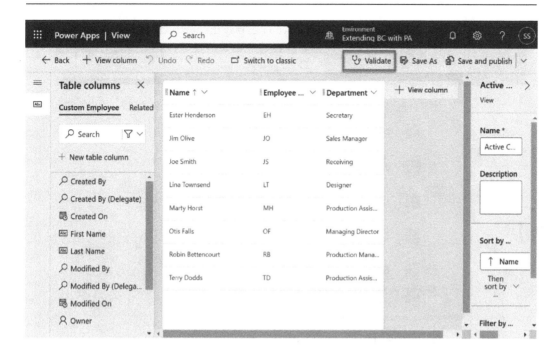

Figure 4.37 – Validate screen

10. Select **Save** at the top right.

11. Select **Back** to go back to the main page.

12. In this step, we will add the following fields to the form. Select **Safety Checklist form** | **Edit form**, then add the following fields to the form by dragging and dropping columns from the left: **Employee No**, **Risk Management**, **Hazard Analysis**, **Program Audit**, **Emergency Planning**, **Certified**, and **Certified Date**.

13. Select **Save** | **Publish**.

14. Select **Safety Checklist views** | **Edit view** – this will show all the available columns in the **Safety Checklist** table. Add the following fields by selecting the view column: **Employee No**, **Risk Management**, **Hazard Analysis**, **Program Audit**, **Emergency Planning**, **Certified**, and **Certified Date**.

15. Select **Save** | **Publish**.

16. Once the app has finished and is published, you can play the app back on the home screen.

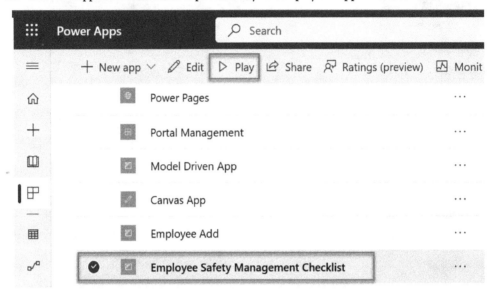

Figure 4.38 – Playing Employee Safety Management Checklist

The next step is to add an advanced filter so the management team can see what employees are certified:

1.   Select **Edit filters**.

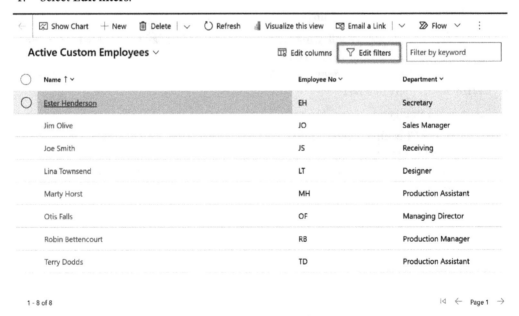

Figure 4.39 – How to set an advanced filter

2. Highlight **Safety Checklists** and then select **Continue**.

3. Change the filter to **Certified | Equals | Yes**.

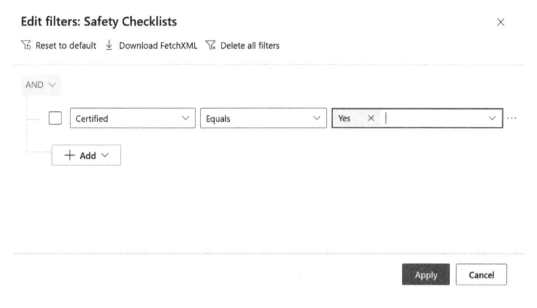

Figure 4.40 – Advanced filter

4. After you select **Apply**, you'll get the following screen:

Figure 4.41 – Filter results

5. The last step is to create a Power BI report to display the data in the dashboard and share it with the users. Select the Power BI icon, **Visualize this view**. Power BI will create a dashboard for you. This gives you a quick summary, and you can save your report.

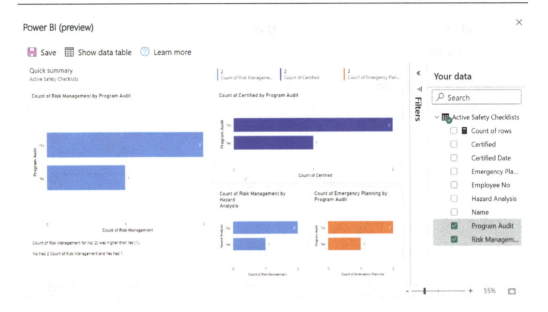

Figure 4.42 – Power BI dashboard

6. Select the **Show data table** option, and this will create a data table visual in the report. Next, select **Save**, enter `Employee Safety` as the name of your report, and for now, leave the Workspace and select **Continue**. Once your report is saved, open it in Power BI by selecting the link provided on the screen.

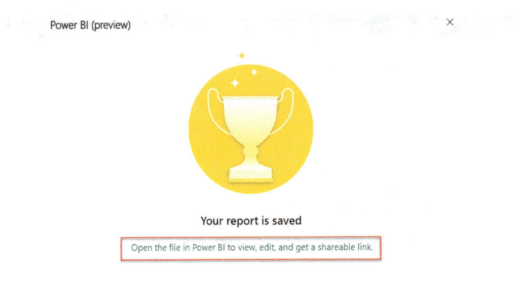

Figure 4.43 – Power BI link

7. Select the link and open the Power BI dashboard. Now, you can share and have an interactive dashboard.

Figure 4.44 – Power BI dashboard

Once you have the foundation, you can add additional features and business rules, process flows, and permissions. I hope this got your creative mind flowing and thinking about all the different types of processes and procedures you could add to expand Business Central and Power Platform.

Summary

In this chapter, we learned about Dataverse and Virtual Table. First, we created a new Power Platform environment and installed the Business Central Virtual Table add-in. Next, we enabled a virtual table inside Dataverse and created a link to the **Vendor** table from Dataverse. Finally, we wrapped up the chapter by creating a model-driven app.

In *Chapter 5*, we will dive into Power Apps, the different types of Power Apps, and when to use each one. Finally, we'll review best practices and build repeatable Power Apps components.

Further reading

- Create and edit virtual tables with Microsoft Dataverse – **Power Apps | Microsoft Learn**: https://learn.microsoft.com/en-us/power-apps/maker/data-platform/create-edit-virtual-entities

- Create your first app in Teams: https://learn.microsoft.com/en-us/power-apps/teams/create-first-app

Part 2 –
Doing the Work of Designing, Building, and Implementing

In the upcoming chapters, we'll explore essential techniques to create efficient and effective Power Apps apps tailored to Business Central's unique requirements. We'll also build seamless workflows and Power Automate, optimizing processes within Business Central and beyond. Lastly, we'll discuss strategies to deliver successful solutions that meet your organization's needs and maximize the benefits of integrating Power Platform and Business Central. Let's dive in and discover the power of these tools in transforming your business processes.

This part contains the following chapters:

- *Chapter 5, Best Practices for Building Power Apps for Business Central*
- *Chapter 6, Building Flow for Business Central*
- *Chapter 7, Delivering Solutions*

Best Practices for Building Power Apps for Business Central

In this chapter, you'll learn about the concept of Power Apps, what types there are, how the different types can be used, and when to use each type. In addition, you will learn best practices and examples of ways Power Apps can extend Business Central's functionality.

By the end of this chapter, you will understand the difference between "citizen developer" app makers versus traditional development, the different types of Power Apps, and how to determine which type of app to create based on requirements. We will discuss connecting to other data sources and repeatable components when creating multiple apps.

In this chapter, we're going to cover the following main topics:

- Citizen developers versus pro developers
- Understanding the different types of Power Apps
- Creating a canvas app
- Repeatable components

Technical requirements

The Creator Kit is a managed solution from Microsoft; once you download the kit, go to **Solutions** and import the solution into your Power Apps environment. This kit was designed to help you speed up your app development and help with designing and creating compatible apps in your organization or clients' environments.

Download and install the Creator Kit from Microsoft: `https://learn.microsoft.com/en-us/power-platform/guidance/creator-kit/overview`.

> **Important note**
>
> Before installing the component framework that enables Power Apps, Microsoft has instructions on enabling the feature, so I won't walk you through it in this book: `https://learn.microsoft.com/en-us/power-platform/guidance/creator-kit/overview`.

This chapter's code examples can be found on GitHub: `https://github.com/PacktPublishing/Extending-Business-Central-with-the-Power-Platform`.

Exercise for creating the Contact canvas app

In this chapter, we will use the following requirements for the exercises.

K&S Solutions Inc. must connect to Business Central contacts when salespeople are on the road. The sales team has requested the ability to update contact information on their phones. Here is the design for the Contact Phone App.

Figure 5.1 – Contact canvas app

Now that we have the design and layout, it is time to review what we need on the software side and the key components we must understand before creating the contact canvas app. Although we will review the foundations of Power Apps and repeatable components in the following sections, we also need to make a simple app that will be used on a phone and take up little space on the screen. Keeping it simple will be the key to creating apps.

Citizen developers versus pro developers

I have always loved development and code. Although I am not a developer by nature, I like to do light coding and can read code. When Kim and I started in Navision, we didn't have all the documentation and YouTube videos, and even Microsoft Learn didn't exist because, at the time, Microsoft wasn't in the picture. I mentioned I used a lot of Access databases to pull data out of Navision and build applications; one application I made was a service management system. We would link tables from Navision to other tables and queries. Back to my point about learning Navision – when we wanted to know how something worked, we would run a debugger and step through the code; I think this is where the love of code came from. I consider myself a citizen developer, not a pro developer.

Several years back, the goal was to take all the external systems, Excel spreadsheets, and databases and combine them into one ERP system. Times have changed, and when we do requirements analysis, we look at the best system for the business requirements. Sometimes, this means doing things outside the traditional ERP system, and if you can connect them all, why not? Approaching a citizen developer and using Power Platform has helped with taking the burden off the IT department and finding a qualified developer that understands NAV code and understands the business requirements, not to mention the fact that often you would have multiple developers and different styles, and this led to many more issues when trying to upgrade a system. In a traditional environment, only pro developers could write code; Power Platform enables other business users, "citizen developers," to build low-code or no-code applications. Both types of developers have their strengths and weaknesses, and the choice between citizen developers and professional developers will depend on the organization's business, projects, and available resources.

> **Important note**
>
> Documentation, testing, and application life cycle management are crucial aspects of software development, regardless of whether you are a professional developer or a citizen developer.

Microsoft has created a new role, app maker. This new role is for someone who has expertise in an organization to build custom apps for their team. App makers also help businesses design, develop, test, and roll out applications.

Microsoft has a certification around app maker skills, and you can take the **PL-100 Microsoft Power Platform App Maker** certification. Head to the app maker learning catalog and select **Power Apps | Microsoft Learn** for more information. This is a great resource for reading up and learning more about the role and certification.

We now know that citizen developers can use Power Platform solutions to increase productivity and allow for additional features to be designed to work alongside the Business Central application. It will be essential to understand the framework and what is possible. I want to first go through the different types of Power Apps.

Different types of Power Apps and deciding which type of app to create

Power Apps has three different kinds of apps – canvas apps, model-driven apps, and power pages. I have built more canvas apps because these apps are available on a mobile device, primarily for warehouse and outside sales teams. Let's look at these three kinds of apps:

- **Canvas apps**: This type of app gives the app maker complete control over the user interface using drag-and-drop elements. You can start with the app first and then pick your data. This app is used for internal tenant-facing functions; typically, you wouldn't release it to your customers or vendors. Due to licensing, data, and security, it is only used for internal resources within your organization. Canvas apps are typically used for more straightforward tasks or data entry. Canvas apps can use any number of connectors to access your data.

Figure 5.2 – Blank canvas app

- **Model-driven**: The app maker starts with the data first when creating a model-driven app. Model-driven apps also require Microsoft Dataverse databases. The app maker has limited control over the user interface since model-driven apps start with a template, and the app maker adds columns. Model-driven apps are good if the business logic is complex and you want to manage business processes easier. For example, in *Chapter 4*, we used a model-driven app to create our Employee Safety Management app.

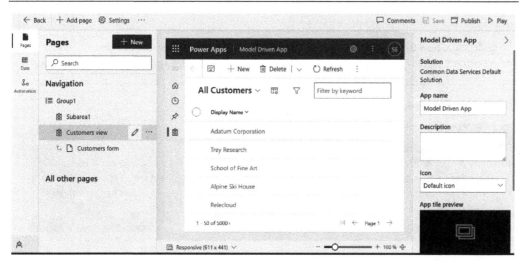

Figure 5.3 – Model-driven app using customer data

- **Power Pages**: Formally known as **portals**. Pages are designed to be built and available to external-facing resources, for example, vendors or customer portals. When you first create a page, you must give it a website URL, and the system checks to ensure the URL is available and not already in use. Then, based on the environment in Power Apps, you can select different templates.

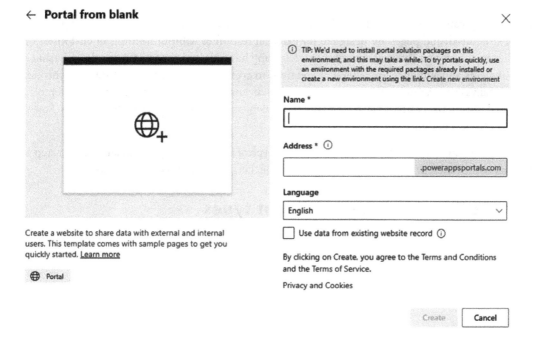

Figure 5.4 – Power Pages blank app

> **Tip**
> To understand how to use portal templates, go to the Learn Microsoft website: `https://learn.microsoft.com/en-us/power-apps/maker/portals/portal-templates`.

To help you understand, here is the Power Apps Decision Flowchart:

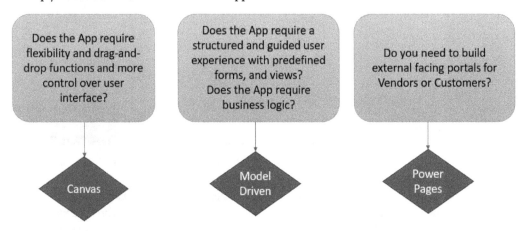

Figure 5.5 – Power Apps Decision Flowchart

In summary, canvas apps provide flexibility and a drag-and-drop function, model-driven apps are more structured, and pages are designed for external resources without needing all customers or vendors to access your internal environment. Each app has pros and cons and depends on business requirements and audience. In general, if you need to create a simple app to capture data, you can create a canvas app. A model-driven app would be best if your business requirements required complex logic and workflows. Lastly, if you need to build a custom app for mostly external-facing users, Power Pages is the best option.

Now that you understand how to determine which type of Power Apps app to create, the next step is to explore the different types of data sources available. Let's dive into this next section.

Data sources and their different types

Power Apps can connect to hundreds of data sources. Here is a list of popular connectors: Dataverse, SharePoint, Business Central, SQL Server, and Excel. To see the complete list of connectors, visit the Microsoft website: `https://learn.microsoft.com/en-us/connectors/connector-reference/`.

Data performance is crucial when building apps and other solutions in Power Platform. Using the right data source can help ensure your app or solutions run smoothly and provide a good user experience. First, it is essential to understand that the data source types, Table or Tabular, mean two different things:

- A **table** is a collection of data stored in rows and columns – for example, in Excel, Dataverse, SharePoint, SQL, and Business Central.

- **Tabular** is action-based; the data isn't stored in tables. Instead, it is all driven by different activities. As an example for an Office 365 user, this can be used to add managers to approve timesheets or expenses. Microsoft Teams is another excellent example of an action-based connector.

Many types of data sources can be used in Power Apps, and Power Apps uses the connections to connect to external data, which can be used to create and manage data in your app. Power Platform has two types of data sources; these types are sometimes used interchangeably, but Table and Tabular mean two different things in Power Platform. Knowing about the other data sources and the different types can help you work more effectively with the entire Power Platform and extend Business Central's functionality.

In the next section, we'll discuss how to create and use components, which can be reused across different screens and save you time and effort in app-building.

Repeatable components

When I started to think about the topics for this chapter, I wanted to go over setting up components that could be reused, or at least talk about and share with you the things that I spent hours (okay, weeks) working on when I first started building apps. I love to be consistent; whether I am making the app for personal use, my 75-year-old dad, or clients, I like to have all the screens look the same and use color to make them stand out and pop for the end users.

I mentioned that most of my apps had been canvas apps, or at least for internal use. With that end in mind, I like to have a little fun with it, and the way I do so is not just to use the out-of-the-box controls – I change up the title colors and maybe sneak in a small logo. So, I planned to share repeatable components. However, I am completely freaking out about the Creator Kit. I can't imagine how many hours this would have saved me. In this section, we will look at what the Creator Kit has to offer. I am sure I won't be able to write about it all, but I encourage you to spend more time on the kit before creating more apps. There are a lot of blogs and YouTube videos on this subject. Here are three top ones I will walk you through so you can get some experience with the Creator Kit and its features.

Reference apps

You need to use best practices and dos and don'ts, plus the code in your app. You get basic inputs with **Auto Width Label**, **SearchBox**, **SpinButton**, Breadcrumb, Pickers, Progress Bar, Navigation, and more. Go to the solution app and open a reference app. It is recommended to make a copy of the Creator Kit since it is a managed solution, and even if you plan to use some of the components or template app, copy those as well.

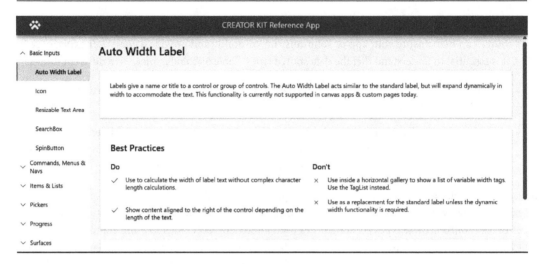

Figure 5.6 – Reference app

Once you find the reference you want to use, select {} **Code** to copy the code into your clipboard and paste it into your app.

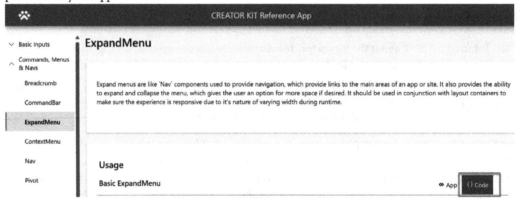

Figure 5.7 – Sample code

If you haven't installed the Creator Kit and reference apps, you can go to the Microsoft Learn website and open the overview of the Creator Kit's components (`https://learn.microsoft.com/en-us/power-platform/guidance/creator-kit/components`), and all the information on reference apps can be seen on this page. It gives you all the code components, when to use them, which apps can the components use, and the code sample. This is an easy way to get ideas and code to copy and paste into your app.

The reference app can be installed and used, or you can go to the Microsoft Learn website and copy the code to use in your app-making process.

Fluent Theme Designer

I pulled this out because we can use it to set up the primary, text, and background colors. I will use my cow app design. I asked my dad, when I started to fine-tune the app, what his favorite colors were, and he loves green. So, I looked up John Deere green and yellow; I didn't the yellow because I felt like it was too much in the app, but I loved the green. Using this theme designer, I could have plugged in the color numbers once and been done. When designing Power Apps, I often ask my clients or use their website color. I do feel like this adds a personal touch. If you have had the opportunity to play with Power Apps, you know that when you first design canvas apps and connect to Business Central or any other data source, the app will create three pages, which I plan to talk through in detail as we make a canvas app in this chapter. I always like to change the blue color in my app. Fluent Theme Designer does help you come up with a color palette; however, you still must copy it into your app at the start. It would be nice for it to be included in the theme and selectable; maybe this be an option in future releases. Either way, it is an excellent tool to have in your toolbox.

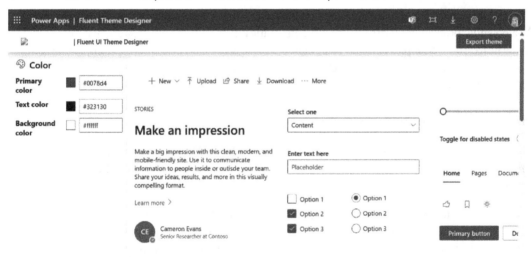

Figure 5.8 – Fluent Theme Designer

It is still fun to go in and play around with the different color themes and see how some of the control will look. It has an **Accessibility checker** function built in.

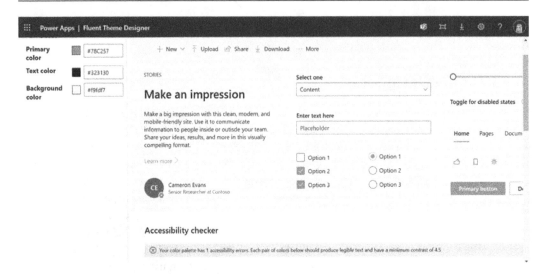

Figure 5.9 – Fluent Theme Designer – Using colors that cause an accessibility error

Accessibility checker is a tool that finds potential accessibility issues and explains why each might be a potential problem for users with specific disabilities. This is an essential feature that I hold close to my heart. Some examples of issues you might see are missing labels, missing captions, and missing helpful control settings. Each one will give you a severity level, how to fix it, and why it is important for you to fix the errors.

How to import components

This is the last section on the Creator Kit, and we will walk through the steps to get more components imported into your library to use. This process is completed inside Power Apps and will require you to go to Power Apps and start a new app:

1. Connect to Power Apps and create a new canvas app. Open Power Apps, select + **New App** | **Canvas**, then in the **App Name** field, enter Import Components, and in the **Format** field, select **Phone**. After that, select **Skip** and you'll see the welcome screen.

2. Select + from the left panel. The **Insert Popular components** panel will be visible, and you can select **Get more components** at the bottom of the options.

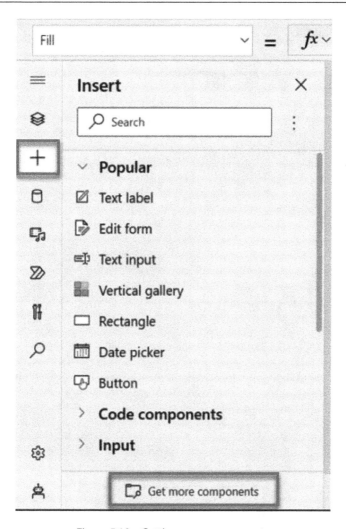

Figure 5.10 – Getting more components

3. The **Import components** screen will be visible on the right hand of the screen and available for you to select the components you want to import. You will notice that if you installed the Creator Kit, you'll see the option to select **Power CAT Component Library**; I selected all four options to make them available for future use.

Import components   ✕

Canvas   Code

Import components created by other people in your environment. After importing, components will show in the
Insert pane. Learn more

↻ Refresh   🔍 Search

⌄ **Power CAT Component Library**
   Last published on 1/16/23 by Shawn Sissenwein.   4 component(s)   **Select all**

○ **Dialog**

○ **Header**

○ **Panel**

○ **ExpandMenu**

Import   **Close**

Figure 5.11 – Import components

Once the components have been imported, they will be available under **Library components**:

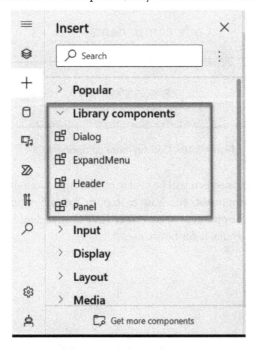

Figure 5.12 – Library components

In this section, we reviewed a few options in the Creator Kit. Using the Creator Kit's pre-built templates and components, you can create powerful and flexible apps with minimal effort, making it easier to build custom apps and save time. In the next section, we will create a canvas app connecting to Business Central contact data.

Creating a canvas app

Canvas apps offer a powerful and flexible way to create a custom phone application that will meet the sales department's requirements by providing an easy way to update and manage contacts. It will also always allow the business to keep a master list of references in Business Central so that it is a shared-access list within the organization. Let's get started with the process of creating a canvas app:

1. Open Power Apps, select + **Create**, On this screen, you will see the **Start from** options, and Business Central is in the **More data sources** section.

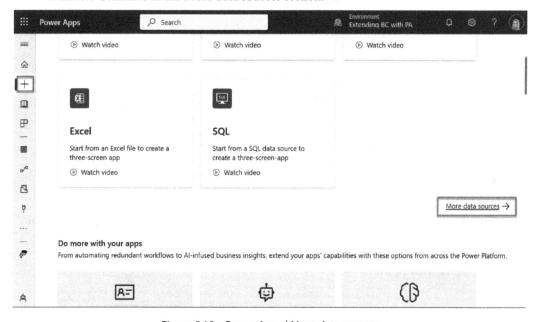

Figure 5.13 – Power Apps | More data sources

2. Select **Dynamics 365 Business Central**. If Business Central isn't on your list, select + **New connection** to connect to Business Central:

Figure 5.14 – Business Central connections

> **Tip**
> If you have connected to Business Central Power Apps, it will keep track of your past connections and you will see them in your **Connections** section. Another tip is that the user must have a Premium license if you see a diamond icon to the right of the connection. Before building or designing your solution, confirm which license your organization or client has; this has burned me in the past when I created an app, and when I went to publish it, my users couldn't view it due to the licensing requirement.

3. Once Power Apps has confirmed your login information, the next option is to select the company, **SANDBOX – CRONUS USA, Inc.**.

Figure 5.15 – Selecting the company

4. In the following list will be an option to select the table you want to connect the app to, so we'll use **contacts (v2.0)**, and then select **Connect**.

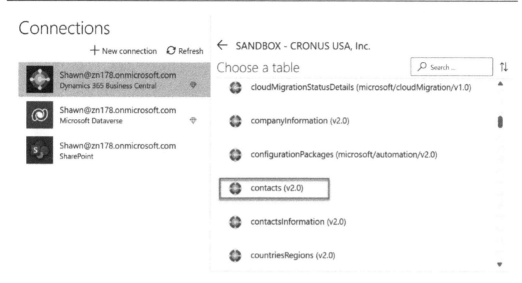

Figure 5.16 – Selecting contacts

5. This process will take a few minutes, and once it is completed, the **Welcome to Power Apps Studio** screen will appear. Select **Skip** unless you want to see a preview of the app; I usually jump right in and start my changes; you also have the option to **Don't show again** if you always skip the preview. I will leave it on for now. That way, if in the future I wanted to see the preview option, I could always show it.

6. The first thing I do before I start any changes is to save the app. Select the floppy disk icon in the top-right corner and save it as a contact app.

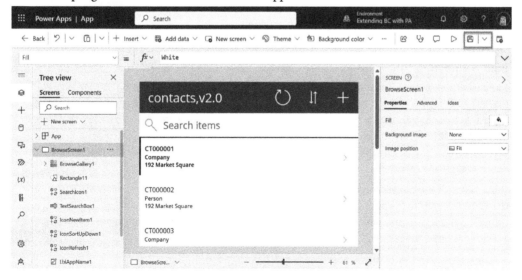

Figure 5.17 – Contact app

Power Apps creates three screens when you use this option to make the app. You get a browse screen, a detail screen, and an edit screen.

7.   Right-click on each of the screens to rename them. Rename all three screens as follows:

- In the **Browse screen name** field, add Home Page

- In the **Detail screen name** field, add View Contact Details

- In the **Edit screen name** field, add Edit Contact Details

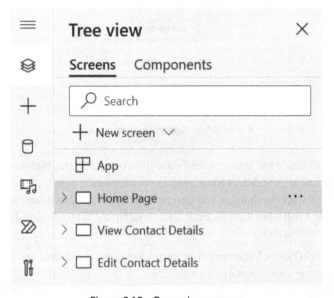

Figure 5.18 – Renaming screens

Important note

Renaming the screens is essential. There are a couple of reasons for renaming the screens; the first is accessibility – if you have people who use screen readers, it will read the name of the screen. For example, change it to Contact Home Screen instead of Screen 1. Also, as you have lots of screens in your app, it helps you know what screen to call on when setting up Fx code formulas. Finally, when you need to go back and make changes to the screens, it keeps everything organized.

Renaming all the controls consistently is just as crucial as renaming your screens. Taking the time to rename them at the beginning of the design will help ensure your app is more understandable, maintainable, and customizable for you and other team members.

8. Use the following renaming control cheat sheet to rename all the controls; this is just a guide I like to use.

Control Name	Abbreviation
button	btn
camera control	cam
canvas	can
card	crd
collection	col
combo box	cmb
dates	dte
dropdown	drp
form	frm
gallery	gal
group	grp
header page shape	hdr
html text	htm
icon	ico
image	img
label	lbl
page section shape	sec
shapes (rectangle, circle, and so on)	shp
table data	tbl
text input	shp
timer	tim

Figure 5.19 – Renaming control cheat sheet

9. Since we used a wizard to create the app, we will want to change a few fields. The wizard guessed what fields to add to the screen, and we want different fields displayed on the home screen. I renamed `BrowseGallery1` to `galContact` using the control cheat sheet as my guide.

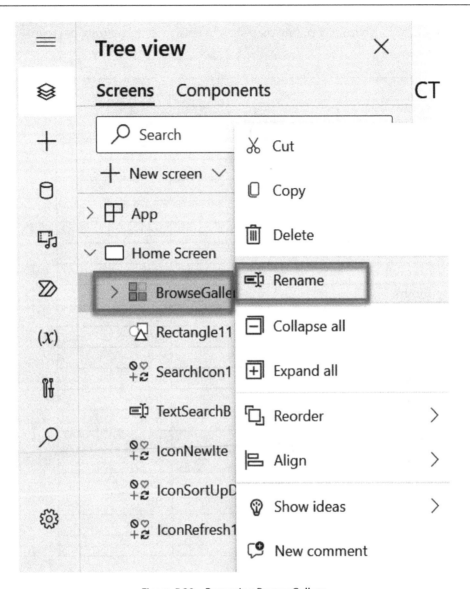

Figure 5.20 – Renaming BrowseGallery

10. Highlight **galContact** on the tree view and the right pane. Select **Edit**, and change the **Body1** field to **Email**, the **Subtitle1** field to **Company Name**, and the **Title1** field to **Search Name**.

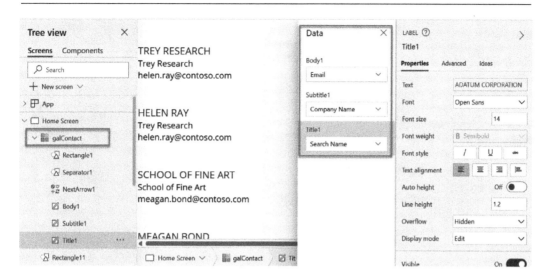

Figure 5.21 – Updating galContact

11. We will add different fields to the **View Contact Details** screen. I renamed `DetailsForm1` to `frmContactDetails`. When you select the form, highlight it in **Tree view** so that the full form is highlighted, and you can see the display properties on the right panel.

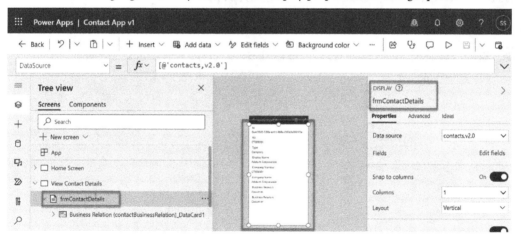

Figure 5.22 – Form properties

12. Select **Edit fields** on the right panel to adjust the fields on **frmContactDetails**. Add the following areas to the screen: **No.**, **Display Name**, **Company Number**, **Company Name**, **Email**, **Mobile Phone No.**, **Address Line 1**, **City**, **State**, and **Zip Code**.

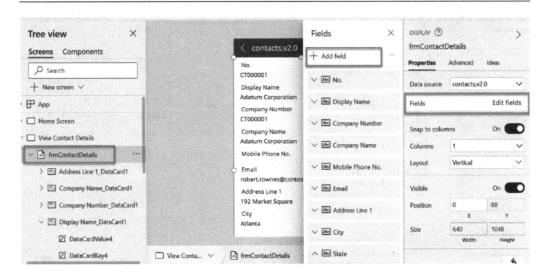

Figure 5.23 – Adding fields to the contact details screen

In the following section, let's look at customizing fields, labels, and descriptions.

Customizing fields, labels, and descriptions

Follow these steps to modify fields, labels, and descriptions:

1. Before changing any fields, you must unlock the label, and each field must be opened. To unlock the field, highlight the label and, from the ellipsis, select **Unlock**:

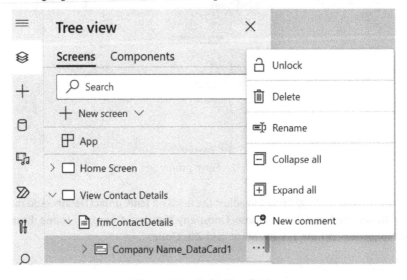

Figure 5.24 – Unlocking fields

2.   I also like highlighting the labels on the screen so it stands out to the user that it is a label and not an input field. I play around with many colors; I will consider the company color or people's favorite colors. Keep in mind color-blind individuals. For each label on the screen, highlight it using a visual background color; to do this in the label properties, select the **Fill** properties and enter the RGBA number for the color you want the labels. If you use the panel on the right, select the color using a color screen, which is useful when you first start.

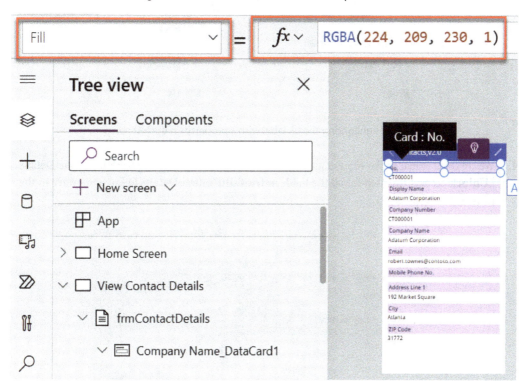

Figure 5.25 – Highlighting the fill label a different color

3.   If you use the panel on the right, select the color using a color screen, which is useful when you first start and gives you the option to use the color wheel to pick a color palette:

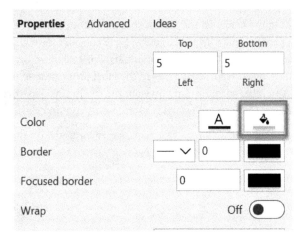

Figure 5.26 – Highlighting the fill label with a property on the left panel

4.   We are going to make a few more adjustments: select **Edit Contact Screen | frmEditContactDetails | Unlock**. Repeat this step for all the fields in **frmEditContactDetails** before you move to the next step.

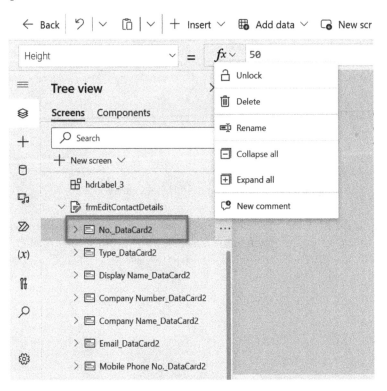

Figure 5.27 – Unlocking the fields on the frmEditContactDetails form

5. Select **Border radius**. To round the fields, enter 25 – this gives you a more rounded edge. Highlight each of the fields and repeat this step:

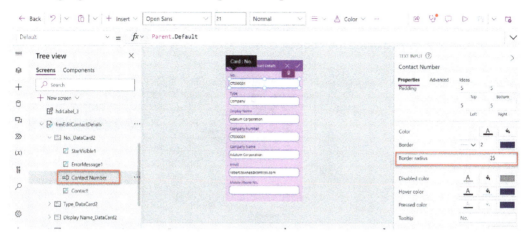

Figure 5.28 – Border radius property

6. Change the **Edit Contact Details** screen to a light color. Select the form under **Edit Contact Details**. I renamed my form `frmEditContactDetails`. Once you have it highlighted and it is unlocked, select the **Fill** properties and enter RGBA (211, 180, 237, 1). As you can see, I used a purple theme, but feel free to use any color you would like to have as your theme for the canvas app.

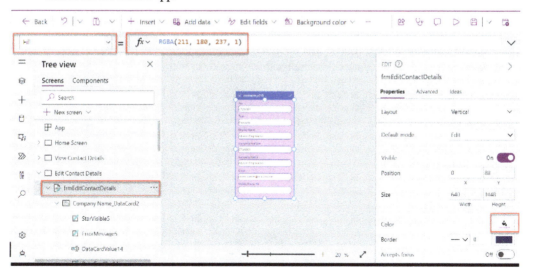

Figure 5.29 – Fill property for form control

7. Now, we'll create a new header component. We will walk through how to create a new component, and I use this one for the headers on all my screens in the app. In **Tree view**, select **Components | + New component | + New custom property** in the right-side panel, change **Display name** to hdrText, and leave the rest of the default values. Rename the component hdrLabel in accordance with the naming conventions.

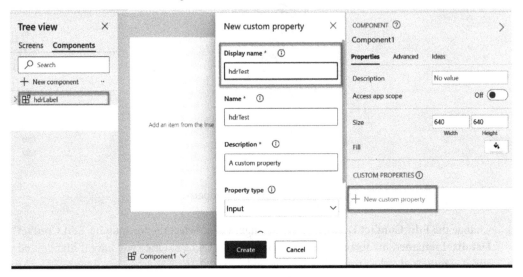

Figure 5.30 – New header component

8. The sizing needs to match the headers on the screen. Enter the **Size** value by selecting the property from the right-hand pane and key in 640 for the width and 88 for the height. We want to have a fill color; select the **Fill** property, and enter in RGBA (109, 49, 162, 1), and since we are using a dark color, change the text color to white.

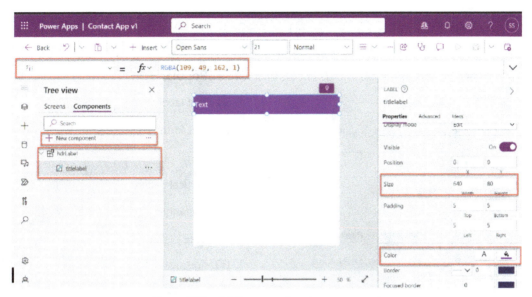

Figure 5.31 – Adding a new header component

9. In the **fx** formula bar, under the **Text** property, we need to link **hdrLabel** to **hdrText**; this will allow us to change the title on each screen of the app. For the **fx** code, start typing hdr and when you see **hdrLabel**, always select the option from the drop-down list. This will ensure that the syntax is always correct. The formula bar should read **hdrLabel.hdrText**:

Figure 5.32 – Text property

10. Using the new component, select **Home Screen**, and click on + **Insert** so that the new component we just created will be an option. Then, select **hdrLabel**, and add **hdrLabel** to all screens.

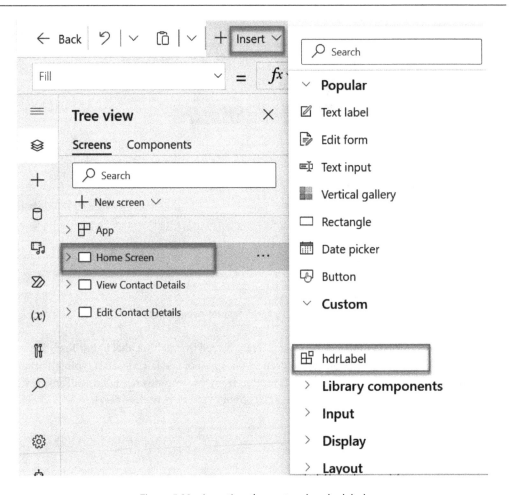

Figure 5.33 – Inserting the custom header label

11. Next, we must show the icons behind the new components. To bring them to the front, highlight each icon, and select **Eclipse | Reorder |Bring to front**. Complete this task for all the icons on each of the screens. On **Home Screen** we have four icons: Refresh, New Item, Sort Up, and Sort Down. On the **View Contact Details** screen, we have two icons: **Delete** and **Edit**. On the **Edit Contact Details** screen, we have two icons: **Accept** and **Cancel**.

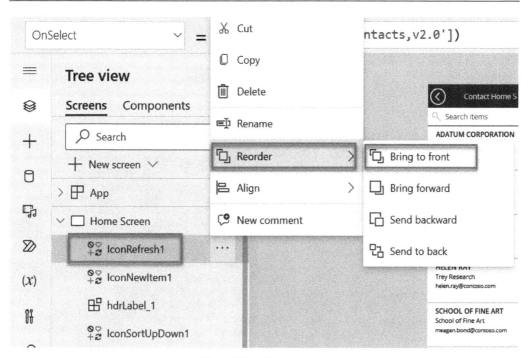

Figure 5.34 – Screen icons

12. When we have multiple screens in the app, the user will need a way to return to the previous screen. To add icons or additional information to **hdrLabel**, select **Components | hdrLabel | + Insert** and add a **Back arrow** option; this will allow the user to go back to each of the screens. Line it up with the top left corner; change the icon's color. Once you add it to the component, it will update everywhere you have it in the app.

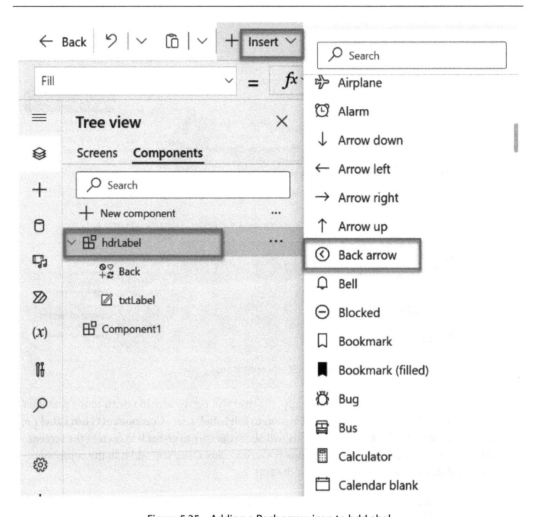

Figure 5.35 – Adding a Back arrow icon to hdrLabel

13. In the top right, select the *stethoscope* to check for any app errors; reviewing all the messages and fixing them before you publish the app is always a good idea. You will also notice that if you didn't update **AccessibleLabel** earlier, you will get a warning to fix it.

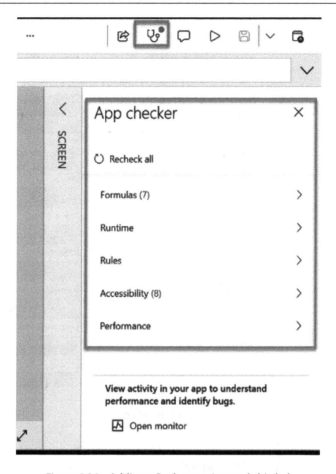

Figure 5.36 – Adding a Back arrow icon to hdrLabel

14. The system will take you right to the property; in the **fx** formula, add the name of the label in double-quotes. Remember that **AccessibleLabel** will be read if the user uses a screen reader.

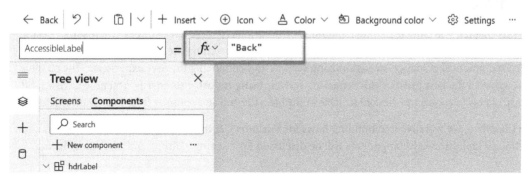

Figure 5.37 – Updating the Back arrow label

15. Preview and publish the app:

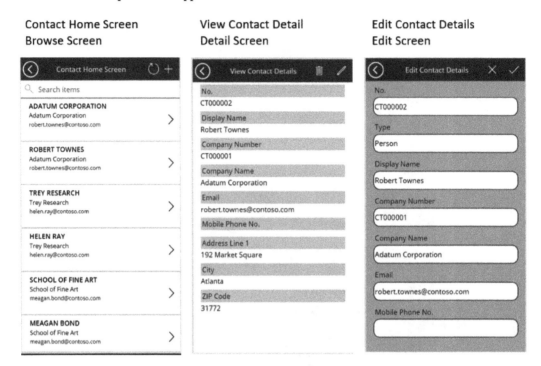

Figure 5.38 – Contact app

Congratulations on building your first canvas app. If this isn't your first, I hope you learned a few tips and tricks. Remember to have a little fun with the layout, and if you are not restricted to a color theme, play around with different colors. I also like to consider whether someone is colorblind and what colors to use; I believe that is why you see many blue apps and logos.

Summary

In this chapter, you gained an understanding of the various types of data sources, Microsoft's Creator Kit, and creating repeatable components. The chapter focused on creating a canvas app, and you received practical guidance on customizing screens and enhancing the user experience. The chapter also covered the best practices for renaming screens using industry standards. You now have a solid grasp of how to connect to the contact table in Business Central and optimize it for maximum efficiency.

In *Chapter 6*, we will dive into building flows for Business Central and learn about flow triggers and actions. Finally, the key components will be discussed for creating, editing, and managing flows.

Further reading

- Creator Kit overview – Microsoft Learn: `https://learn.microsoft.com/en-us/power-platform/guidance/creator-kit/overview`

- Power Apps: `https://powerapps.microsoft.com/en-us/`

- Power Apps Community: `https://powerusers.microsoft.com/t5/Power-Apps-Community/ct-p/PowerApps1`

- Power Apps accessibility standards and guidelines: `https://pahandsonlab.blob.core.windows.net/documents/Power%20Apps%20Accessibility%20Standards%20and%20Guidelines.pdf`

- Controls and properties in canvas apps: `https://learn.microsoft.com/en-us/power-apps/maker/canvas-apps/reference-properties`

- Understanding delegation in canvas apps: `https://learn.microsoft.com/en-us/power-apps/maker/canvas-apps/delegation-overview`

I get many ideas and much inspiration from YouTube; I usually will go through the exercises along with the person presenting. One of my best practices is to do research to see whether another person has developed an app or layout that you are trying to create so that you don't have to reinvent the wheel. I like to say don't do what I did and make a cow app from scratch. When I started the app, I did not even look to see what was available; I am glad I did that because I learned so much, but there is always an easier way.

6

Building Flows for Business Central

In this chapter, we will explore Power Automate and its potential to transform business processes with Business Central. We will dig into how you can utilize Power Automate to create solutions that will help automate processes in your business. The goal of this chapter will be to equip you with the knowledge and insights to be able to take advantage of its capabilities.

In this chapter, we're going to cover the following main topics:

- Well-documented business process flows
- Triggers and actions
- Advanced Power Automate setup and best practices

Technical requirements

You can set up automated workflows by referring to **Business Central | Microsoft Learn**: `https://learn.microsoft.com/en-us/dynamics365/business-central/dev-itpro/powerplatform/automate-workflows?tabs=blank`.

Well-documented business process flows

Shawn and I have worked in IT as end users and consultants for over 20 years, and, if there is one thing we have learned, it's that a good process flow is even more important when you are trying to automate a process. If a company has a business process that is not well documented and all over the place, the chance of automating this process is not good. Let's take the example of a scenario in which five different people in a company create five different items by following five different processes. If we take the preceding example and plot it in a flow chart, the work process flow will look as shown in *Figure 6.1*.

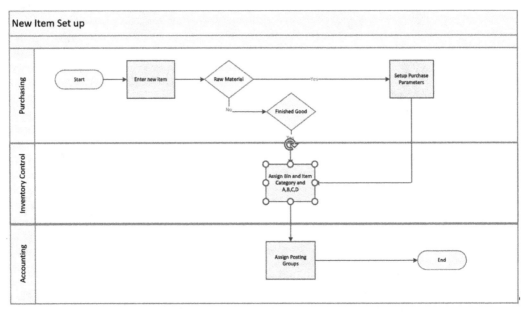

Figure 6.1 – New item setup process flow

When it comes to documenting process flows here are some key things to keep in mind:

- **Start with a clear objective**: Make sure you can clearly define the objective or purpose of the process. This will help you focus on the essential steps and ensure that the documentation accurately reflects the intended outcome.

- **Understand the existing business process**: Analyze the current workflows, procedures, and activities for the process. As you do this, a lot of the time, the inefficiency and areas for improvement will become apparent to you.

- **Break down the process into smaller more manageable steps**: Begin with a high-level overview and gradually drill down into more detailed subprocesses or tasks. Use concise descriptions and clearly identify each step.

- **Include decision points and any conditional logic**: Indicate the decision points in your process flows and document the criteria that determine the course of action to be followed. This is often a place where we discover some eye-opening things. The reason for this is that people commonly make decisions based on knowledge that only they have.

- **KISS – Keep it simple, stupid**: Simple is better, especially if we are trying to automate things. If a process has evolved over time, we as people are good at overcomplicating things that don't need to be complicated.

- **Review and revise the process a couple of times**: We also find that it's easy to forget part of a process because you do it so automatically. Make sure you review and revise a couple of times.

- **Use flow charts or a visual representation of the process**: For me, I find it is easier to identify gaps when looking at a visual representation – if there are many steps in the process, it will highlight the inefficiency in the process.

- **Maintain up-to-date versions of your processes**: Processes will evolve over time and it's important to review them on a regular basis.

> Tip
>
> To learn more about Visio, go to https://support.microsoft.com/en-us/visio.

Triggers and actions for Power Automate

Power Automate offers a lot of different options for creating flows and automating business processes. There are a couple of things to talk about as we dive into this topic in more depth. There are three ways to create flows in Power Automate. In the screenshot in *Figure 6.2*, you can see two of the choices when you select the **Create** menu from your Power Automate home page.

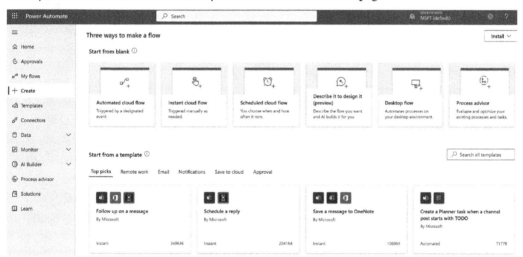

Figure 6.2 – Choices when you select + Create from the Power Automate Menu

Let's look at the three ways to create flows:

- **Start from blank**: If you start from blank, there are six choices on how to start from there. You can start with an automated cloud flow, an instant cloud flow, or a scheduled cloud flow; describe it; design it; implement a desktop flow; or use the process advisor.

- **Start from a template**: There are hundreds of different templates that you can start with and then adjust to your needs. We would encourage you to use these as you start your journey. Using these is a wonderful way to make sure you understand the concepts.

- **Start from a connector**: This will allow you to choose the connector that you want to start with first and then walk you through selecting the trigger to start the flow.

There are many important concepts to keep in mind when building flows with Power Automate. One of these is the concept of **Triggers** and **Actions**. The following are things to keep in mind regarding Triggers and Actions:

- Every flow is made up of a trigger and one or more Actions.

- Triggers are the starting action for a flow. This can be a new vendor being created, a customer record being edited, or someone requesting approval in Business Central.

- When a trigger is invoked, Actions will be what you want to happen. For example, when a new vendor is created in Business Central (trigger), then I would like a message posted in Teams (action).

While this is a high-level view, these two things are going to allow you to create more complex flows as you learn more. Let us dig in a little more about Triggers.

> Tip
> Since Triggers are the foundation of a flow, one of the most important things you need to make sure of is that you pick the right trigger. Nothing is worse than starting your flow with the wrong trigger and then having to go back and fix it or having to just start over.

When it comes to selecting the correct Triggers, you have a few options to consider.

- **Instant/manual Triggers** give you the ability to manually start a flow by simply tapping a button on your mobile device. They offer immediate control and are great for initiating flows on demand.

- **Scheduled Triggers** are perfect for running flows at specific times and frequencies. For example, you can use them to automatically send out a weekly project report without any manual intervention.

- **Automated Triggers** are designed to perform tasks automatically based on external events. For instance, you can set up a trigger to detect a change to a customer record in Business Central and then have it send you an email notification in response. This can be handy for keeping up with important updates or interactions with your customer records.

When you are building your flows, you can edit a trigger for an existing flow or customize Triggers by adding conditions. These two things tend to lend a lot of flexibility to the solutions you can build. Adding a trigger to an existing flow is something you may do, especially if you're starting with a template. One example of this may be if you want to build a flow to notify you when a vendor record in Business Central is blocked. This template doesn't currently exist, but there is a template named Block the selected Customer in Dynamics 365 Business Central. You will be able to choose this and see how it works for the customer and then follow it and edit it for a vendor record. We could also customize this by adding an action that also sends a message in Teams when someone does this. We will examine how to do this in the next exercise, and you will gain experience firsthand of creating a notification when a new vendor is created in Business Central.

Exercise – creating a flow for a new vendor

K&S Solutions needs to know when someone blocks a vendor. It would like to be notified by email and then want the same information posted in a Teams channel. Also, it would be nice if the Power Automate functionality to block the vendor could be run from the Vendor Card in Business Central. One option that we can do to solve this is to look for a template in Power Automate. To do this, open Power Automate and then select **Templates**. When we search through the options, there, we see one for Blocked Customers, but not Blocked Vendors. Since customers are similar to vendors but just in different tables, it makes sense to start there and modify it for a vendor. The other appeal of this template is it already has the notification for an email in it. Also, in this template, there is a setup of an instant flow using the manual trigger **"For a selected record (V3),"** which means it will show up in the Automate menu in Business Central from the Customer Record. In theory, this would give us a 75% head start on what we needed to build. Let's begin creating that flow for a new vendor:

1. Open Power Automate, select **Template** from the menu, and type `Business Central` into the search bar. Select the **Block the select customer in Dynamics 365 Business Central** template. See *Figure 6.3*.

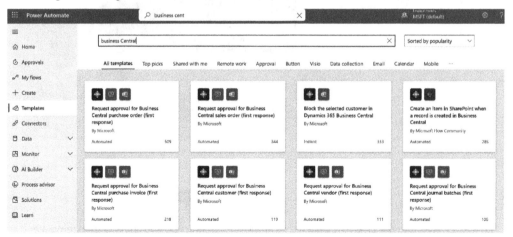

Figure 6.3 – Selecting Block the selected customer in Dynamics 365 Business Central

2. The template window will open. Select **Continue**.

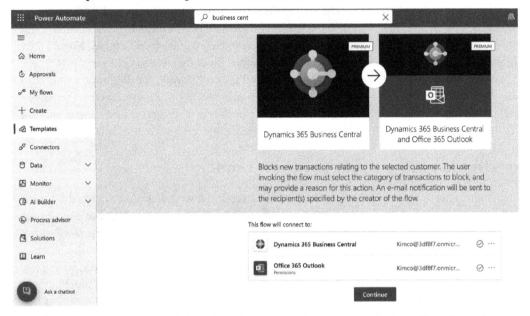

Figure 6.4 – Selecting the Block the selected customer in Dynamics 365 Business Central template

3. Select your email on the next screen and select + **Create**.

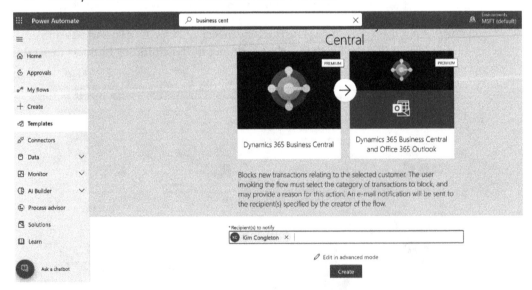

Figure 6.5 – Selecting the Block the selected customer in Dynamics 365 Business Central template

4. Select **Edit** on the next screen.

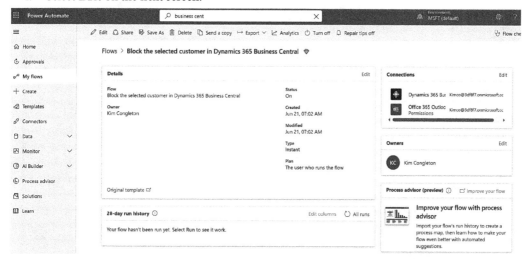

Figure 6.6 – Main page for the Block selected customer in Dynamics 365 Business Central flow

5. Click on the word **customer** in the name at the top for the flow. Delete this and replace it with **vendor**. Click on the **For a selected record (V3)** trigger to edit it.

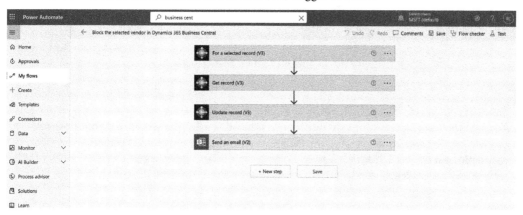

Figure 6.7 – Power Automate window for editing the flow

6. Select **Environment name** and **Company name** for your environment and company. Under **Page or table**, update the value to TABLE23 (vendor) instead of **TABLE18** (customer). Under **Drop-down list of options**, change **Shipment** to **Receive**.

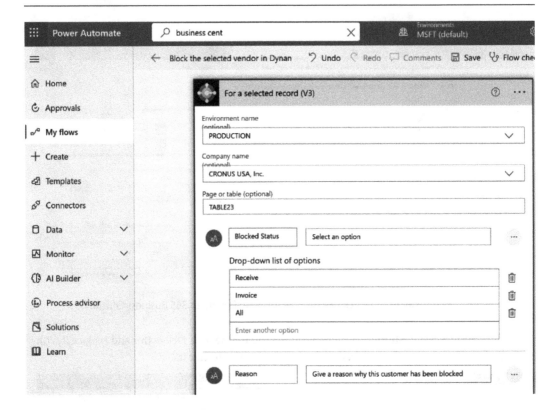

Figure 6.8 – Editing an existing trigger in a flow

Environment variables

You are able to use variables for your environments and this will allow you to build one flow and point it to either your sandbox or your production environment. To do that, you can follow the instructions at this URL from Microsoft: `https://learn.microsoft.com/en-us/power-apps/maker/data-platform/environmentvariables`.

7.   Select **Get record (V3)** and change **Table name** from **customers** to `vendors`.

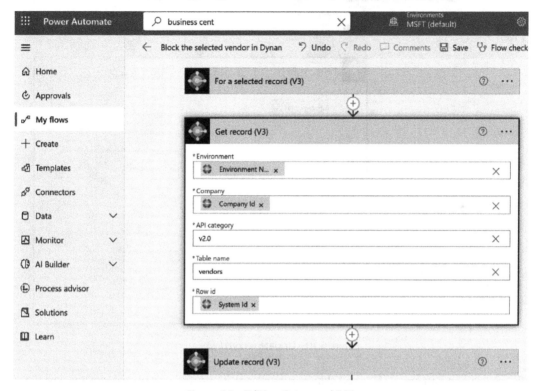

Figure 6.9 – Editing Get record (V3)

8.   Select **Update record (V3)** and change **Table name** from **customers** to `vendors`.

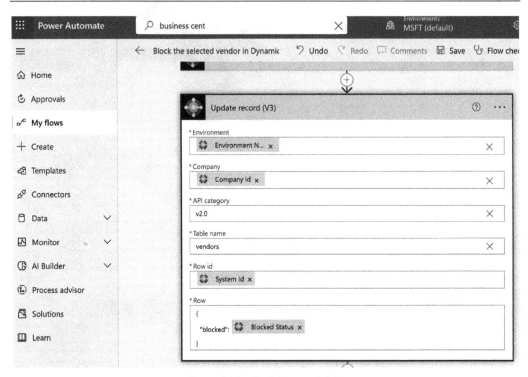

Figure 6.10 – Update record (V3)

9. Select **Send an email (V2)** and change `customer` to `vendor` in the subject line and the body of the email.

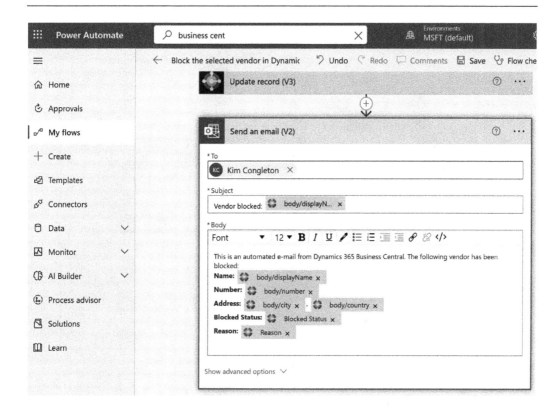

Figure 6.11 – Send an email (V2)

10. Select + above the **Send an email** action and select **Add a parallel branch**:

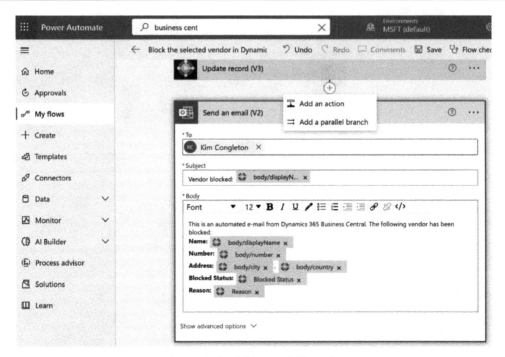

Figure 6.12 – Add a parallel branch

11. Search for Teams and then select **Post message in a chat or channel**.

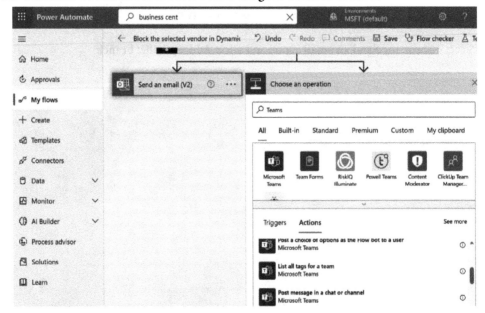

Figure 6.13 – Searching for Teams and selecting Post message in a chat or channel

12. Select the dropdown for **Post in** and select **Channel.**

Figure 6.14 – Selecting the channel to post the message in

13. Select the respective **Team** and **Channel** from the dropdowns.

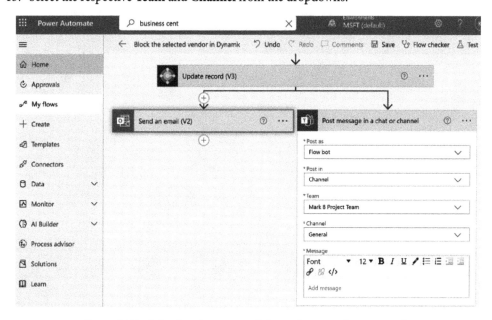

Figure 6.15 – Selecting the team and channel to post the message in

14. Click the **Send an email (V2)** action to expand the window. Copy the text in the body of the email and paste it into the body for the Teams message.

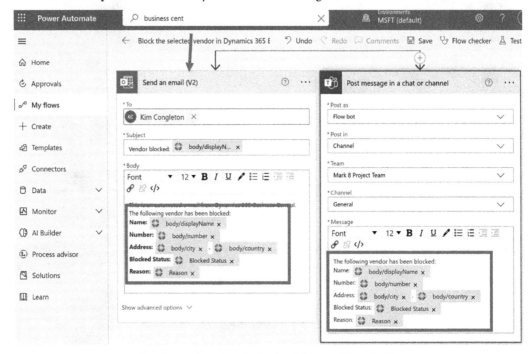

Figure 6.16 – Copying and pasting the body of the email into the Teams message

15. Select **Save** and then select **Flow checker** to check the flow.

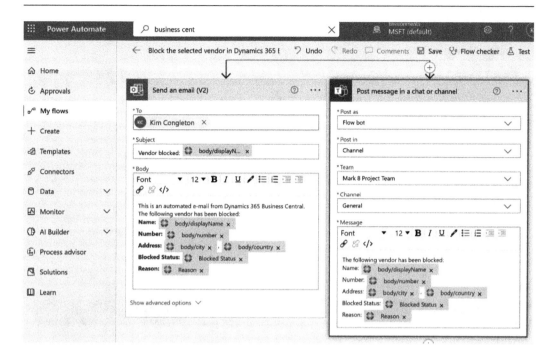

Figure 6.17 – Saving the flow and running Flow checker

16. After **Flow checker** runs, make sure there are no errors.

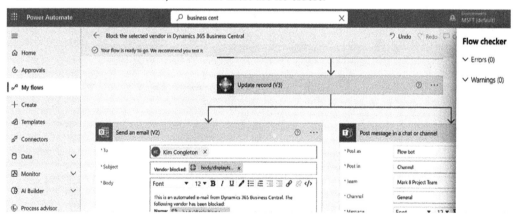

Figure 6.18 – Results of Flow checker

17. To test this flow, we will have to open Business Central. Open Business Central and then select **Vendors**.

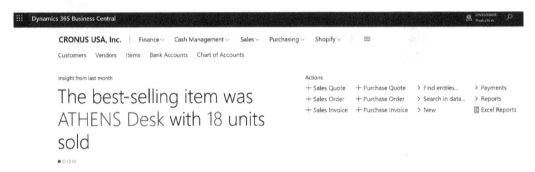

Figure 6.19 – Opening Business Central and selecting Vendors

18. From the **Vendors** list, select a vendor and go into the record.

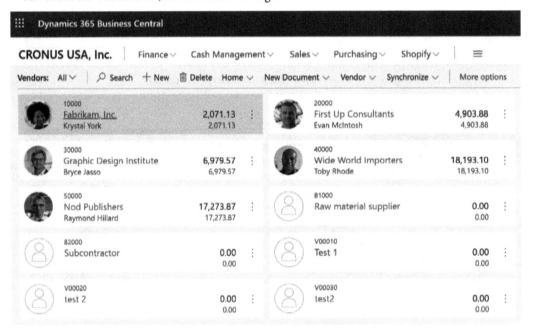

Figure 6.20 – Select a vendor record to open it

19. Select **Automate** and you'll see the flow list in the dropdown. Select **Block the selected vendor in Dynamics 365 Business Central**.

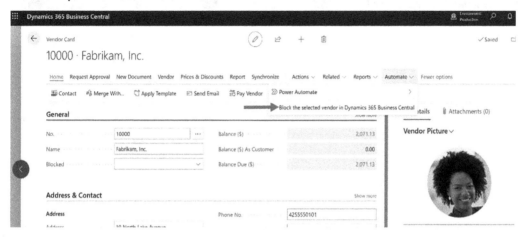

Figure 6.21 – Selecting Automate and then selecting the correct flow

20. A window will open to run the flow. Select **Continue**.

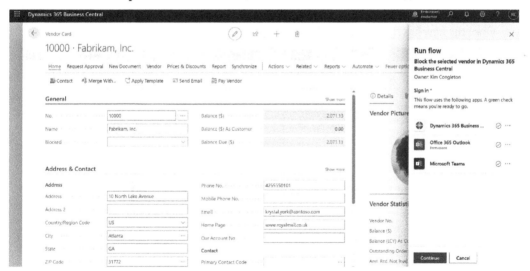

Figure 6.22 – Run flow window that shows the connections that will be made

21. Select **Blocked Status**. Fill in **Reason** and select **Run flow**.

Figure 6.23 – Entering the values for Run flow and then running it

22. Once the flow has run properly, select **Done**.

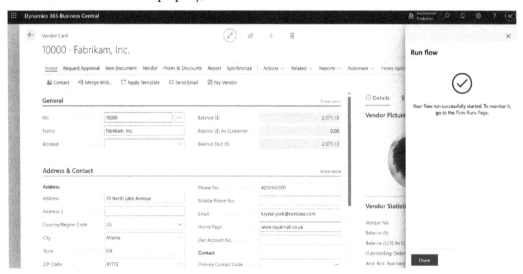

Figure 6.24 – Verifying the flow ran properly and selecting Done

23. Open Outlook and verify that you received an email.

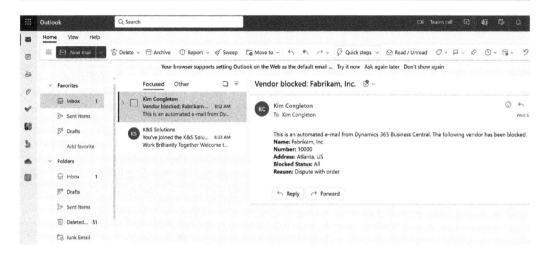

Figure 6.25 – Verifying that you received an email

24. Open Teams and verify a message was posted in Teams in the channel you selected.

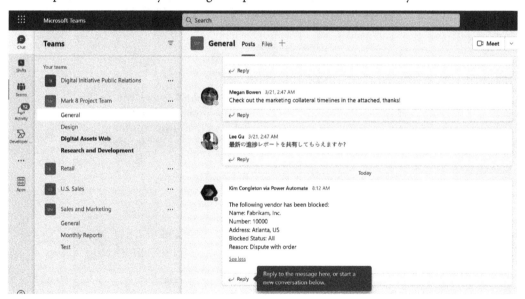

Figure 6.26 – Verify the message for the blocked vendor in Teams

As you can see, it is easy to take an existing template and edit the Triggers and Actions and create a new flow. Whenever you can start with a template, I would recommend doing that. I have learned a great deal by reviewing all the existing steps in the template and seeing how a proper flow is created. Then, once you see how to build different parts of a flow, you'll find it easier when you start building your own. It is also easy to start from scratch with flows to create solutions. Let's look at how you could create a flow from scratch.

Building a Power Automate flow from scratch

For our next flow, we'll use the example of creating a notification for a new vendor. For example, we have a lot of clients that are not public companies, but they get audited once a year and have some specific requirements around tracking changes to Vendors. It's one of the key places where auditors want to see what controls you have in place to prevent theft from a company. One example of this is the need to know when an address change happens within a vendor record. Let's look at building this from scratch and see how easy it is. To create a Power Automate functionality that will notify us when a vendor changes, we would take the following steps. First, we would check to see whether there was already a template for the solution we needed. In this case, we are going to assume there is none. The next thing we would do is to figure out what the trigger that we want to start with is and what our Actions are. In the example shown in *Figure 6.27*, you can see a rough sketch of my Power Automate flow.

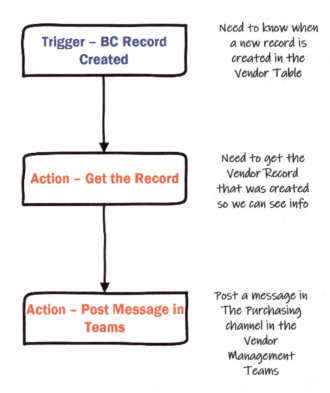

Figure 6.27 – Rough draft of the flow design for new vendor notification

Let's get into creating the flow through Power Automate. Follow these steps to create your flow:

1.   Open Power Automate and select + **Create**.

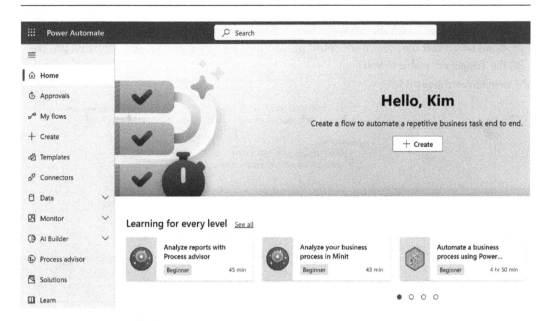

Figure 6.28 – Creating a new flow

2.   Select **Automated cloud flow**.

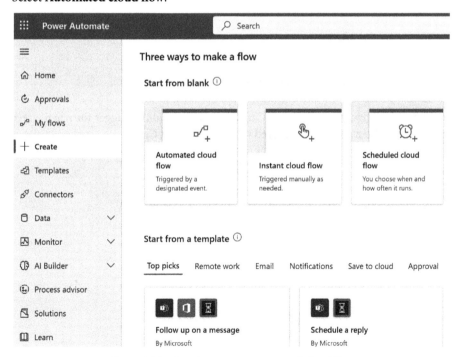

Figure 6.29 – Creating a new automated cloud flow

3. The window will open the wizard, which will walk you through setting up your automated cloud flow. Enter the name under **Flow name**. Then, search for Business Central to see the Triggers available to you.

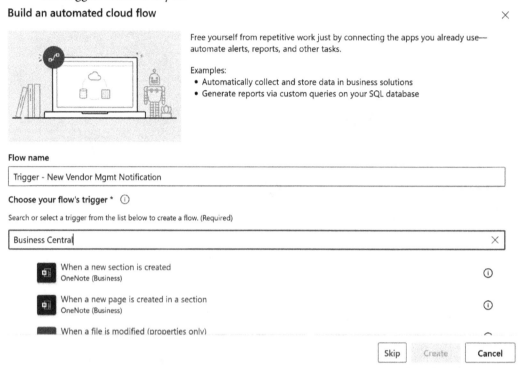

Build an automated cloud flow   ✕

Free yourself from repetitive work just by connecting the apps you already use—automate alerts, reports, and other tasks.

Examples:
- Automatically collect and store data in business solutions
- Generate reports via custom queries on your SQL database

Flow name

Trigger - New Vendor Mgmt Notification

Choose your flow's trigger * ⓘ

Search or select a trigger from the list below to create a flow. (Required)

Business Central   ✕

When a new section is created
OneNote (Business)   ⓘ

When a new page is created in a section
OneNote (Business)   ⓘ

When a file is modified (properties only)

Skip   Create   Cancel

Figure 6.30 – Building an automated cloud flow

4. Scroll down the Triggers for Business Central until you find the trigger for when a record is created. Select **When a record is created (V3)**. Then, select **Create**.

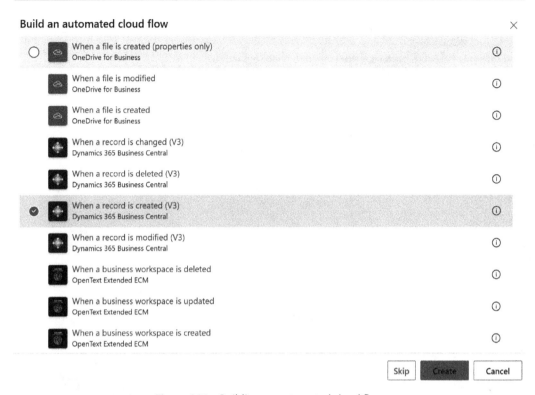

Figure 6.31 – Building an automated cloud flow

5.   Fill in the information for your trigger like in the screenshot in *Figure 6.32* and select **+ New step**.

Figure 6.32 – Filling in the information for the trigger

6.   Search for `Business Central` and select it.

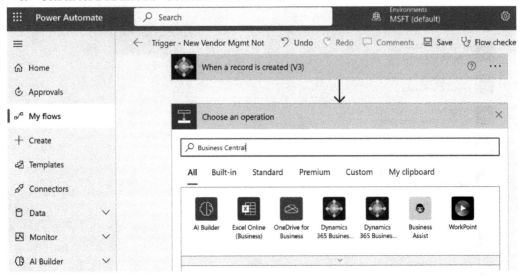

Figure 6.33 – Searching for Business Central

7.   Select **Get record (V3)**.

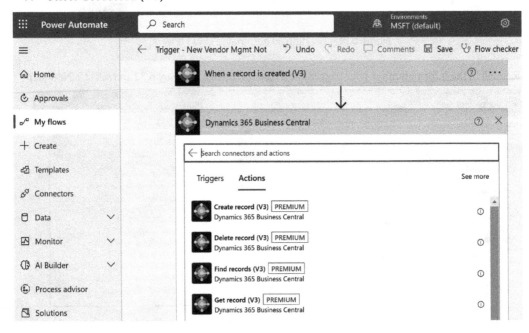

Figure 6.34 – Select Get record (V3) for Business Central

8. Fill in the information for the action as follows and select + **New step**.

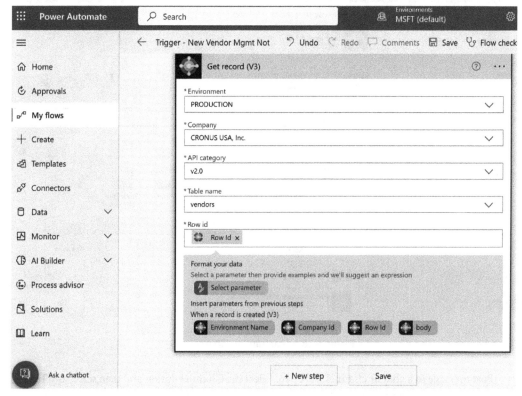

Figure 6.35 – Filling in the information for Get record (V3) for Business Central

9. Search for Teams and select **Post message in a chat or channel**.

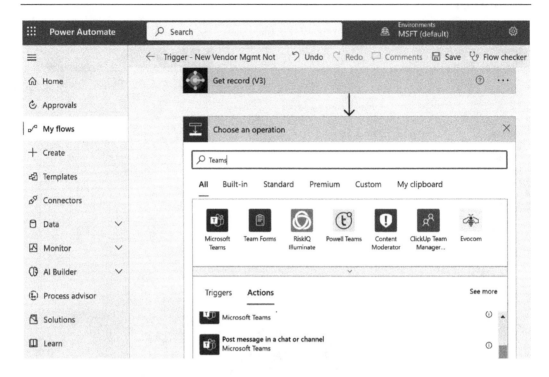

Figure 6.36 – Searching for Teams

10. **Post message in a chat or channel** will open. Select the **Channel** option and then select any **Team** you would like to post it in. I added a **Purchasing** channel to my teams. Once you select a team, you will have to select a channel in that team. Next, insert the text you would like to post as your message and select the **No.** and **Display Name** information to show in the message. Select **Save**.

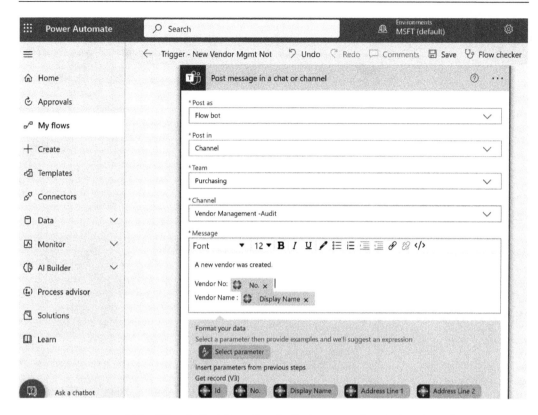

Figure 6.37 – Filling in the information for Post message in a chat or channel

11. Select **Flow checker**.

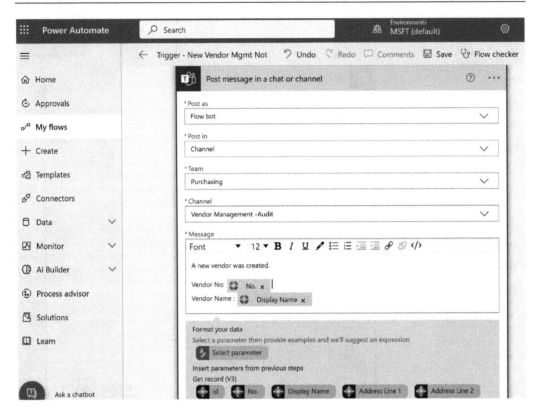

Figure 6.38 – Selecting Flow checker to check your flow for errors

12. Verify that there are no errors or warnings in **Flow checker** and close the **Flow checker** screen.

Figure 6.39 – Verifying there are no warnings or errors in Flow checker

13. Select **Test** to manually test the flow.

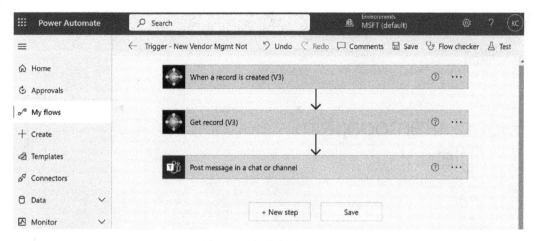

Figure 6.40 – Selecting Test

14. Select **Manually** and **Test**.

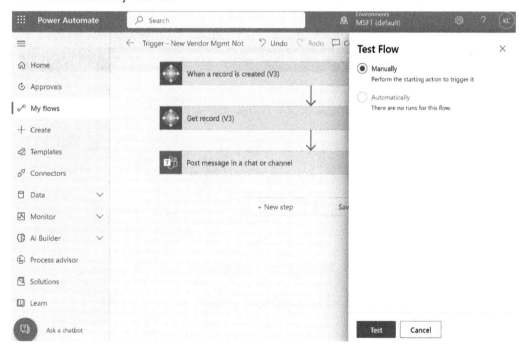

Figure 6.41 – Selecting Manually and Test to test your flow

15. Open Business Central and select **Vendors**.

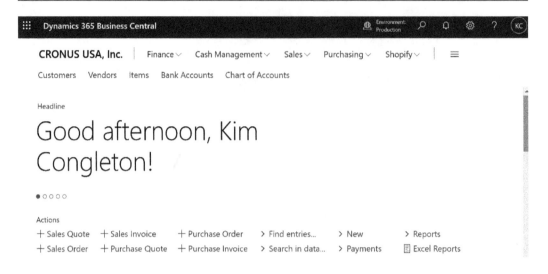

Figure 6.42 – Opening Business Central and then selecting Vendors

16. Select **+ New** from the **Vendors** list.

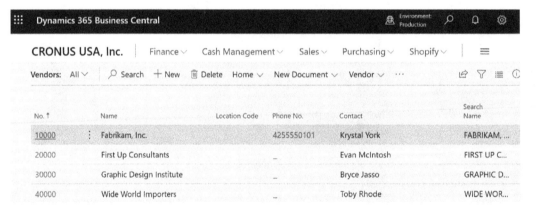

Figure 6.43 – Selecting New to create a new vendor

17. Enter the **Name** and **Address** information for the new vendor.

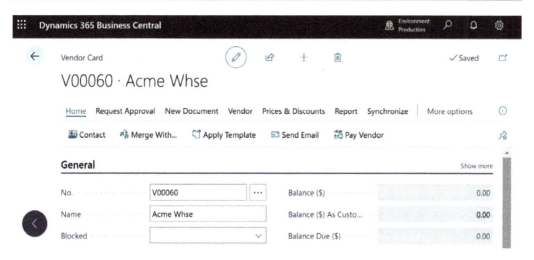

Figure 6.44 – Entering a name and address for the new vendor

18. Open Teams and verify that your message is in Teams.

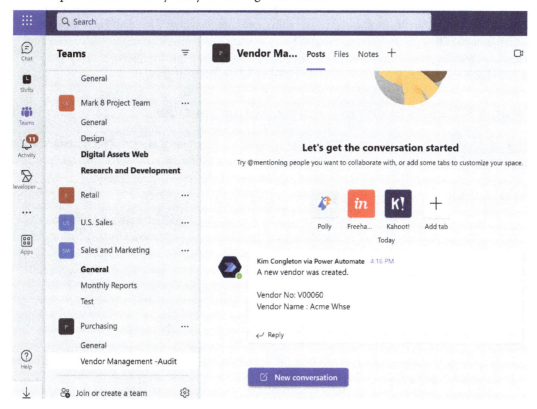

Figure 6.45 – Opening Teams and verifying your notification of the new vendor

19. Verify that your flow ran successfully in Power Automate:

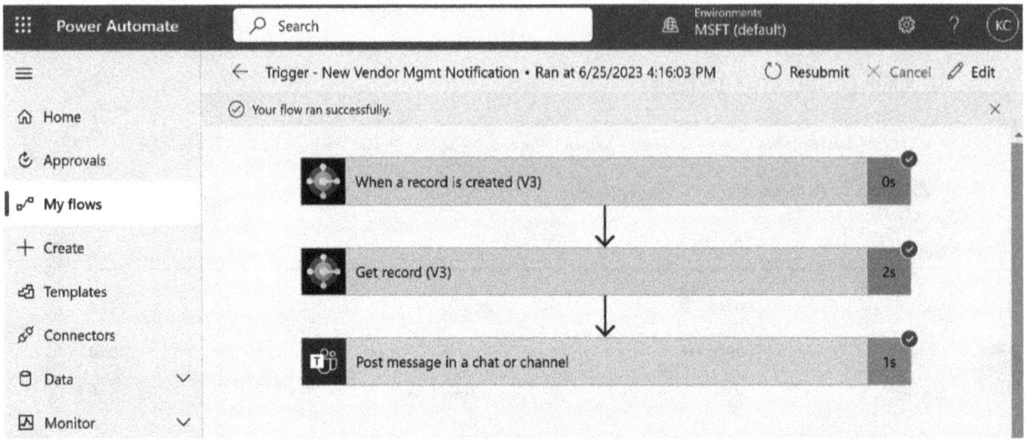

Figure 6.46 – Verifying the flow ran successfully

We can see from the previous example how easy it is to create a flow from scratch. This was a simple example, but you can see how you could easily build more complex flows if needed. There are several Actions and parallel branches you can use to build a much more robust solution. We've seen two examples of building Power Automate flows, one from a template and one from scratch, using Triggers related to records. Let's look at one of the other starting places for your flow.

Using a Business Event in a Power Automate flow

Microsoft provides a set of business events that we can access through the Business Central Connector. These are events that happen in the system that we can use as a trigger for some other action to take place.

> **Learning more about Business Events in Business Central**
>
> You can learn more about Business Events at the following URL: `https://learn.microsoft.com/en-us/dynamics365/business-central/dev-itpro/developer/business-events-overview`.

Let's look at how to use one of the business events in a flow. To do this, we would use the following steps:

1. Log in to **Power Automate** and select **+ Create**.

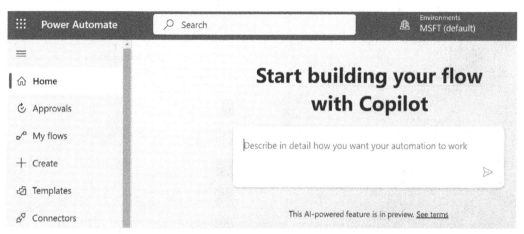

Figure 6.47 – Creating a new flow

2. Select **Automated cloud flow**:

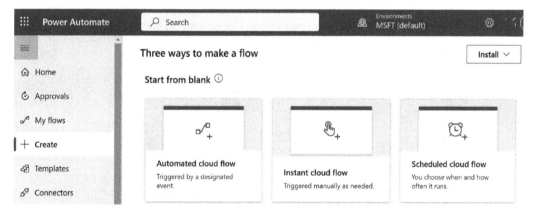

Figure 6.48 – Creating a new flow

3. Enter **Flow name** and type Business Central into the search box:

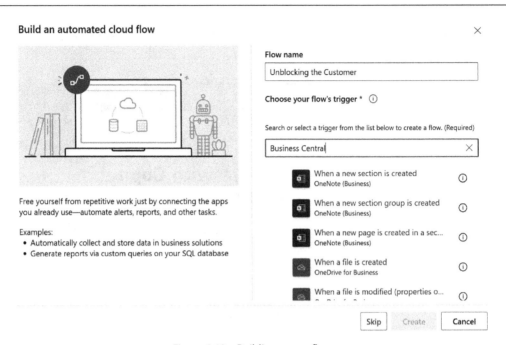

Figure 6.49 – Building a new flow

4.   Scroll down to find **When a business event occurs (V3)**, select it, and then select **Create**.

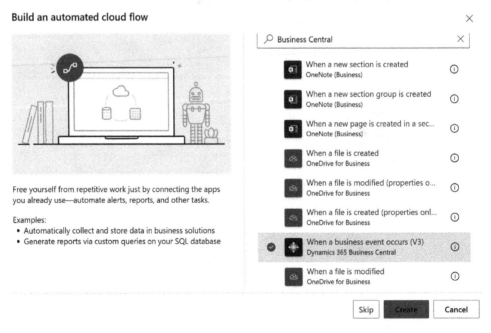

Figure 6.50 – Creating the new flow

5. Select the **Environment** name and then select **Event** to see the list of events available. Scroll through this list to see them all and then select **Customer unblocked (Microsoft)**.

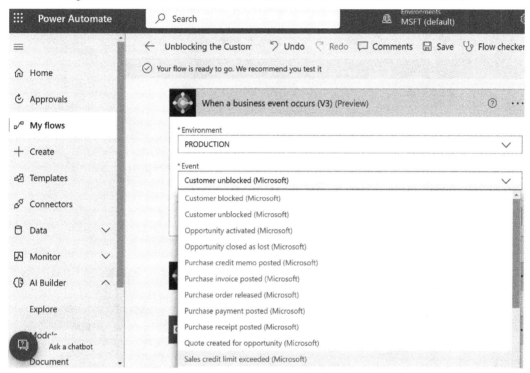

Figure 6.51 – List of events available

6. Select your company and then select + **New step**:

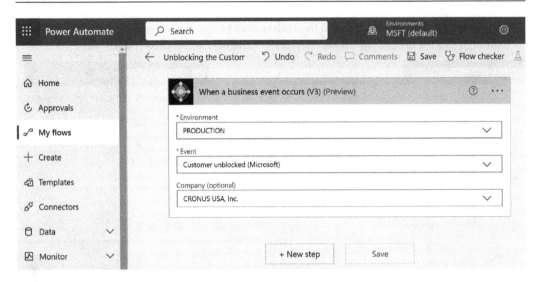

Figure 6.52 – Trigger with complete information

7. Type Business Central into the search bar and select **Dynamics 365 Business Central Connector**.

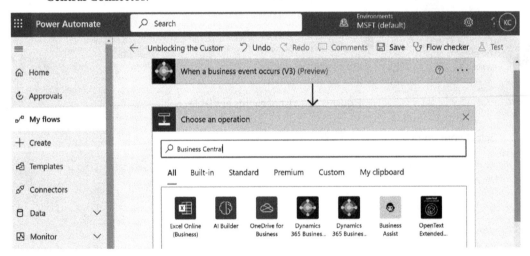

Figure 6.53 – Creating the new action

8. Find and select **Get record (V3)**:

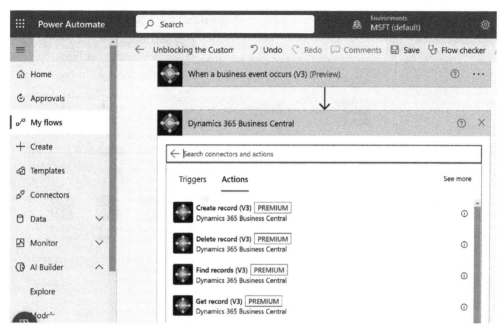

Figure 6.54 – Selecting Get record (V3)

9. Select your **Environment, Company, API category, Table name**, and **Row id** like in the following figure and select **+ New step**.

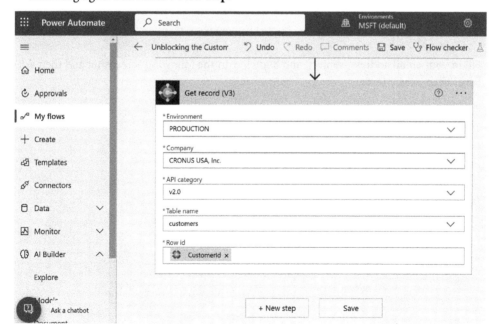

Figure 6.55 – Get record (V3) completed

10. Type `Office` into the search bat and then scroll down and select **Send an email (V2)**.

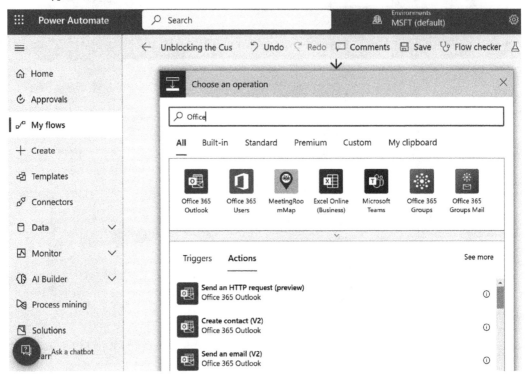

Figure 6.56 – Choose an operation screen

11. Fill in your email address, subject, and body like in the following screenshot and then select **Save**. Then, select **Test**.

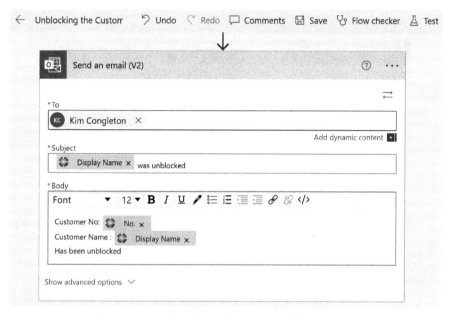

Figure 6.57 – Completed Send an email (V2) screen

12. Select **Test Flow** and then **Manually** and **Test**.

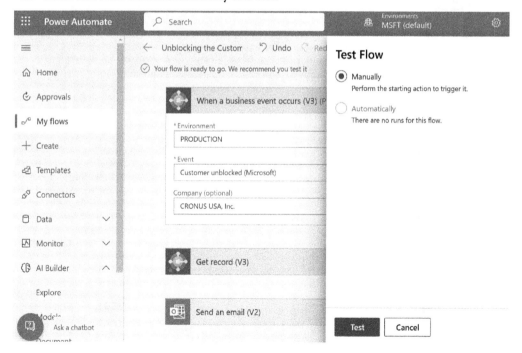

Figure 6.58 – Testing the flow manually

13. Log in to Business Central and select **Customers**.

Figure 6.59 – Selecting customers in Business Central

14. Select a customer.

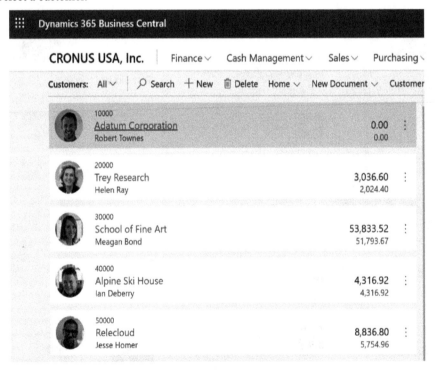

Figure 6.60 – Customer list in Business Central

15. Set the customer to **Blocked** – **All** and then set it to **Unblocked**.

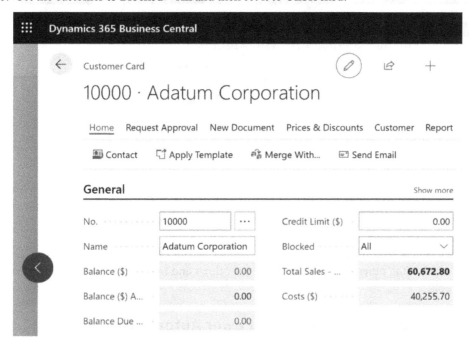

Figure 6.61 – Customer card in Business Central

16. Verify that the flow ran successfully.

Figure 6.62 – Results of the test flow

17. Next, validate that the email was successfully sent.

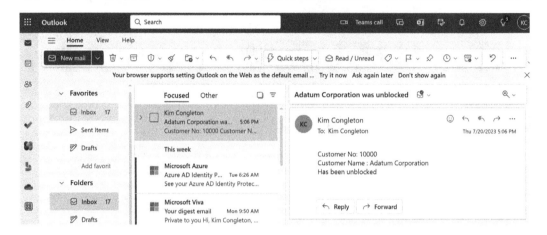

Figure 6.63 – Verifying the email has been successfully sent

This is one example of using a business event and, through this example, you can begin to see the possibilities for using other Business Events in your flows and in conjunction with other Power Platform tools.

Inserting a record into BC using Power Automate

The next example we will look at is how we can insert records into Business Central using Power Automate. In this example, we will use the Business Central **Create record (V3)** action. This is an important action to understand because it will allow us to add records to Business Central using Power Automate. This can be combined with other Power Platform solutions to build more complex solutions. To do this, you will need to follow these steps:

1. Log in to **Power Automate**, select + **Create**, then select **Instant cloud flow**.

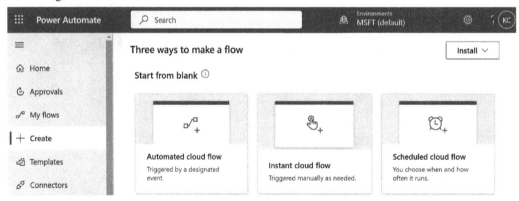

Figure 6.64 – Creating a new instant flow

2. Give the flow a name, then select **Manually trigger a flow**, and select **Create**.

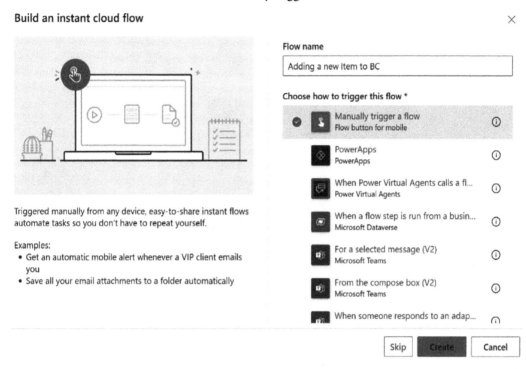

Figure 6.65 – Creating a new instant flow

3. Select + **Add an input** to begin filling out the input fields.

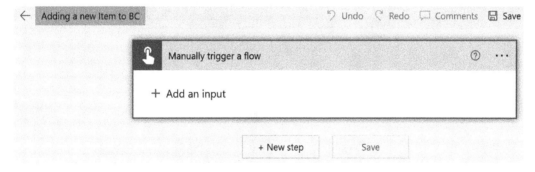

Figure 6.66 – Add an input screen

4.   Select **Text** for the type of user input:

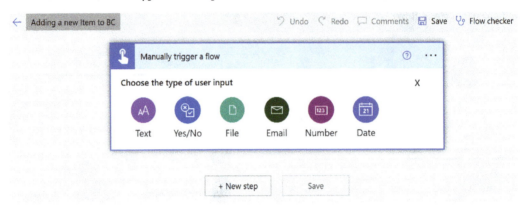

Figure 6.67 – Adding a text input

5.   Create three text inputs like the following:

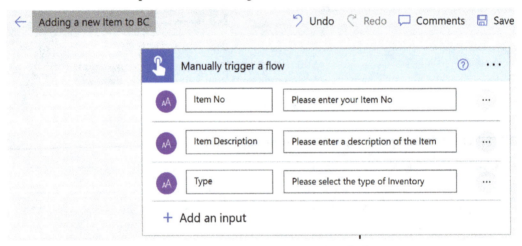

Figure 6.68 – Adding inputs to the trigger

6.   For the **Type** field, select the three dots to the far right and then select **Add a drop-down list of options**. When you are done, select + **New step** to add the next step.

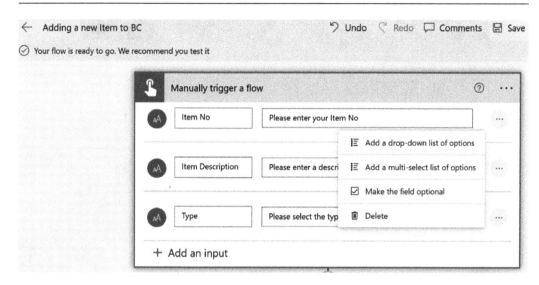

Figure 6.69 – Adding a drop-down list to an input

7. Enter the exact values from the **Type** field in Business Central. If you are unsure what the values are, be sure to check the field on the item card to look at them.

8. The following screenshot shows where you can find the exact values in Business Central for the **Type** field.

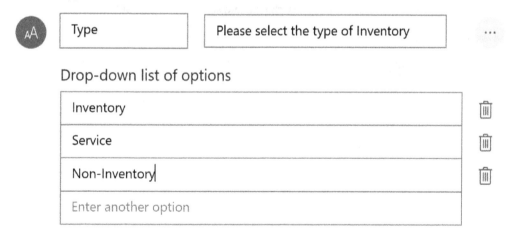

Figure 6.70 – Adding the values to the drop-down list for an input

9. Here is an example of values for **Type** in Business Central:

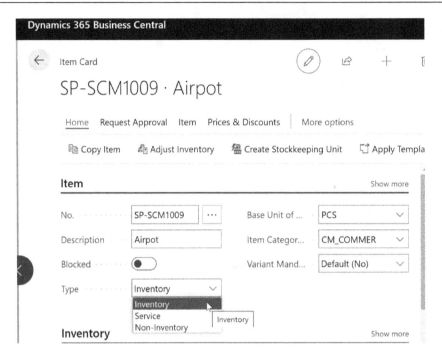

Figure 6.71 – Example of values to use for Type from Business Central

10. Enter Business Central in the search field and select **Dynamics 365 Business Central**.

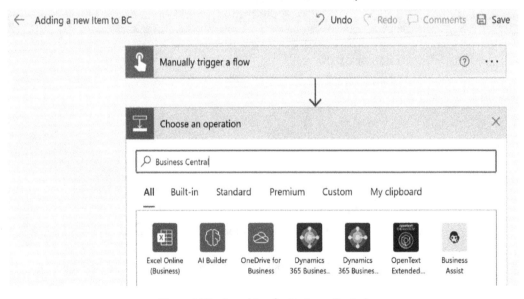

Figure 6.72 – Searching for Business Central

11. Select **Create record (V3)**:

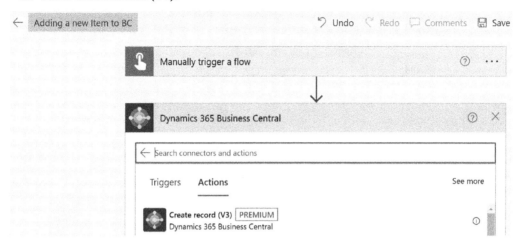

Figure 6.73 – Selecting Create record (V3) for Business Central

12. Fill in **Environment**, **Company**, and **API category** and then select **items** under **Table name** like so:

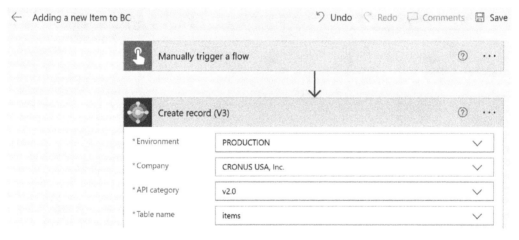

Figure 6.74 – Selecting Create record (V3) for Business Central

13. Map the **No.**, **DisplayName**, and **Type** fields to the input fields you just added. You can also hardcode values to be written when the new record is created. You can automatically set the new item to **Blocked** so that the setup can be completed. Also, if you have an Item category created for new items in Business Central, you can add that as well. Select **Save** and then **Test** to test the flow.

Figure 6.75 – Filling in the values for Create record (V3)

14. In the screenshot here, you can see where I created an item category called **New** so that I could use it to filter records in Business Central based on this value.

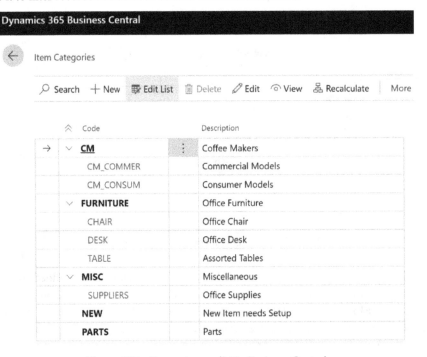

Figure 6.76 – Item category list in Business Central

15. Select **Manually** and then select **Test**.

Figure 6.77 – Testing the flow

16. You will be prompted to log into Business Central. Select **Continue**.

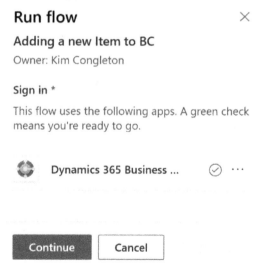

Figure 6.78 – Connecting to Business Central

17. The **Run flow** screen will open and you can see the prompts:

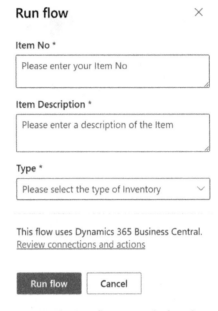

Figure 6.79 – The Run flow screen before data entry

18. Fill in the fields for the new item and select **Run flow**.

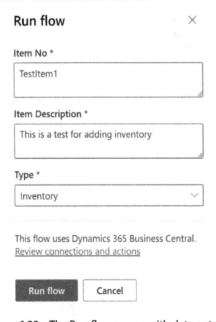

Figure 6.80 – The Run flow screen with data entered

19. Verify that the flow ran successfully in Power Automate.

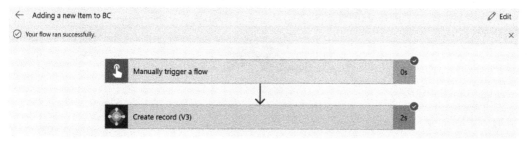

Figure 6.81 – Verifying the results of the test

20. Log in to Business Central and verify that the new item was created.

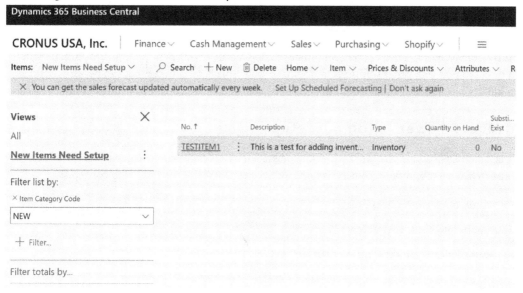

Figure 6.82 – Verifying the new item is in Business Central

21. Open the item card and then confirm it is blocked.

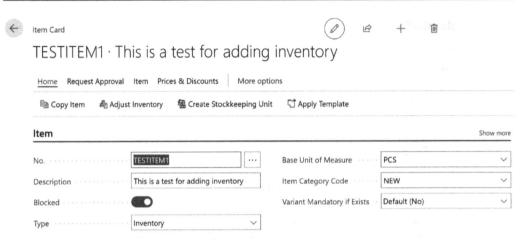

Figure 6.83 – Verifying the new item is blocked in Business Central

In this example, we have used Power Automate to add records to Business Central. This functionality can be combined with other solutions to do this as well. This is something that can be very useful as you build solutions using other tools but need to be able to create records in Business Central as well.

Advanced Power Automate setups

Power Automate is a powerful tool and, as such, there is a lot of functionality to explore in the advanced setups. When we talk about advanced setups, we need to talk about the following concepts:

- Conditions and expressions
- Loops and iterative processes
- Error handling and exception management

Conditions and expressions

Implementing **IF/ELSE logic** within flows allows you to create powerful conditional branching scenarios in Power Automate. By evaluating certain conditions, you can direct the flow to take different paths based on the outcome. This enables you to build more dynamic and flexible workflows. To define the conditions, you can utilize expressions and comparisons. These expressions can be constructed using variables, dynamic values from previous Actions, or static values. The IF/ELSE logic empowers you to execute specific Actions based on whether a condition evaluates as true or false, providing granular control over your flow's behavior.

In addition to basic IF/ELSE statements, Power Automate also offers the capability to handle complex decision-making scenarios. With advanced expressions and functions, you can create intricate conditions to guide the flow's execution. Logical operators, such as **AND**, **OR**, and **NOT**, allow you to combine multiple conditions and create more sophisticated branching logic. Furthermore, functions such as **SWITCH** and **CASE** enable you to handle multiple branching options based on different values or conditions. These advanced decision-making capabilities empower you to design flows that cater to complex business requirements.

> **More information on expressions and conditions**
>
> For a tutorial on expressions and conditions, see the following URL: `https://learn.microsoft.com/en-us/power-automate/use-expressions-in-conditions`.

Loops and iterative processes

Loops are a fundamental component of Power Automate that allows you to perform iterative processes and handle collections of items. Understanding the concept of loops and their usage in Power Automate is essential for building efficient and scalable workflows. Power Automate offers several types of loops, each serving different purposes. The most used loops are the **Apply to Each** and **Do Until** loops.

The Apply to Each loop is designed to iterate over an array or collection of items. It allows you to process each item individually, perform Actions on them, and gather the results. This loop is particularly useful when working with tables, arrays, or data retrieved from connectors such as SharePoint or SQL Server.

On the other hand, the Do Until loop repeats a set of Actions until a specified condition is met. This loop is beneficial when you want to iterate until a specific condition becomes true, allowing you to perform Actions repeatedly until the desired outcome is achieved.

By leveraging loops, you can automate repetitive tasks, process multiple items, handle arrays or tables efficiently, and achieve iterative processing of data within your flows.

> **More information on loops**
>
> For more information on loops inside of Power Automate, see the following URL: `https://learn.microsoft.com/en-us/power-automate/desktop-flows/use-loops#simple-loops`.

Error handling and exception management

When working with flows, it is crucial to manage potential errors and exceptions effectively. Flows can encounter errors or exceptions during their execution, which may disrupt the intended workflow. Implementing error-handling mechanisms ensures that your flows can gracefully manage such situations and prevent flow failures.

Power Automate provides various features for managing errors and exceptions within flows. By using Actions such as **Configure run after**, you can specify alternative paths based on the success or failure of previous Actions. This allows you to define different Actions to be taken depending on the outcome of a specific action, providing flexibility in error handling.

In addition to handling errors, it is essential to implement **retry mechanisms** and **error notifications**. Retry mechanisms help manage transient errors or recoverable failures. You can configure Actions to automatically retry failed Actions for a specific number of attempts or within a certain time interval. This ensures that your flows have built-in resilience to overcome temporary issues.

Moreover, setting up error notifications can alert the relevant stakeholders when critical errors occur during flow execution. This allows for timely awareness and enables a quick response to resolve issues and minimize disruptions.

To assist with troubleshooting, logging and monitoring flow executions is crucial. Power Automate provides features such as run history, flow analytics, and connectors to external monitoring tools for comprehensive flow monitoring. By logging relevant information and capturing detailed error messages, you can identify and resolve any issues or bottlenecks. These insights enable you to improve the overall performance and reliability of your flows, ensuring the smooth automation of your business processes. Now that we have looked at some examples of error handling, let's look at how we avoid getting errors in the first place by learning about some best practices.

Best practices

Whenever we are working with technology solutions, we do want to follow standard best practice guidelines when creating solutions. As we move to low-code/no-code solutions, which put the creation of solutions in the hands of citizen developers, there is an important need to make sure we are also not creating scenarios where we have a bunch of extensions that no one understands or that are not well thought out. The following is a list of things to keep in mind when building solutions.

Ensuring scalability and performance

Ensure scalability and performance by optimizing flow design for efficiency and speed. To ensure optimal scalability and performance of Power Automate flows in Business Central, consider the following best practices:

- **Simplify flow design**: Streamline the flow logic by removing unnecessary Actions or conditions. Minimize the number of steps and branches to improve execution speed.

- **Leverage parallelism**: Utilize parallel branches to perform independent tasks concurrently, maximizing efficiency and reducing processing time.

- **Avoid excessive looping**: Minimize the use of loops and iterations whenever possible. Excessive looping can impact performance, especially when dealing with large datasets.

Manage large datasets and batch processing when dealing with large datasets in Power Automate flows within Business Central by adopting the following approaches to enhance scalability and performance:

- **Implement batching**: Divide large datasets into smaller chunks or batches for processing. This strategy helps prevent performance degradation and enhances overall efficiency.

- **Leverage pagination**: When working with APIs or data sources that support pagination, fetch data in smaller chunks instead of retrieving the entire dataset at once. This approach reduces memory usage and improves flow performance.

To ensure that Power Automate flows in Business Central can handle increased demands and perform efficiently, it's important to optimize their design. This means streamlining the flow logic by removing unnecessary Actions and conditions, minimizing steps and branches, and making the execution faster. Employing parallelism allows independent tasks to be carried out simultaneously, maximizing efficiency and reducing processing time. It's advisable to avoid excessive looping, especially when dealing with large datasets, as it can negatively impact performance. To enhance scalability and performance, it's recommended to divide large datasets into smaller batches for processing, preventing performance issues. Additionally, when working with APIs or data sources that support it, fetching data in smaller chunks through pagination improves the flow performance by reducing memory usage.

Security considerations and data privacy

It is critical to protect sensitive data within the flows you build. There are many ways to do this but one of the most important things to keep in mind is to make sure you configure the appropriate permissions and access controls. Follow the principle of least privilege. Grant users or service accounts the minimum required permissions to perform the task within the flows. Be sure to evaluate the permissions thoroughly to ensure they do not have any potential security risks.

Also, make sure you also do the following when building flows.

- **Use secure connectors**: When accessing external services or systems, utilize connectors that support secure communication protocols (such as HTTPS) and provide robust authentication mechanisms.

- **Apply data loss prevention (DLP) policies**: Define and enforce DLP policies to prevent accidental or unauthorized exposure of sensitive data. Use Actions such as data redaction, encryption, or masking to safeguard sensitive information within flows.

DLP

DLP is an important topic to learn about. It is defined as the comprehensive approach to protecting your company's data from outside and inside threats. Your company should have a policy to deal with this. You can learn more about this at the following URL: `https://www.microsoft.com/en-us/security/business/security-101/what-is-data-loss-prevention-dlp`.

Protecting sensitive data within workflows requires configuring appropriate permissions and access controls, following the principle of least privilege. Secure connectors should be used for accessing external services, supporting secure communication protocols and robust authentication mechanisms. Implementing DLP policies is crucial to prevent accidental or unauthorized exposure of sensitive data, employing Actions such as data redaction, encryption, or masking. Adhering to these security considerations and data privacy measures ensures the protection of sensitive data, minimizing the risk of data breaches and unauthorized access throughout workflows.

Testing and debugging flows

We like to say "test now or pay later when things don't work." Make sure you have created test scripts for the solution and tested them thoroughly. It is also critical to have the end user execute the test scripts. By doing this, you will identify any gaps that may exist in the solution.

To effectively test and validate the behavior of Power Automate flows in Business Central, employ the following techniques:

- **Use input/output validation**: Validate inputs and outputs at various stages of the flow to ensure the expected results. Incorporate assertions or conditions to verify the correctness of data transformations or calculations.

- **Test with sample data**: Utilize sample data representative of real-world scenarios to validate the flow's functionality. Test boundary cases and exceptional scenarios to ensure the flow handles different scenarios correctly.

When encountering issues or errors in Power Automate flows within Business Central, employ the following troubleshooting strategies:

- **Utilize error-handling mechanisms**: Implement error-handling Actions within the flow to catch and handle exceptions gracefully. Include informative error messages or notifications to aid in troubleshooting.

- **Check flow history and logs**: Review the flow's execution history and logs to identify potential issues or bottlenecks. Analyze any reported errors or warnings to pinpoint the root cause of problems.

Testing is a critical aspect of preventing future complications. It is highly recommended to develop comprehensive test scripts for solutions and actively involve end users in executing them to uncover any potential gaps. Specifically pertaining to Power Automate flows in Business Central, employing validation techniques such as input/output validation and thorough testing with diverse datasets becomes paramount to ensure seamless functionality. When encountering issues, employing effective error-handling mechanisms and meticulously examining the flow's history and logs allows for precise troubleshooting and root-cause analysis. By diligently following these practices, businesses can significantly enhance solution reliability and performance, and mitigate potential risks.

Version control and flow management

Version control and managing your flows are key components of the proper administration of your solutions. We will talk about this in the chapter on the center of excellence further; however, to maintain and update Power Automate flows in Business Central efficiently, adhere to the following best practices:

- **Use version control**: Employ a version control system to track changes and revisions to flows. This enables easy rollback to previous versions, facilitates collaboration, and provides a historical record of modifications.

- **Document changes and updates**: Maintain thorough documentation of changes made to flows, including reasons for modifications and any potential impacts. This documentation helps maintain clarity and enables smooth collaboration among team members.

When implementing changes to Power Automate flows in Business Central, consider the following strategies for rollback and change management:

- **Create backups before making changes**: Before implementing any significant changes to flows, create backups or export the current working versions. This precautionary measure ensures that you can revert to a stable state if issues arise.

- **Test changes in a controlled environment**: Deploy changes to a test or staging environment first to evaluate their impact. Verify the modified flow's behavior and performance before deploying it to production.

- **Follow change management protocols**: Adhere to established change management processes and procedures within your organization. Implement proper approval workflows and review mechanisms to ensure seamless deployment and minimize potential disruptions.

Efficiently managing version control and flow management is essential for administering Power Automate flows in Business Central. To ensure effectiveness, it is recommended to utilize version control systems, maintain comprehensive documentation of changes, and adhere to best practices. When implementing modifications, creating backups and testing in controlled environments help mitigate potential risks. Furthermore, following established change management protocols, including approval workflows and review mechanisms, facilitates smooth deployment and reduces disruptions. By incorporating these practices, businesses can effectively maintain and update their Power Automate flows, foster collaboration, and easily revert to previous versions if necessary.

Summary

In this chapter, we learned about Power Automate and how well-documented business process flows are essential when creating Power Automate solutions. We learned about some tips and tricks for creating and documenting business process flows.

We found out about Triggers and Actions and how they are the foundations for all the flows you will build. We saw examples of starting to build a Power Automate flow with a template and then from scratch. We also explored Power Automate advanced setups and best practices. We saw how there are a lot of advanced setups that will enable you to build more complex flows.

We learned about the importance of following best practices when creating flows to ensure that we have solutions that are easy to support and manage over time.

In the next chapter, we will discuss delivering solutions and introduce the application life cycle management concept to you. This will include how to create solutions, an environment overview, and an explanation of solution components.

7

Delivering Solutions

In this chapter, we'll introduce you to **Application Lifecycle Management** (**ALM**) for Power Platform. We will review solution concepts and the two types of solutions: managed and unmanaged. We will also discuss environments and the different types of environments, the importance of always having at least two environments, and some key points on the default environment you get when installing your environment. To support seamless solution delivery, we'll also introduce the role of pipelines, which automate and streamline various aspects of the ALM process.

Lastly, in this chapter, I will walk you through creating a solution and how to deploy the solution to other environments.

In this chapter, we're going to cover the following main topics:

- ALM for admin, citizen, and pro developers
- Environment overview
- Solutions
- Creating solutions

ALM for admin, citizen, and pro developers

ALM involves the holistic management of the complete lifecycle of an application, encompassing various stages, starting from the initial planning and development phases and extending all the way to deployment and ongoing operations. ALM includes various activities such as version control, integration, and delivery, testing and **Quality Assurance** (**QA**), and project management, as illustrated in the following diagram:

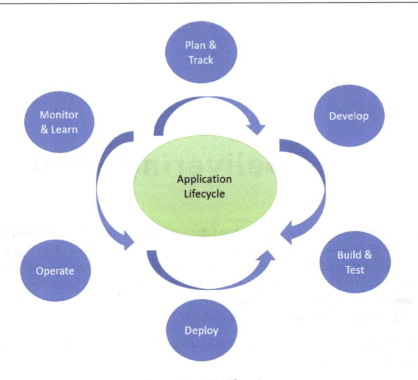

Figure 7.1 – ALM lifecycle

There are many different approaches to ALM methodology or frameworks; however, the stages are the same, as you see in *Figure 7.1*. Waterfall and Agile are a few of the common methodologies companies like to use to track the lifecycle of an application.

Let's have a look at the stages in more detail:

- **Plan & Track**: This stage involves identifying the business requirements, defining the scope, and estimating resources. Common tasks in this area include analysis and design.

- **Develop**: This stage involves the development and coding to create the software application or enhancement to the system.

- **Build & Test**: This stage involves testing the application. You and the team will conduct functional and non-functional testing, commonly known as unit test scripts and acceptance testing. Having a test script or plan for testing and working with the business, especially the end user, is a very important step.

- **Deploy**: This stage involves deploying the application to the production environment.

- **Operate**: At this stage, the application is actively used by end users. This is (hopefully) the happy stage.

- **Monitor & Learn**: This stage is important to ensure that the application is performing as expected and supporting the user if anything comes up. At this stage, it is important to be able to respond to any issues quickly.

I wanted to give you a layout of ALM and the whole lifecycle. Since, in this chapter, we are focusing on solutions, it is important to take a deep dive and break down the **Develop** stage of ALM.

By understanding each component of the **Develop** stage—solutions, Dataverse, source control, Azure DevOps, and pipelines—you can streamline your development processes and improve the overall quality of your applications. We discussed **Dataverse** in *Chapter 4*, so we will cover solutions, source control, Azure DevOps, and pipelines in this chapter, as follows:

- **Solutions** are containers for organizing and deploying components in Power Apps. They allow developers to package customizations and configurations into a solution file that can be easily moved between environments. Another critical component is ensuring you don't forget to move a piece of the solutions when moving components. There are two different types of solutions: managed and unmanaged (these are explained in the *Types of solutions* section).

- **Source control** is a method of managing changes to code. It allows developers to track changes to code over time, collaborate with team members, and revert to previous versions if necessary.

- **Azure DevOps** is a cloud-based platform for software development that provides a suite of tools for managing the application lifecycle. It includes source control, project management, and deployment. Leading companies will use this tool to manage projects, especially integration projects.

- **Pipelines** significantly impact the ALM cycle, particularly in the develop, test, and deploy stages. Pipelines enable the automation and orchestration of various processes, including building, testing, packaging, and deploying applications.

I will not go through each of Microsoft's scenarios in implementing and maintaining a healthy ALM system, but we will talk about a few of them. A link to this is provided in the *Further reading* section; this will come in especially handy if you have a new project and this is your first time going through the process. This chapter will cover the environment overview strategy, solution publishers, solution types, components, pipelines, and solution creation and deployment.

Environment overview

A Power Platform environment is a space or container to store, manage, and share your organization's business data, apps, chatbots, and flows, along with permissions and security. Environments are crucial in ALM, and establishing a strategy is critical.

Every tenant has a default environment, and in *Chapter 4*, we discussed that you shouldn't use this environment unless it is your personal development environment. It is recommended to rename that environment `Personal Productivity` or add your company's name and personnel to the name of the environment. This will help everyone in your organization know it is for personal productivity; also, most times, IT will only want to manage specific environments.

> **Did you know?**
>
> *Key facts about the default environment*: Do not put critical apps in the default environment. Everyone in your organization has access to the default environment, and there is no way to block Environment Maker role assignments.

There are six types of environments: default, trial, sandbox, developer, production, and Microsoft Dataverse for Teams. We will focus on sandbox and production as we build solutions and move from one environment to another.

> **Tip**
>
> More details on each type of environment can be found at `https://learn.microsoft.com/en-us/power-platform/admin/environments-overview#the-default-environment`.

Having at least three environments is key: development, test (**User Acceptance Testing (UAT)**), and production. In some cases, if you have large critical projects, I have seen companies have separate environments for each project or multiple **business unit** development environments with shared testing. I have created three environments to show you how you can select and go from one environment to another. In this screenshot, you will see **Dev**, **Extending BC with PA**, and **Test**:

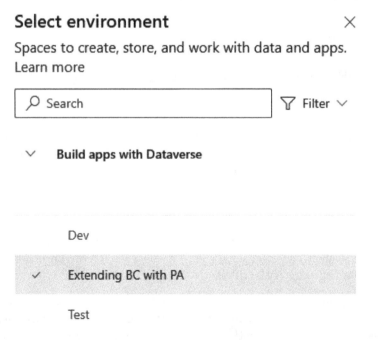

Figure 7.2 – Select environment

Environments have built-in roles, and two that provide access within an environment are **Environment Admin** and **Environment Maker**. Let's take a closer look at these roles:

- **Environment Admin** can perform all administrative actions on the environment, including create, read, write, and delete actions, customizations, database backups, **Data Loss Prevention (DLP)** policies, and administering security roles

- **Environment Maker** has customization privileges and can create and manage apps, custom APIs, gateways, and flows using Power Automate

I encourage you to review all the predefined security roles and make sure that before moving solutions into production, all users test all solutions and components. This has been the tricky part, and it just takes me back to one of my rules: have everyone test before rolling out. I'm aware everyone knows this, but you will be surprised how often this is missed, and with all the different components involved, security and roles have been my number-one lesson learned. We will review this in more detail later in the chapter.

Although we have discussed the environment overview, the types of environments, and the two basic built-in roles for your environment, we must also remember that having a secure environment is important. If this is part of your role at your company, here is a short checklist of how to establish a secure environment to get you started:

- Assign your administrators the Power Platform **Service Admin** role

- Restrict the creation of new trial and production environments to administrators

- Treat the default environment as a "personal productivity" environment

- Establish a process for requesting access to create environments

- Establish tenant- and environment-level DLP

In summary, to follow the application lifecycle, you'll need to have separate environments. Treat the default environment as a personal productivity environment, know that everyone has access to this environment, and do not develop critical apps or solutions in the default environment. It is essential to at least familiarize yourself with the different roles' permissions. This will help with troubleshooting issues. Follow a straightforward process from development, through test (UAT), to production.

Solutions

A **solution** is a container that holds related assets or components such as Power Apps, Power Automate, chatbots, tables, and connectors. Consider it the next level down from the environment; one environment can have many solutions. Therefore, the solution can transport and move customizations from environment to environment. In addition, solutions can be managed using version control.

> **Important note**
>
> Always build in a solution; it is essential to start a solution and create everything in the solution or create the solution and add all the components to your solution. This will ensure you don't miss pieces when you transport the solution to another environment and will keep everything contained together.

Solutions allow developers to package customizations and configurations into a solution file that can be easily moved between environments. Let's now look at the types of solutions we have in Power Platform.

Types of solutions

There are two types of solutions in Power Platform: **unmanaged** and **managed**. First, it is essential to understand the differences between the two types. Unmanaged solutions can be exported and imported between environments, allowing for easy migration of customizations. In unmanaged solutions, the components can be modified. Unmanaged solutions are typically used in development environments. Managed solutions are typically packaged for distribution and are intended to be deployed to production environments. The user can't modify managed solutions—they can't be exported or changed. The primary difference between the solutions is the level of control that they provide. When developing, it is essential to consider which type of solution is appropriate for your requirements based on the level of control and security.

Figure 7.3 displays the differences between managed and unmanaged solutions:

Solution Types		
	Managed Solutions	**Unmanaged Solutions**
Nature	Sealed and controlled by the solution publisher	Customizable and modifiable by the solution owner
Changes	Changes made by the publisher are not editable	Changes made by the owner can be modified anytime
Updates	Updates are released by the publisher	Updates need to be manually applied by the owner
Sharing	Can be distributed to other environments and users	Can be distributed to other environments and users
Security	Limited customizations to prevent unintended changes	Full customization allows complete control
Deployment	Installed as a single package	Requires manual selection and deployment of components
Collaboration	Collaboration with publisher-controlled access	Collaboration with flexible access and customizations

Figure 7.3 – Differences in the types of solutions

In summary, with unmanaged solutions, you can add components, remove components, delete, export, and import solutions. With managed solutions, you can't add, remove, delete, export, or import solutions; you may be able to customize the solution's components if the creator has enabled this, and this is managed using the object-level properties and is set on components individually. Just to be aware of the property—the solution provider might have this disabled as well.

Solution components

Power Platform solutions have several components: Power Apps, Power Automate, Power BI, connectors, and the **Common Data Service** (**CDS**). Think about anything that can be added to a solution as a solution component. In *Figure 7.4*, you will see a list of all the types of components and objects listed in a particular solution:

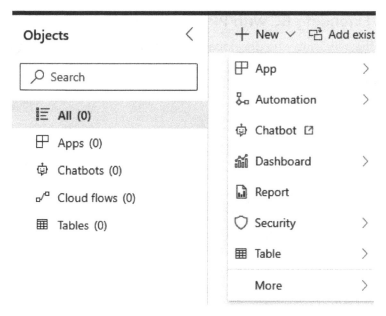

Figure 7.4 – List of components and objects in a solution

Next, let's look at how to create solutions.

Creating solutions

To create a new solution, you can make the solution first and add existing components, but the best option is to create the solution first as a shell and use the new function to develop Power Apps apps, tables, and Power Automate solutions.

Adding existing components to a new solution

In this section, we will add an existing component to a new solution. This will allow us to add the Contact app we created in *Chapter 5* to a solution. Follow these steps:

1. Go to `make.powerapps.com` and log in to your Dev environment. Then, select **Solutions | Create a new solution** and give it a display name; I've used `Existing Solution` as my display name and the name of the solution.

2. Then, select **Publisher** or create a new publisher; this is used as your company name, or if you have a specific name you want to use as the developer of the solution, use a name that will be meaningful. Select the **+ New Publisher** button to add a new publisher, then create a new publisher as `Extending BC with PP`, and use `ebcpp` for **Prefix**, as shown here:

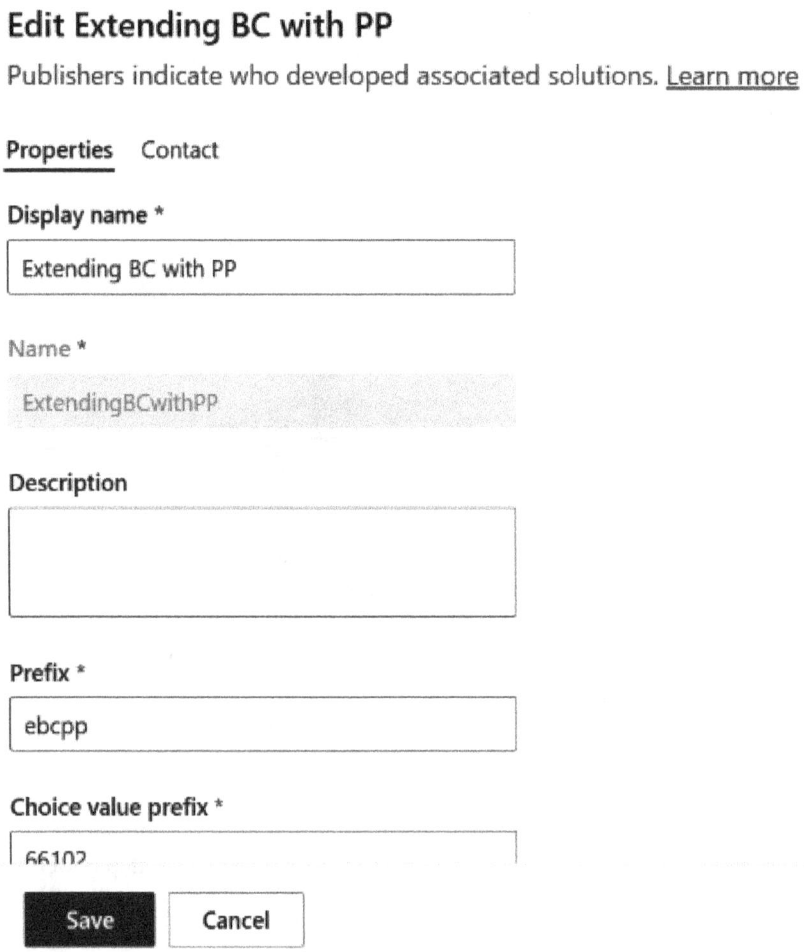

Edit Extending BC with PP

Publishers indicate who developed associated solutions. <u>Learn more</u>

Properties   Contact

Display name *

Extending BC with PP

Name *

ExtendingBCwithPP

Description

Prefix *

ebcpp

Choice value prefix *

66102

Save   Cancel

Figure 7.5 – Creating a new publisher

3. After you've created the new publisher in *step 2*, your last step is to save the publisher and create a solution. The **Version** field can be used for version control; for the first solution, leave the version at 1.0.0.0:

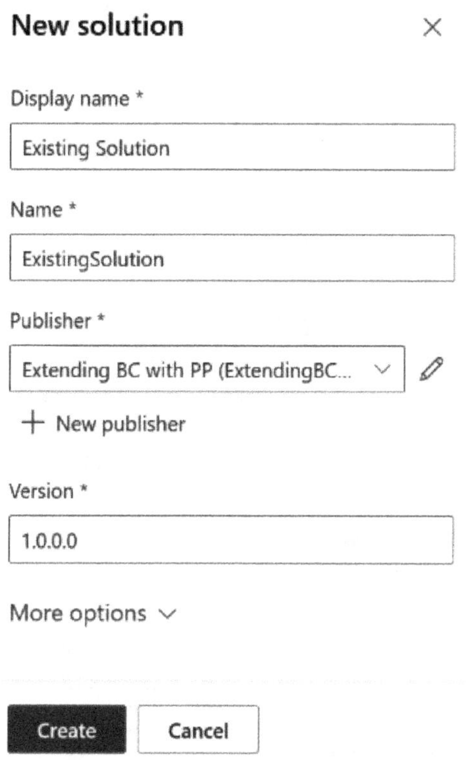

New solution   ✕

Display name *

    Existing Solution

Name *

    ExistingSolution

Publisher *

    Extending BC with PP (ExtendingBC...   ∨   ⬚

    ＋ New publisher

Version *

    1.0.0.0

More options ∨

    Create   Cancel

Figure 7.6 – New solution

4. Add existing apps to the solution by selecting **Add Existing | Select Apps | Canvas App**. A list of all the canvas apps created in the environment will be listed once the section has **From Dataverse** and **Outside Dataverse** displayed:

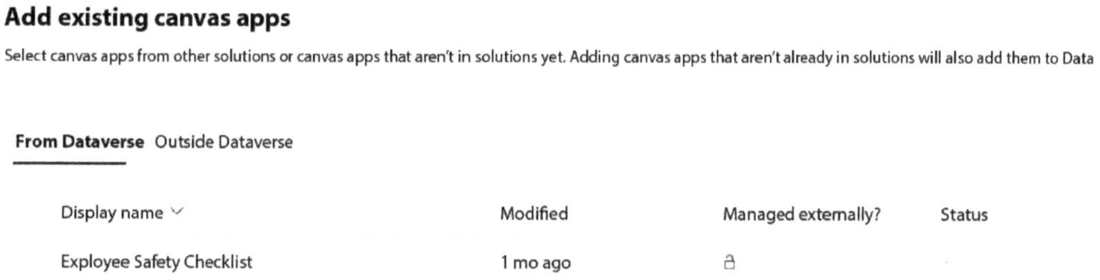

Add existing canvas apps

Select canvas apps from other solutions or canvas apps that aren't in solutions yet. Adding canvas apps that aren't already in solutions will also add them to Data

From Dataverse Outside Dataverse

Display name ∨	Modified	Managed externally?	Status
Exployee Safety Checklist	1 mo ago	⬚	

Figure 7.7 – List of canvas apps from Dataverse

Here is the list of all the canvas apps created under **Outside Dataverse**:

Add existing canvas apps

Select canvas apps from other solutions or canvas apps that aren't in solutions yet. Adding canvas apps that aren't already in solutions will also add them to Dataverse.

ⓘ Some canvas apps are currently not available to add to solutions. Learn more

From Dataverse   **Outside Dataverse**

Display name ⌄	Modified	Managed externally?	Status
Contact App v1	4 d ago	🔒	-
Contact App	2 wk ago	🔒	-
Canvas App	3 wk ago	🔒	-
Import Components	1 wk ago	🔒	-

Figure 7.8 – List of canvas apps from outside Dataverse

5. Add the Contact app created in *Chapter 5* by selecting **Contact App v1** and clicking **Add**:

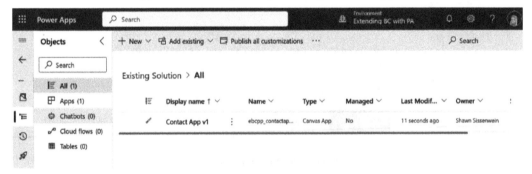

Figure 7.9 – Existing solution

6. Continue to add all the components to the solution and click on **Publish all customizations**:

Figure 7.10 – Published solution

Notice in the **Name** column, the publisher prefix is added to the app name.

7. The next step is to export the solution to your test environment to have users test the solution. Select a solution and click **Export solution**:

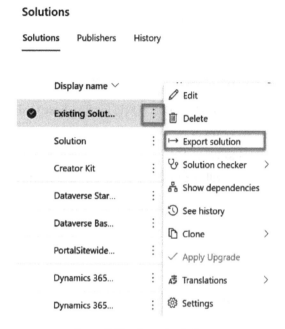

Figure 7.11 – Export solution

8. On the next screen, you can publish all changes if you haven't already done so, as we did in *step 6*. It's a good idea to check for any issues; if you have any problems, review the issue and download the results.

    I prefer to download the report and open it in Excel, giving you details of the issues you need to fix:

Figure 7.12 – Sample error report

9. Update all the errors and export the solution. Save the solution, open the test environment, and import the solution. After the testing is completed, export, and then import into production.

Creating a new solution

Let's create a new solution by following these steps:

1. Create a new solution by clicking **+ New Solution**, then enter Quality Inspection in the **Display Name** and **Name** fields, select **Extending BC with PP** for the publisher, and click **Create**.

2. Create a new table by clicking **+ New Table** and then enter Quality Inspection as the display name.

3. Add the following fields to the Quality Controls table:

    A. PurchaseOrder: This will be a lookup field for **Purchase Order** in Business Central

    B. Pass: Set the options to **Yes** or **No**

    C. Fail: Set the options to **Yes** or **No**

    D. InspectorName: This will be a lookup field for the **Azure Active Directory (AAD)** user

    The fields are shown in the following screenshot:

Figure 7.13 – Quality Controls table and new fields

4. Add a new model-driven app with the name Quality Purchase Order Receiving:

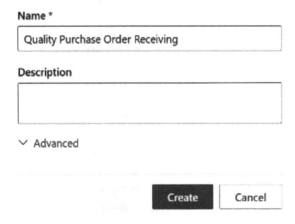

Figure 7.14 – Quality Purchase Order Receiving app

5. Add a few pages to the app. Select **+ New**, then select **Dataverse Table**; this option gives you two pages: a view and a form. Select **Quality Control** and rename the **Title** field `Quality - Purchase Order - Receiving`:

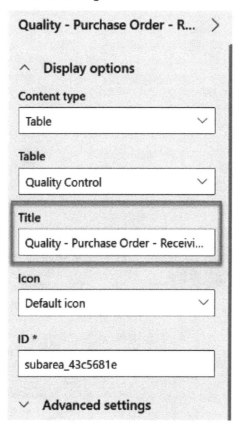

Figure 7.15 – Renaming the title

6. Save and publish the app.

7. Users can add the fields they want to see on the app. I will add **Purchase Order**, **Pass**, **Fail**, and **Inspector Name** fields by selecting **Edit columns**, highlighted in the following screenshot:

Figure 7.16 – Edit columns

You will see all the components and objects attached to the solution:

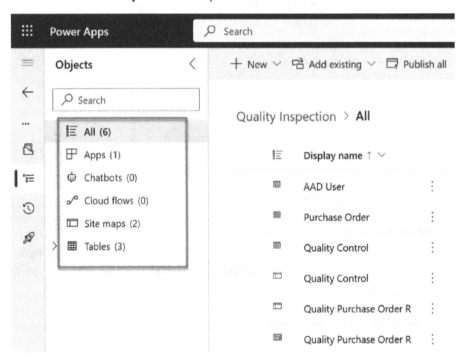

Figure 7.17 – Solution components (objects)

8. The final step is to export the solution to your test environment to have users test the solution. Select a solution and click on **Export solution**.

> **Tip**
> By default, the system creates a default solution that will have all components in your environment added to this master solution or container. Power Platform likes to have containers to hold all the resources needed to build solutions.

In your environment, if you open the **Default Solution** option, you will see all the components that you have created listed in the **Default Solution** screen under **All**:

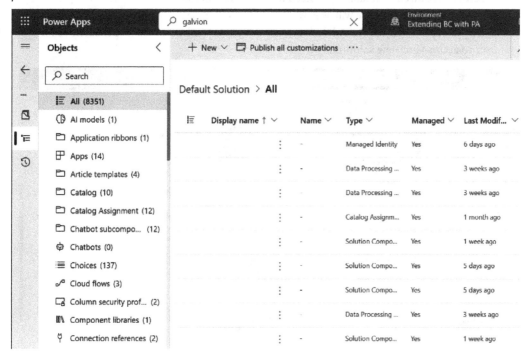

Figure 7.18 – Default Solution

In the last two sections, we covered how to create a solution, add components, create the answer first, and design everything inside the solution. Both methods work, but the recommended way is to always start with a solution.

Reviewing security and permissions

Now that we have created a solution, ensuring the users have the correct Power Platform license to run solutions is essential. Confirm and assign a license to each of the users along with sharing objects with them by following these steps:

1. Select **Active users** in the admin center to assign a license.

2. When you create custom tables, you need to set up custom roles. Since we created a Quality Controls custom table, we will need roles to assign to the users that need access to the solution. In this example, I will use the **Adele Vance** user to show you how to assign permissions for the user to access your new solution:

Figure 7.19 – Assigning Power Apps and Power Automate licenses

3. Select **Power Apps Admin Center**—the gear icon at the top right of the screen. You will want to get familiar with this admin center.

4. Select the environment; in this case, you should be in your **Extending BC with PA** environment. You will notice that when you go into the admin center, you will see a list of all your environments:

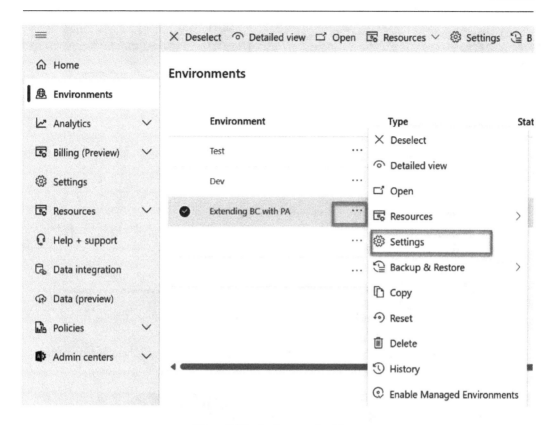

Figure 7.20 – Environment settings

5. In **Settings**, select **User + permissions | Security roles**.

6. You can create a new role from scratch, but I find it easier to copy one. Select one of the roles; for that, I am using **App Opener**. Then, select **Copy** and enter the name of the role, **Quality Control App**, and again select **Copy**. When the process is finished, you will get a success message.

7. Select the new role you just created, **Quality Control App**.

8. You can select **Table | Show all tables**, **Show only assigned tables**, or **Show only unassigned tables**; this helps to narrow down the list of options. You have the opportunity to search by table name:

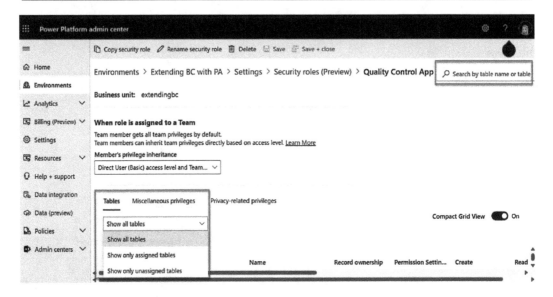

Figure 7.21 – Filter list of available tables

9.   I will grant **Full Access** to the table in this role. Be sure to read about all the different settings on the Microsoft website—a link to this is provided in the *Further reading* section:

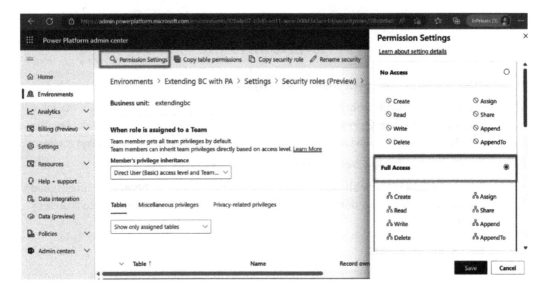

Figure 7.22 – Permission Settings

10. Add members to the role by selecting the role and three dots to open the screen to assign members. Select **Members** | **+ Add people**. This will open a screen to search by name, email, or team name:

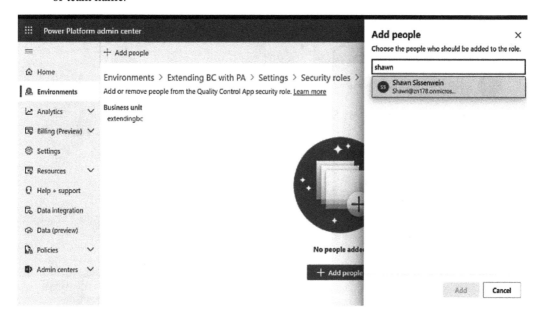

Figure 7.23 – Add people

11. Another way to assign a user to a role for an app in the Power Apps screen is to select **Share**:

Figure 7.24 – Sharing the Quality Purchase Order Receiving app

12. Enter a team member in the **People** search bar; once you find the user, select **Share**:

Share Quality Purchase Order Receiving   ✕

Add people and assign security roles so that they can use your app.

App

Ⓠ Quality Purchase Order Receiving

People

Current

ⅅA Delegated Admin

Shawn Sissenwein

Select your app to manage which security roles are used.

Select someone to assign their security role.

Share   Cancel

Figure 7.25 – Sharing the Quality Purchase Order Receiving app (continued)

In this section, we have covered how to assign the appropriate license for users needing access to Power Apps and Power Automate. In addition, we learned how to copy a basic role and created a custom role that we assigned to the custom `Quality Controls` table we made in our solution.

Pipelines

Pipelines in Power Platform strive to democratize ALM for Power Platform and Dynamics 365 customers. They achieve this by directly introducing ALM automation and **continuous integration/ continuous delivery (CI/CD)** capabilities within the service, making them more accessible to all makers, administrators, and developers.

The goal is to provide a user-friendly and approachable experience for ALM, ensuring that all stakeholders can effectively leverage automation and CI/CD practices. Pipelines empower users to streamline their ALM processes, from development to deployment and beyond, without requiring extensive technical expertise or specialized knowledge.

By incorporating ALM automation and CI/CD capabilities, pipelines within Power Platform democratize these practices. They remove barriers, making it easier for makers, administrators, and developers to adopt and integrate ALM best practices into their workflows. This promotes collaboration, efficiency, and the ability to deliver high-quality solutions within the Power Platform ecosystem.

The aim of pipelines is to democratize ALM by making it accessible, intuitive, and inclusive. By bringing ALM automation and CI/CD capabilities directly into the service, Power Platform and Dynamics 365 customers can benefit from enhanced ALM in a manner that is more approachable and user-friendly for all stakeholders involved.

Setting up pipelines for Power Platform

It is recommended to create a host environment to manage the layer of all pipeline security. This should be a dedicated environment separate from your other environments—development, test, and production.

The host should be of type production and requires a Dataverse database. This environment doesn't have to be managed, but all the other environments that will be part of it will need to be set as managed.

DevOps

In the context of ALM for Power Platform, DevOps refers to integrating development and operations practices to streamline application development, deployment, and management processes. DevOps principles aim to foster collaboration, communication, and automation among development teams, operations teams, and other stakeholders involved in the ALM process. By embracing DevOps in Power Platform ALM, organizations can achieve faster delivery cycles, improved quality, and enhanced collaboration. It involves implementing CI/CD pipelines, automating testing and deployment processes, and fostering a culture of collaboration and shared ownership. DevOps practices enable seamless collaboration between developers, IT operations, and business stakeholders, ensuring the efficient delivery of high-quality solutions that meet the organization's and end users' evolving needs.

Consider adopting a source code control system such as Azure DevOps. Azure DevOps provides developer services for support teams to plan work, collaborate on code development, and build and deploy applications.

Export a solution from your development environment containing your apps and customizations, unpack your solution, and store the components in your source control system. Use Azure Pipelines to manage your components, and then deploy them to the target environment for testing. Finally, deploy to the production environment for user consumption.

Summary

This chapter taught us about ALM and the components of implementing a healthy solution. ALM has many elements, but we touched on a few main ones. Then, we discussed the environment overview and strategy based on ALM recommendations. Finally, we discussed managed and unmanaged solutions, created a solution, added an already-built app to the new solution, and created an object within the solution. This chapter's last important note is to ensure the users have the correct license and permission roles to run the solution.

Throughout the ALM process, collaboration, communication, and documentation play vital roles. Tools such as project management software, version control systems, issue tracking systems, and collaboration platforms facilitate effective ALM.

In the next chapter, *Chapter 8*, we'll see how to connect Business Central and Power Automate, the advantages of combining a Business Central workflow, and the functionality of Power Automate. Finally, we'll also learn about common troubleshooting errors and reasons for Power Automate flows not running.

Further reading

- Learn more on ALM on the Microsoft website: `https://learn.microsoft.com/en-us/power-platform/alm/overview-alm`

- *ALM Accelerator for Power Platform*: `https://learn.microsoft.com/en-us/power-platform/guidance/alm-accelerator/overview`

- Learn about healthy ALM in many different scenarios: `https://learn.microsoft.com/en-us/power-platform/alm/implement-healthy-alm`

- Learn about multiple solution layering and dependencies: `https://learn.microsoft.com/en-us/power-platform/alm/organize-solutions#multiple-solution-layering-and-dependencies`

- *Secure the default environment*: `https://learn.microsoft.com/en-us/power-platform/guidance/adoption/secure-default-environment`

- *Backup and restore environments*: `https://learn.microsoft.com/en-us/power-platform/admin/backup-restore-environments`

- *Security roles and privileges*: `https://learn.microsoft.com/en-us/power-platform/admin/security-roles-privileges#team-members-privilege-inheritance`

- Configure user security to resources in an environment: `https://learn.microsoft.com/en-us/power-platform/admin/database-security`

Part 3 – Common Business Cases in Business Central for the Power Platform

The chapters in this section will focus on streamlining and enhancing your business processes using Power Platform solutions. In the upcoming chapters, we will explore how to automate approval processes, reduce manual interventions, and increase efficiency. We'll also guide you through connecting to Power BI and constructing insightful reports to gain valuable data-driven insights. Additionally, we'll demonstrate how you can extend the functionality of your solutions by integrating multiple Power Platform tools, empowering your organization to reach new heights of productivity and success. Let's dive in and unlock the full potential of Power Platform.

This part contains the following chapters:

- *Chapter 8, Automating Approvals and Reducing Manual Business Processes*
- *Chapter 9, Connecting Power BI for Business Central Data*
- *Chapter 10, Extending Functionality by Using Several Power Platform Solutions*

Automating Approvals and Reducing Manual Business Processes

In this chapter, we will explore automating approvals in Business Central using Power Automate. This is one of the first places a lot of Business Central users will start using Power Automate. Microsoft has made this easier to do by including templates of approval flows and they can be leveraged as a starting point; we can add additional functionality as needed after.

We are going to cover the following main topics related to approvals in Business Central and Power Automate:

- Setting up approvals in Business Central
- Setting up Power Automate integration with Business Central
- Setting up an approval purchase order flow
- Common troubleshooting tips

After reading this chapter, you will gain the knowledge necessary to implement approvals using Power Automate and Business Central. This chapter will lay the foundation so that you understand what needs to happen in both Business Central and Power Automate for approvals to work.

Technical requirements

You can find out more information about setting up approvals in Business Central at `https://learn.microsoft.com/en-us/dynamics365/business-central/dev-itpro/powerplatform/automate-workflows?tabs=blank`.

Setting up approvals in Business Central

Understanding these key components is crucial for effectively utilizing approvals in BC and optimizing workflow efficiency. So, let's dive in and explore the world of approvals and Power Automate templates in BC.

Approvals in Business Central refer to the process of granting or denying authorization for specific actions, such as purchase orders, expense reports, or time off requests. These actions typically require validation from designated individuals or roles within an organization to ensure compliance, accuracy, and adherence to company policies. The approval workflow in BC involves routing the request to the appropriate approver(s), capturing their decision, and updating the system accordingly. By implementing approvals, businesses can establish control mechanisms, enhance accountability, and maintain consistency in their operational processes.

Power Automate, a comprehensive workflow automation platform, plays a crucial role in simplifying and expediting the approval process in BC. Power Automate offers a wide range of pre-built templates specifically designed for managing approvals that can be seamlessly integrated with Business Central. These templates provide a foundation for creating customizable approval workflows tailored to the organization's unique requirements.

The use of Power Automate templates for approvals brings several advantages. Firstly, it reduces the need for manual intervention and minimizes the chances of errors or delays as the templates automate the entire approval process. Additionally, these templates offer flexibility, allowing businesses to define complex approval hierarchies, multi-step workflows, and conditional logic based on specific criteria. With Power Automate templates, organizations can optimize their approval workflows, improve response times, and streamline decision-making.

Furthermore, Power Automate integrates with various communication channels, such as email, Microsoft Teams, or mobile notifications, enabling approvers to conveniently review and respond to approval requests from anywhere, at any time. The ability to access approvals on different devices enhances productivity and ensures timely actions, even for on-the-go personnel.

Configuring your environment for approvals

To set up approvals in Business Central, there are some core things we will have to do to get our developer's environment ready and configured for approvals. The first thing we will need to do is make sure we have multiple users set up in the Business Central environment. To do this, we will need to do the following:

1. Log into Office 365 and select **Admin**:

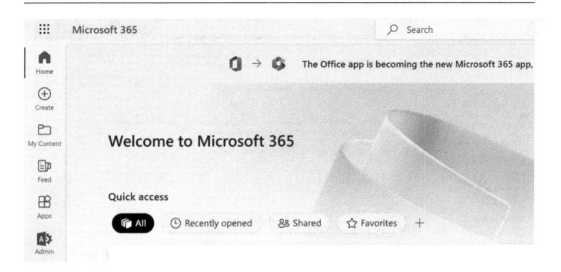

Figure 8.1 – Selecting Admin from the home screen for Office 365

2. Select **Billing**:

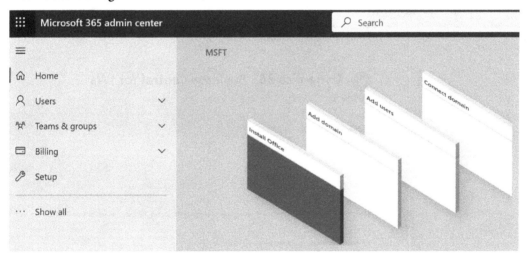

Figure 8.2 – Selecting Billing from the admin center

3. Select **Licenses** and then **Dynamics 365 Business Central for IWs**:

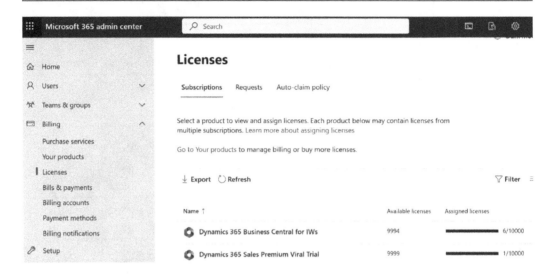

Figure 8.3 – Selecting Dynamics 365 Business Central for IWs

4.   The Dynamics 365 Business Central license screen will open. Select + **Assign licenses**:

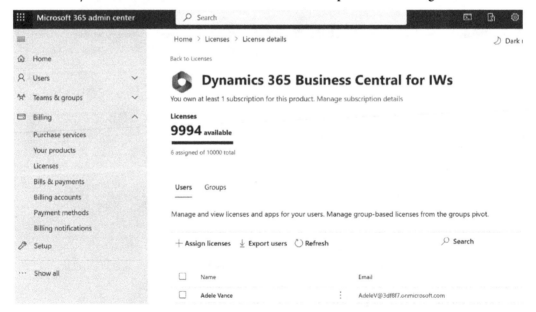

Figure 8.4 – Selecting Assign licenses

5.   When the **Assign licenses to users** page opens, click in the box to see a drop-down list of all the users available in your environment. Select a few users that do not have a license:

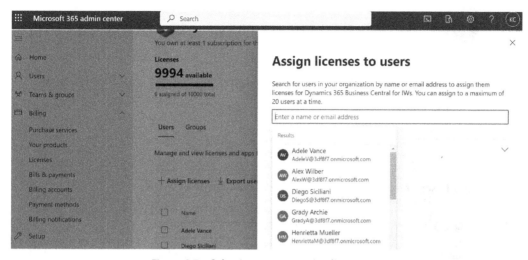

Figure 8.5 – Selecting users to assign licenses to

6. Once you have selected your users, select **Assign**. I've selected three users for this example:

Assign licenses to users

Search for users in your organization by name or email address to assign them licenses for Dynamics 365 Business Central for IWs. You can assign to a maximum of 20 users at a time.

Turn apps and services on or off   ⌄

Figure 8.6 – Assign licenses to users

7. A message will appear, notifying you that you have assigned a license to three users:

These users now have licenses
- Adele Vance
- Diego Siciliani
- Alex Wilber

Figure 8.7 – Assigned licenses user notification

Now, let's import users into BC.

Importing users into Business Central

Now that we have added the licenses to the users in Office 365, we can log into Business Central and then begin setting up the approval process. This process follows a lot of the same steps that you would follow if you were using the base Business Central approval functionality without Power Automate. Let's look at the steps involved in importing the users we just created and then setting up the approvals in Business Central:

1. Log into Business Central, search for `users`, and select **Users**:

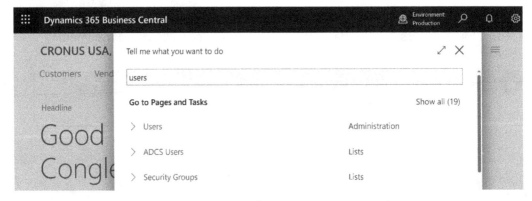

Figure 8.8 – Searching for users in Business Central

2. When the **Users** screen opens, select **Home**, and then select **Update users from Microsoft 365** to import the users we just assigned licenses to:

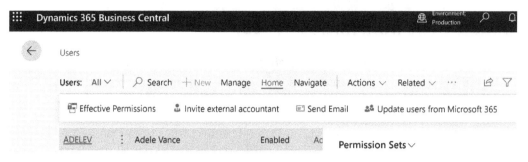

Figure 8.9 – Selecting Update users from Microsoft 365 from the Users screen

3. The **Update users from Microsoft 365** screen will appear and notify you that it could take up to 72 hours for changes to be available. I have not experienced this yet, but the new user may not be available for 72 hours. This is standard Microsoft verbiage. Select **Next** to import the new users:

Update users from Microsoft 365

Bring changes to user information from your Microsoft 365 organization to Business Central. Update license assignments, name changes, email addresses, preferred languages, and user access.

Note:

It can take up to 72 hours for a change in Microsoft 365 to become available to Business Central.

Before you get started

You might want to configure custom permissions for each license type to speed up how you configure users.

Configure permissions per license

Figure 8.10 – The Update users from Microsoft 365 screen

4. Once you select **Next**, the next message will let you know how many updates will take place. Click **Finish** to complete the process:

Update users from Microsoft 365

Number of updates ready to be applied: 20. These can be name, email address, preferred language, and user access changes. Choose View changes to see the list.

Cancel	View changes	Finish

Figure 8.11 – The Update users from Microsoft 365 screen

Configuring the approval process in Business Central

Now that we have the users that we added to Business Central, we can go ahead and set up the approval process in Business Central. There are a couple of steps that we must take to get the system ready so that we can add the Power Automate functionality. We'll need to take the following steps to do this:

1. While we are still on the **Users** screen, verify that our users have been added to Business Central, not the emails for the users that were added. We'll need them later as part of the setup:

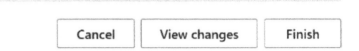

Dynamics 365 Business Central

← Users

Users: All ∨   🔍 Search   + New   Manage   Home   Navigate | More options

🔲 Effective Permissions   🎗 Invite external accountant   📧 Send Email   👥 Update users from Microsoft 365

User Name ↑	Full Name	Status	Authentication Email
ADELEV	Adele Vance	Enabled	AdeleV@3df8f7.onmicrosoft.com
DIEGOS	Diego Siciliani	Enabled	DiegoS@3df8f7.onmicrosoft.com
HENRIETTAM	Henrietta Mueller	Enabled	HenriettaM@3df8f7.onmicrosoft.com
ISAIAHL	Isaiah Langer	Enabled	IsaiahL@3df8f7.onmicrosoft.com
KIMCO	Kim Congleton	Enabled	Kimco@3df8f7.onmicrosoft.com

Figure 8.12 – The Users screen in Business Central

2. Select **search**. Then, enter `user setup` and select **User Setup**:

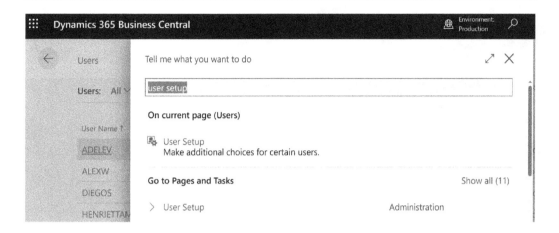

Figure 8.13 – Searching for user setup

3. The **User Setup** window will open. This is where we will set up each user with their email address. Select the **User ID** field and then the drop-down list. Select the first user you want to add and then enter their email address. Do this for each of the users you added:

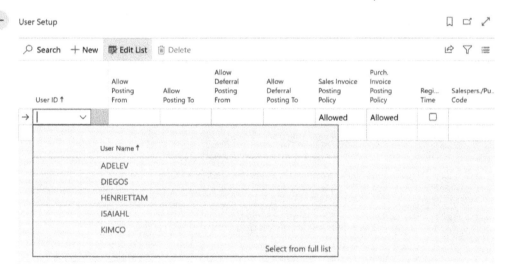

Figure 8.14 – The User Setup screen in Business Central

4. The next step is to do the approval setup. To do this, select **Search** and then search for Approval User. Select **Approval User Setup**:

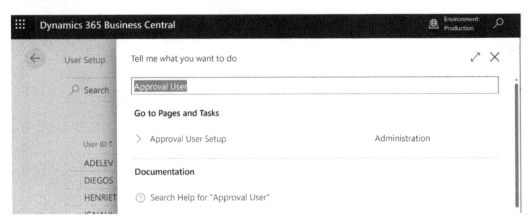

Figure 8.15 – Searching for Approval User

5. Select the **User ID** field and select your users. Set **Approver ID** to yourself and then enter your email. For yourself, make sure you check the checkbox for **Approval Administrator** and that you have the **Unlimited Sales Approval** and **Unlimited Purchase Approval** checkboxes checked. In this example, **KIMCO** is the approval administrator:

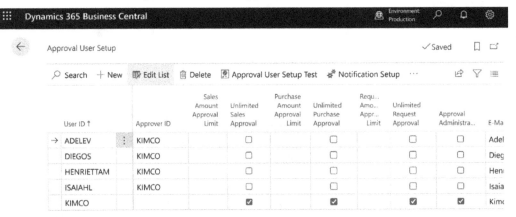

Figure 8.16 – Approval User Setup for your users

6. The notification setup for each user will default to **Notification Type** = **New Record**, **Notification Method** = **Email**, and **Schedule** = **Instantly**. We recommend leaving this to start executing and changing it if needed after:

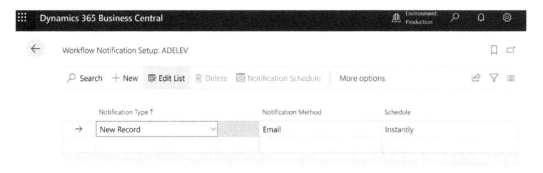

Figure 8.17 – Notification setup defaults for Business Central

Next, we will look at the workflow user groups. We can use these to determine the engagement order of the participants in an approval workflow by assigning a number in the sequence number field. This can be used to establish a chain of approvers. For this example, we'll set up one user to start with.

7.   Select **Search** and then enter `workflow user` to find **Workflow User Groups**. Select this option:

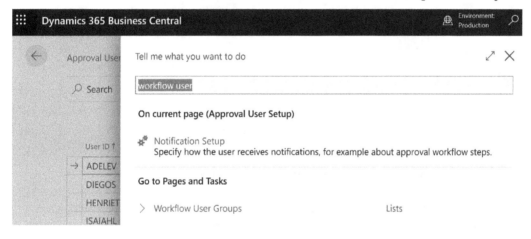

Figure 8.18 – Searching for workflow user

8.   Select + **New** from the **Workflow User Groups** page:

Figure 8.19 – Selecting + New for Workflow User Groups

9. When the next screen opens, enter a code and description for **Workflow User Group**. For now, enter yourself and set **Sequence No.** to 1:

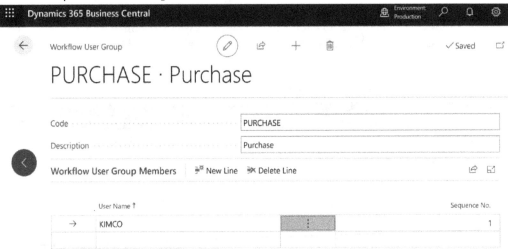

Figure 8.20 – Creating a new Workflow User Group and assigning users

This is the final step in setting up the approval flow in Business Central using the core Business Central functionality. In the next section, we'll set up the Power Automate integration with Business Central.

Setting up Power Automate integration

To use Power Automate integration in Business Central, we must do some basic setup. You can control access to Power Automate's features that will allow users to create and run instant flows from inside the Business Central client. This is an advanced feature and one that you would only want to turn on if users are trained in how to create flows and understand the ramifications of what they are building. Controlling access to users who are building solutions according to the development policies of the organization is critical to preventing a bunch of disparate solutions.

There are a few key things to keep in mind about Power Automate in BC:

- Administrators can hide the **Automation** action group and its actions from all users or individual users.

- All users, by default, have access to all Power Automate features.

- These features are included under the **Automate** action group on most lists, cards, and pages.

- Users must agree to the privacy notice and terms when they select **Automate** from any menu and then get started with Power Automate and run the Power Automate-assisted setup. Running this setup will enable users to create flows and manage flows.

- Power Automate's features can be turned on or off at the company level via the privacy notice agreement.

How to enable Power Automate in Business Central by user

Let's look at how we would do a couple of the points mentioned previously. As an administrator, you have the power to control automation access. To do this, you need to do the following:

1. Search for `privacy` and select **Privacy Notices Status**:

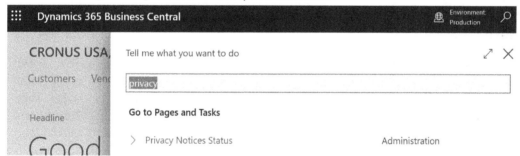

Figure 8.21 – Searching for privacy

2. On the **Privacy Notices Status** screen, find the entry for **Microsoft Power Automate**. This is where you can change the settings for Power Automate. You can choose **Agree for Everyone** or **Disagree for Everyone**. It will default to **Let Users Decide**:

Figure 8.22 – Settings for Microsoft Power Automate on the Privacy Notices Status screen

This is a decision you need to make while implementing Business Central or Power Automate regarding whether you want to allow Power Automate to be used by one person or everyone. We recommend starting with a few users first, especially those that are building flows or need to execute them.

How to enable Power Automate permission in Business Central by user(s)

To grant permissions to individual users or groups in terms of Power Automate's features, you need them to have the **Allow Action Automate ID 9630** system permission in a permission set. Users will default to having the correct permission when they are added to Business Central. If you don't want them to have it, you will have to take away their permission. You can see the permission that's been assigned when you look at the users we added in the first part of this chapter. To do this, do the following:

1. Log into Business Central. Then, search for `users` and select **Users**:

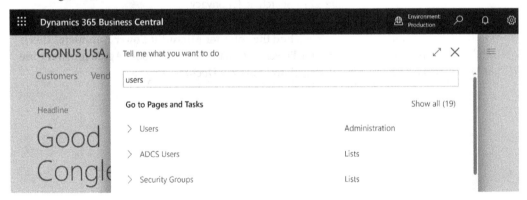

Figure 8.23 – Searching for users in Business Central

2. Select the first user and the user card; the following screen will appear. They have **User Group Memberships** set to **AUTOMATE ACTION** and **User Permission Sets** set to **Automate-Exec**. This will give them the right to use Power Automate in Business Central:

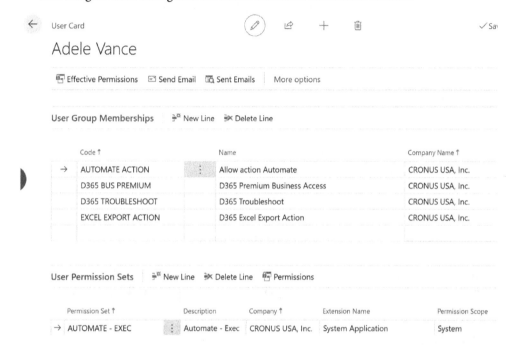

Figure 8.24 – Permissions in Business Central that are required for Power Automate

Now that we have Business Central configured with users, approval setups, and Power Automate integration, we are ready to create our first approval workflow using Power Automate and Business Central.

Exercise for setting up purchase approvals using a Power Automate template

K&S Solutions has a requirement to set up approval notifications for purchase orders, and they would like to take advantage of using Business Central's functionality and Power Automate. They have three people in their purchasing department and one manager (you). The manager will approve everyone's purchase orders.

These requirements are straightforward, so you decide to use one of the existing Power Automate templates for approvals.

To do this, follow these steps:

1. Open Power Automate and select **Templates**:

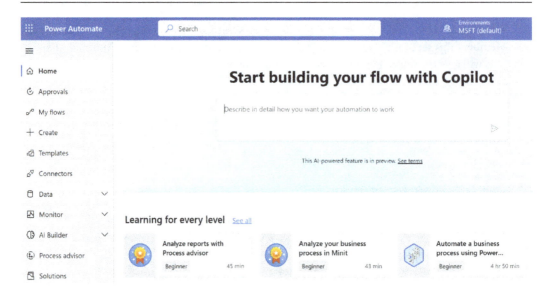

Figure 8.25 – Selecting Templates from the Power Automate home screen

2. Enter Business Central in the search bar to find all the available Business Central templates. Find and select the one that says **Request approval for Business Central Purchase order (first response)**:

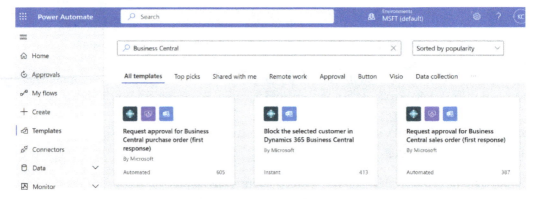

Figure 8.26 – Selecting a Business Central template

3. The **Templates** window will open. Here, you'll see the description at the top and the connections that will be made using the template. Scroll to the bottom of the screen and click **Next**:

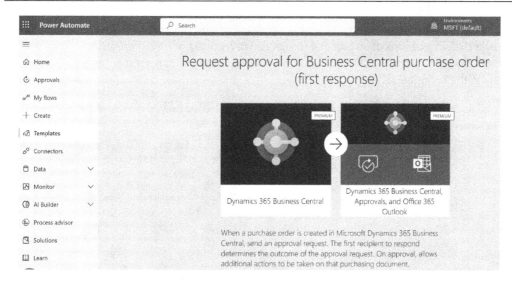

Figure 8.27 – Selecting a Business Central template

4. The next screen will prompt you for your production environment, company name, and approval request recipients. Enter this information and click **Create**:

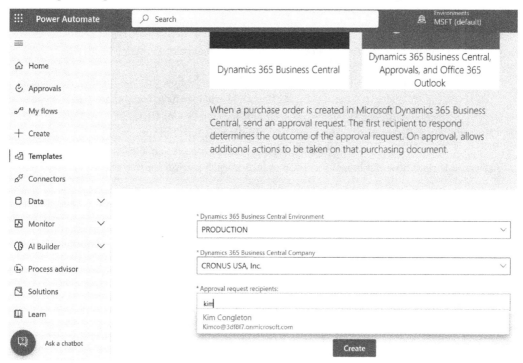

Figure 8.28 – Filling in the information required for the Business Central template

The template will be created for you, and the information will be defaulted into the Power Automate flow. Let's drill in and look at a couple of things that are worthy of note. For example, the flow is automatically set to a status of **On**, and that is a type of automation, meaning it is always on and running in the background.

1. To do this, select **Edit** and then **Edit with designer** so that we can see the rest of the information about the flow:

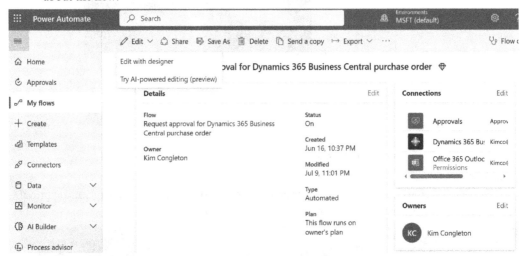

Figure 8.29 – Editing the Power Automate flow that has been created

The Power Automate **Edit** window will open and show us the flow that was created. As you can see, this template contains a more complex flow than what we have seen before. This flow uses some different actions that we have not seen before, such as **Get URL**, **Start and wait for an approval**, **Initialize response summary**, and **Finalize response summary**. If you click on each action, you can expand them and see what settings have been set to make them work. We'll look at a couple right now, but I encourage you to look at each section and see how it is configured:

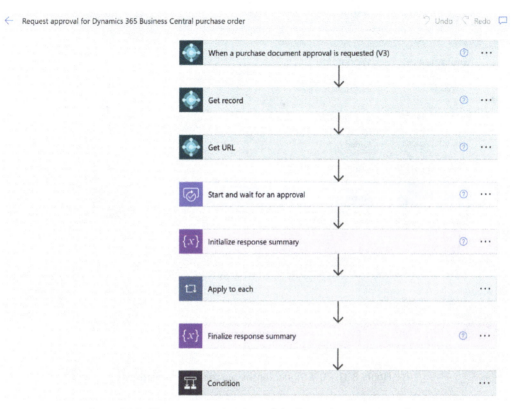

Figure 8.30 – The trigger and actions of the Power Automate template

2. Select the **When a purchase document approval is requested** trigger. You will see that the trigger has some conditions that have been set for approval to be requested. We'll take the defaults for now, but you can see how easy it would be to build a more complex scenario if you needed one:

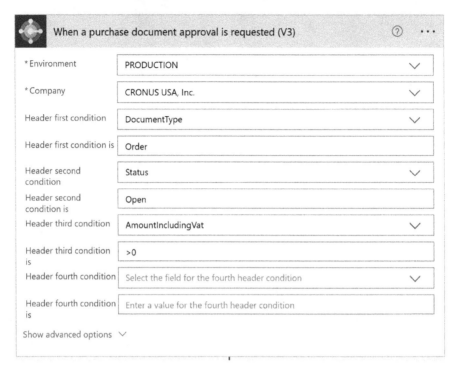

Figure 8.31 – The trigger for the purchase document

3.   The other thing we should look at is the **Condition** action. Select the **Condition** action and notice how the condition is built. You can define a condition and then the action you want based on if the condition is met. This is very helpful for functionality but also troubleshooting:

Figure 8.32 – An example of a condition with a yes action

Once we have saved our template and it is ready to use, we can test it in Business Central. For this, you will need to log in as one of the other users you created in Business Central. I logged into Business Central as *Adele* and then entered a purchase order, and submitted it for approval. To do that, I executed the following steps:

1. Log into Business Central and search for `Purchase`. Select **Purchase Orders**:

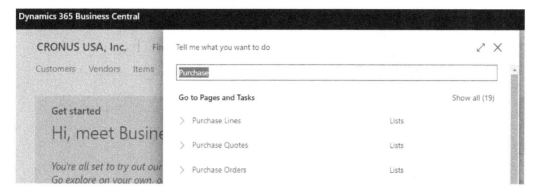

Figure 8.33 – Searching for Purchase in Business Central

2. Select + **New** from the **Purchase Orders** page:

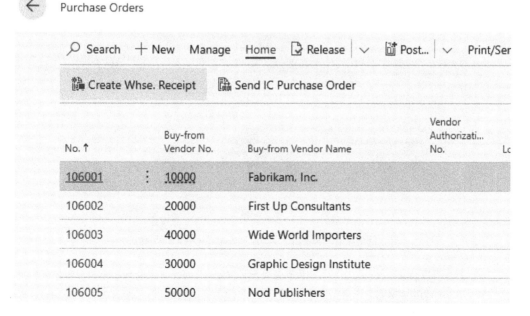

Figure 8.34 – Selecting + New to create a purchase order

3. Enter the **Purchase Order** information for **Vendor Name** and then **No.**, **Location Code**, and **Quantity**. Select **Request Approval** and **Send Approval Request**:

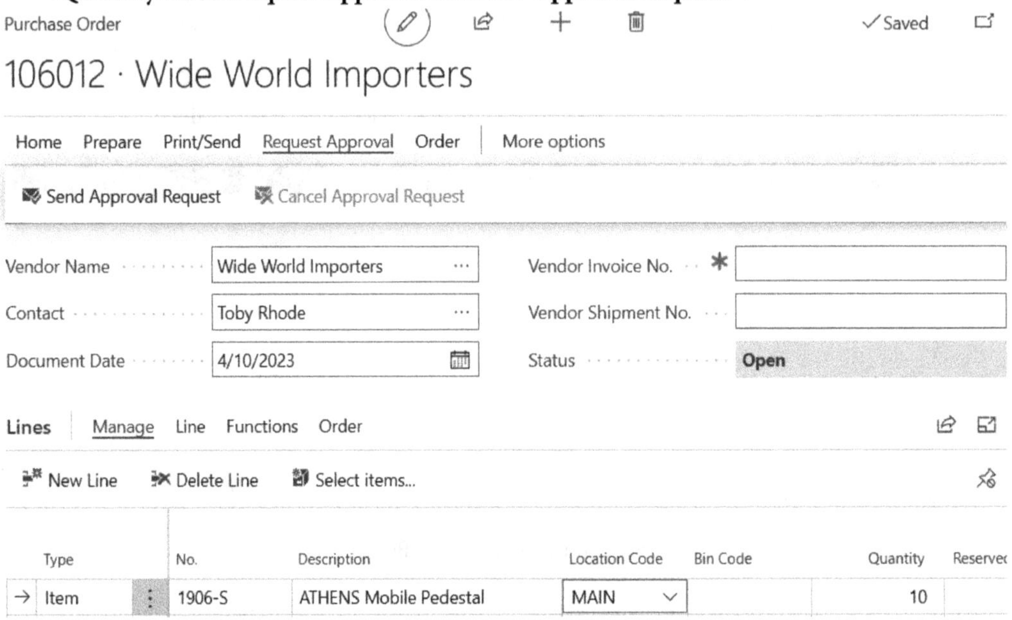

Purchase Order   (✎)   ☚   +   🗑   ✓ Saved   ⌐

106012 · Wide World Importers

Home	Prepare	Print/Send	Request Approval	Order	More options

📨 Send Approval Request   📪 Cancel Approval Request

Vendor Name	Wide World Importers ···		Vendor Invoice No. ✳	
Contact	Toby Rhode ···		Vendor Shipment No.	
Document Date	4/10/2023 📅		Status	**Open**

Lines	Manage	Line	Functions	Order		☚ 🔀

➕ New Line   ✖ Delete Line   🗒 Select items...   ⤢

Type	No.	Description	Location Code	Bin Code	Quantity	Reserved
→ Item	1906-S	ATHENS Mobile Pedestal	MAIN ⌄		10	

Figure 8.35 – Entering a new purchase order and requesting approval

4. **Purchase Order** will be sent for approval, and its status will be updated to **Pending Approval**:

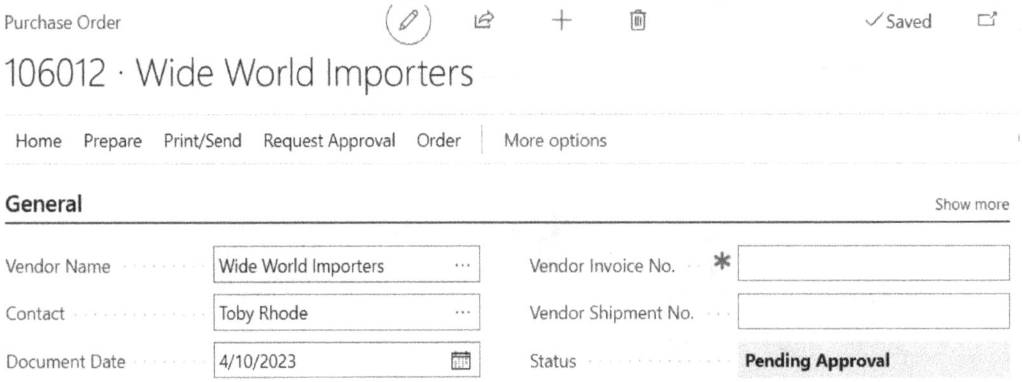

Purchase Order   (✎)   ☚   +   🗑   ✓ Saved   ⌐

106012 · Wide World Importers

Home	Prepare	Print/Send	Request Approval	Order	More options

General   Show more

Vendor Name	Wide World Importers ···		Vendor Invoice No. ✳	
Contact	Toby Rhode ···		Vendor Shipment No.	
Document Date	4/10/2023 📅		Status	**Pending Approval**

Figure 8.36 – Entering a new purchase order and requesting approval

5. The approval request comes in two different forms. We will get a notification in Teams, and we can pin the approvals app to our shortcut bar so that we can go in and approve our request. We will also get an email so that we can approve the request. Since we are in Teams, let's go ahead and approve it. Select **Requested**; the **Approvals** window will open:

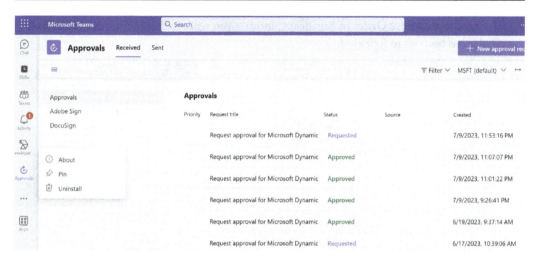

Figure 8.37 – Approvals app in Teams showing approvals that need to be done

6. From the **Approvals** app, you can accept or reject the request and make comments. In this case, we will select **Approve**:

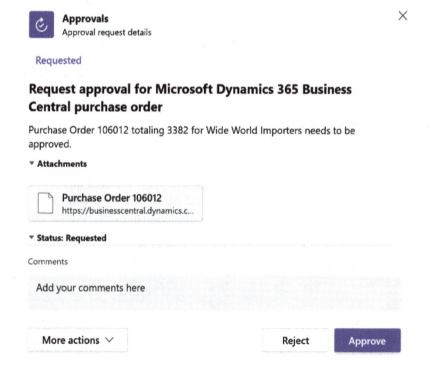

Figure 8.38 – Approvals app in Teams showing approvals that need to be done

7.   Go back to **Purchase Order** in Business Central – you will see that the status of **Purchase Order** has been set to **Released**:

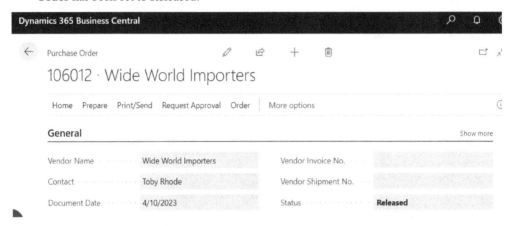

Figure 8.39 – Purchase Order with its released status after purchase approval

Your purchase approval is now working and running behind the scenes in your environment. Once you have verified that the template runs, you will be able to modify it as needed.

Common troubleshooting tips for approvals

There are some common errors that you may run into when working with approval templates or building flows from scratch. The first thing I do when building these flows is to keep it simple. I focus on getting the flow to work, and then I start laying in the complexity in small increments. It's easier to have a working base than build something where you are not sure where it is broken.

> **Tip**
>
> Another tip is to use a condition to help you determine where a flow is failing. For example, I was trying to build a flow that notified me when someone had submitted a timesheet. I could not get the flow to run, and when I tested it, it never returned a failure. So, what I had to do was add my trigger and one action and then create a condition to check if I met the condition. If the condition was yes, then it sent me a notification stating that it had been met, while if it was no, then it told me that I still had a problem. I did this with each action until I found my issue and resolved it.

Microsoft also has a list of common errors regarding Power Automate. You can find this list at `https://learn.microsoft.com/en-us/troubleshoot/power-platform/power-automate/common-errors-creating-and-assigning-flow-approvals`.

This list is technical and it would be best if you refer to their documentation for explanations of these errors.

When my flows do not work, I follow the following checklist each time until I find the error:

1. Verify the approval user setup in Business Central.

2. Verify whether the person has the correct approver assigned.

3. Verify the Business Central user permissions.

4. Verify the settings in the Power Automate flow:

    A. Check the environment.

    B. Check the inputs and outputs.

5. If the flow fails, drill into the flow to see where it breaks or if there is an error.

6. See when it last ran successfully and verify whether there have been any changes in Business Central or modifications to the Power Automate flow.

Summary

In this chapter, we explored the seamless integration of Power Automate approvals with Business Central. We learned that setting up and configuring these is quick and requires minimal time and effort. While it is easy to set up, the integration provides a robust and efficient approvals engine to use for not only purchase orders but other workflows as well.

We walked through the step-by-step instructions for configuring your Office, Power Automate, and Business Central environments. We also looked at how to set up a purchase order approval workflow. Finally, we identified some common troubleshooting tips for you to use when doing approvals.

In the next chapter, we will explore connecting Power BI to your Business Central environment. We'll explore how to enable Power BI reports inside of Business Central and then learn about data modeling to get your data out of Business Central so that you can create powerful dashboards using Power BI.

9
Connecting Power BI for Business Central Data

In this chapter, you'll use the skills you learned in *Chapter 2* on connecting to Business Central and out-of-the-box APIs to connect data to Power BI. In addition, we will walk through connecting Power BI to an Excel file. Finally, we will review setting up parameters in the report to connect to different databases and companies, along with basic best practices in data modeling. In this chapter, we will use Power BI Desktop and publish it to a workspace and Business Central.

Lastly, we will review different visuals and give hints on which visuals to use for what story you are trying to tell. It is essential to have clean data and excellent data modeling skills, and you will want your report to tell a story and make sense to the report consumers. Knowing your audience is critical in this process.

In this chapter, we're going to cover the following main topics:

- Enabling Power BI reports within Business Central
- Connecting to data in Power BI using out-of-the-box APIs
- Best practice data modeling
- Reviewing different visuals and publishing reports
- Creating a dashboard

Technical requirements

If you didn't install Power BI Desktop in *Chapter 2*, you will want to have it installed before going through the exercises in this chapter. You can download Power BI Desktop at `https://powerbi.microsoft.com/en-us/downloads/`.

This chapter's code examples can be found on GitHub: `https://github.com/PacktPublishing/Extending-Business-Central-with-the-Power-Platform`.

Exercise for creating a Power BI report and dashboard

K&S Solutions requires a Power BI report to manage Customer Credit Limits effectively. This chapter will focus on creating a comprehensive Customer Credit Limit report and a corresponding dashboard. The report that you'll generate in this chapter will be utilized in *Chapter 10* to integrate a Power Apps app, enabling users to review customer activities, modify Credit Limits, and block customers when necessary:

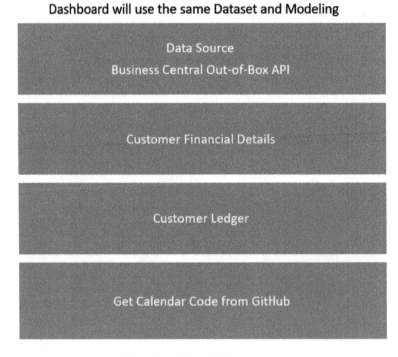

Figure 9.1 – Power BI data sources

We have the report layouts and lots to cover in this chapter. When I first started in Power BI, I thought I would have fun doing all the visuals, but I realized I am a data geek through and through; data modeling has been one of my favorite things, but having amazing visuals that tell a story is also a lot of fun. So, if this is your first time getting started with Power BI, have fun with it and embrace the whole process; this will make you a Power BI rock star. So, let's get started on building amazing Power BI reports/dashboards.

Enabling Power BI reports within Business Central

In this section, we will cover setting up Business Central with Power BI demo reports and having them available for the user on the Business Central home page:

1. Log in to Business Central and, on your **Home** page, scroll down to the **Power BI Report** section. Generally, this can be found on the bottom right:

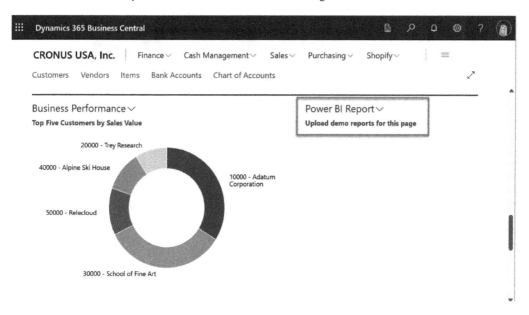

Figure 9.2 – Business Central home page

2. Select **Upload demo reports for this page**; the following screen will inform you that the demo reports to Power BI will run in the background. If you already have reports in your workspace, which means this isn't the first time you have loaded reports in this section, a message box will appear for you to select the reports instead. This is the first time it has been run, so it will run in the background. Select **refresh** or hit *F5*; the report will appear once it has finished downloading. Once it has been refreshed, it will show you **Top 5 Items Sold by Quantity**. See *Figure 9.4*:

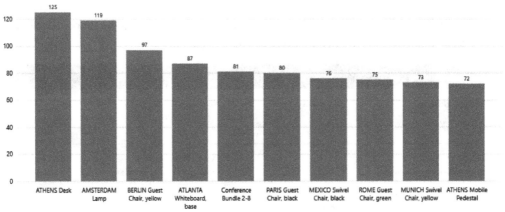

Figure 9.3 – Top 5 Items Sold by Quantity

3. This will give you your first Power BI report inside of Business Central. Here, you will see **Select Report, Expand Report, Previous Report, Next Report, Manage Report, Refresh Page, Upload Report**, and **Rest All Reports** upon selecting the dropdown under **Power BI Report**:

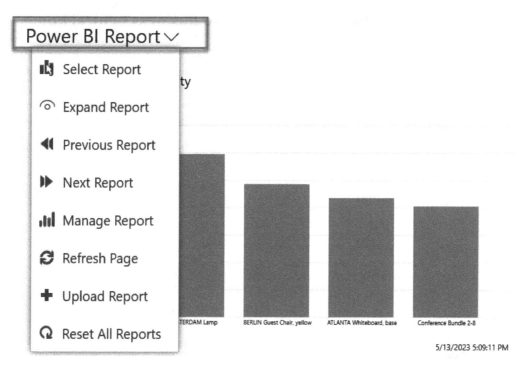

Figure 9.4 – Power BI Report Options

Most of these options are self-explanatory, but I want to point out a few. The first one is **Upload Report**; by selecting this option, if you have a Power BI report file with the **PBIX** extension, you can upload the file right into Business Central; once this has been added and deployed, it will appear in the list of selections of Power BI reports. The **Select Report** option will show you a list of all the Power BI reports that are available to you to add to Business Central. The list will show you all the Power BI workspaces you have been granted access to.

Power BI workspaces

It is essential to understand the workspace concept in Power BI. **A workspace** is a spot in Microsoft Power BI Platform that's used to collaborate with other users and share reports across the organization. Power BI has two workspaces: **My Workspace** and **Shared Workspace**. Shared Workspace admins can assign different permissions and access to the report and dataset. My Workspace is just for you; I use this one as a test or development environment. I will add some links in the *Further reading* section at the end of this chapter for additional resources on workspaces and users permission and access.

Adding additional Power BI reports to the Business Central home screen

Having the ability to embed additional Power BI reports into your Business Central home pages allows users to create Power BI reports and also share them with other team members within the organization. By integrating additional reports into your Business Central home page, you can access additional information and metrics. By following these steps, you can add additional reports to your home page.

Select a report to see all the Power BI reports available to add to your home screen. An option will appear stating all the available reports:

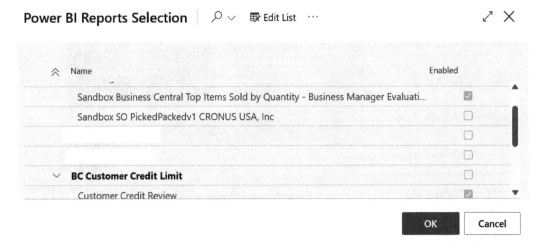

Figure 9.5 – Reports Selection

Adding user-specific reports to the home screen saves the user time; it allows them to stay in one application – Business Central – to do the day-to-day tasks and have the reports available to them. In the next session, we will step through connecting to your Business Central data in Power BI using APIs and how to connect to data that is stored in Excel files.

Connecting to data in Power BI using out-of-the-box APIs

In Power BI, you can connect to different data sources and use Power Query to create relationships and model data. So many data source options include **files**, **databases**, **power platforms**, **Azure**, and **online services**. There being so many options to connect data is one of the reasons Power BI is such a powerful tool. This section will focus on two options: **Online Service** and **File**. We will use Business Central to bring data into Power BI in our examples. If you need a refresher on accessing the Business Central API, refer to *Chapter 2*; with so much to cover in this chapter, I will get right to it. Here are the steps for connecting to data in Power BI:

1. Open Power BI Desktop and ensure you are logged in under the user that you have access to in Business Central. Select **Get data** on the home page ribbon | **Business Central** under **Online Services** and select **Connect**. Once the navigator screen is available, you will see Business Central and the database and companies you have access to. Navigate to **SANDBOX | CRONUS USA, Inc. | Standard APIs v2.0**:

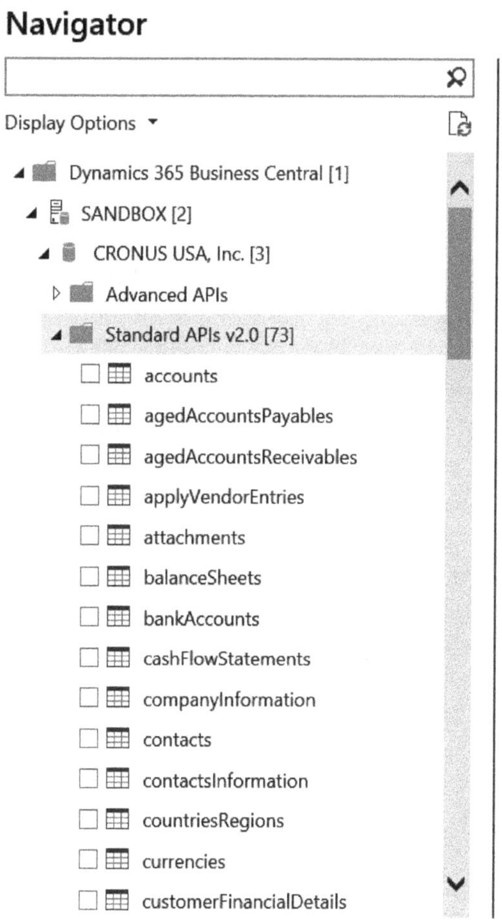

Figure 9.6 – Standard APIs

2. Scroll down or use the search bar to find a Customer API and transform data; this is where the data modeling magic happens. As we walk through the data modeling process, I would like to use a few rules that I incorporate every time I do this exercise; it keeps my data modeling consistent.

3. Rename the table; I named mine `Customers Details`:

   I.   Remove the columns you don't need; in this step, you will want to use the **Choose Columns** step on the **Home** page under **Manage Columns**. You will only want to do this step once – you will notice that **APPLIED STEPS** on the right will keep track of all the changes you make to the data. I have learned that you want to try and do this methodically and not go back and insert steps because it can cause issues down the road. Keep the **number**, **balance**, **totalSalesExcludingTax**, and **overdueAmount** fields:

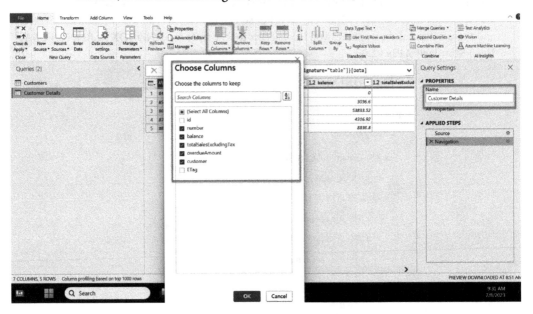

Figure 9.7 – Choose Columns

   II.   The API in **Customer Details** has several links to other tables; the first is the **customer** table. We want to show a few of the fields from the **customer** table by selecting the icon to the right of the **customer** field to expand all the columns:

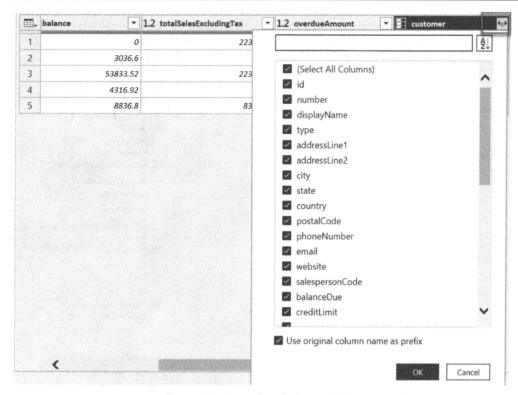

Figure 9.8 – Expanding Customer Fields

III.   Once the list appears, the first thing we need to do is uncheck **Use original column name prefix** because, in the next step, we plan to rename the fields. The second thing we need to do is uncheck all the fields since we only want to select a few of them: **displayName**, **city**, **state**, **salespersonCode**, **creditLimit**, **blocked**, and **paymentTerms**.

IV.   Expand the payment terms code so that we have some of the details for the report. Keep **dueDateCalculation**.

V.   Rename the columns – remember that users will be using them, and they don't always know the database field names. Also, embrace the space you have and put spaces between the column labels. Keep in mind that as you perform data modeling, the dataset will be turned over to users to build reports; having spaces between words is easier for the user as they build visuals and filter the data. This one was the hardest for me, and I still have to say it in my head when I am doing data modeling. If you are like me and used to removing space, using it will be challenging, but you do it over time. Double-click each column and rename **number** to `Customer`, **balance** to `Customer Balance`, **totalSalesExcludingTax** to `Total Sales`, **overdueAmount** to `Over Due Amount`, **displayname** to `Display Name`, **city** to `City`, **state** to `State`, **salespersonCode** to `Sales Rep`, **creditLimit** to `Credit Limit`, **blocked** to `Blocked`, and **duedateCalculation** to `Payment Terms`.

- he **Blocked** data comes through with a blank value set to _x0020_; this is commonly displayed when a value is blank or contains spaces. In this case, the blank value in Business Central shows up as **_x0020_**. To replace the value, select **Blocked**, right-click and select **Replace Values…**, and change _x0020_ to Not Blocked:

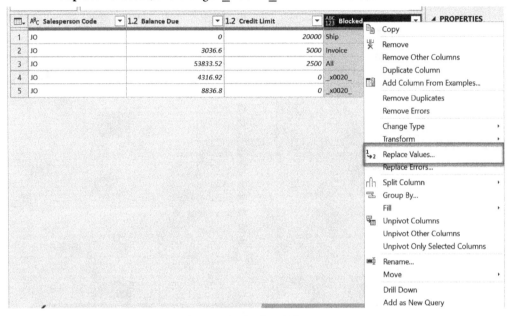

Figure 9.9 – Replace Values…

VI.   Create a column with available credit first as we need a column to subtract the credit limit from **Balance Due**. Select the **Credit Limit** field. Once highlighted, go to the top menu and select **Add Column | Standard | Subtraction**:

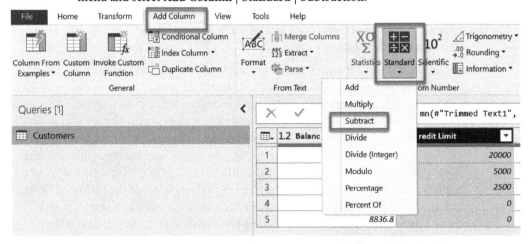

Figure 9.10 – Adding a Subtract column

VII. Set **Value** to **Balance Due** and select **OK**:

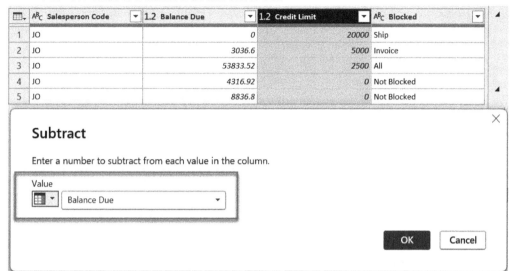

Figure 9.11 – Selecting Balance Due

VIII. To add the **Credit Available** column, select **Add Column | Conditional Column**; the new column's name will be **Credit Available**. Set **If** to Subtraction, **Operator** to is less than, **Value** to 0, **Output** to 0, and **Else** to Subtraction. Then, select **OK**:

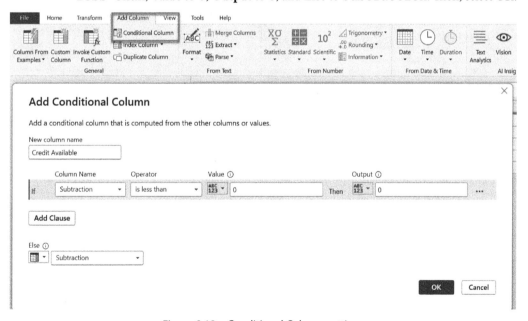

Figure 9.12 – Conditional Column settings

4. The next table or data we need is the **Customer Ledger Entry** table. Select **Recent Sources** on the **Home** ribbon; since we already got the Customer Details API from Business Central, we can use **Recent Sources**, select **Business Central**, then navigate to **Standard API** and scroll or search items and select **customerLedgerEntries**. Then, click **OK**:

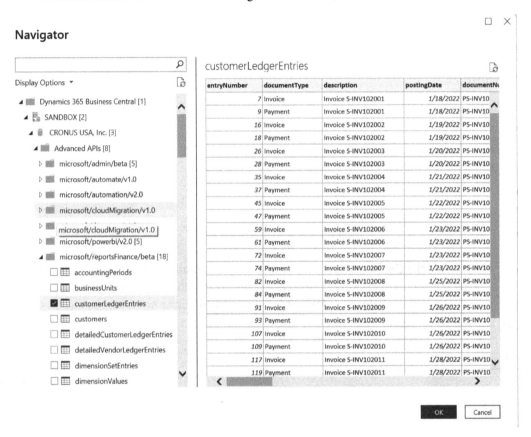

Figure 9.13 – customerLedgerEntries

5. Rename this `Customer Ledger Entries`.

6. Select **Choose Columns** and keep `documentType`, `customernumber`, `postingDate`, `open`, `amount`, `debitamount`, and `creditamount`.

7. Rename the columns so that **documentType** is Document Type, **customernumber** is Customer Number, **postingDate** is Posting Date, **debitAmount** is Invoice Amount, and **creditAmount** is Credit Amount.

8. Right-click **Posting Date** and select **Date**:

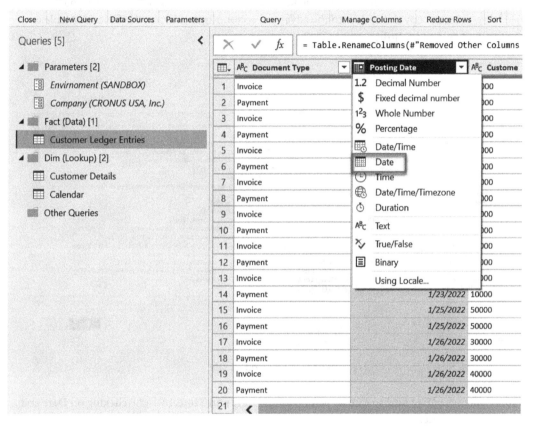

Figure 9.14 – Posting Date

9. The next step is that we need a calendar, and Business Central doesn't have a lovely calendar for us to use; I keep this step in my OneNote tips and copy this repeatedly. There's no reason to reinvent the wheel with every report. First, we need to create a table to store the calendar information, select **Enter Data** on the **Home** ribbon, leave the table empty, and enter a name. I usually name it `Calendar`. Download the Calendar code from GitHub. Once you've done this, you can copy the code into the advanced editor. Right-click on the **Calander** table and go to **Advanced Editor**:

Figure 9.15 – Calendar code

10. Update the **Date** field so that it's just **Date**, not **Date and Time**, by right-clicking on **Date** and selecting **Date**:

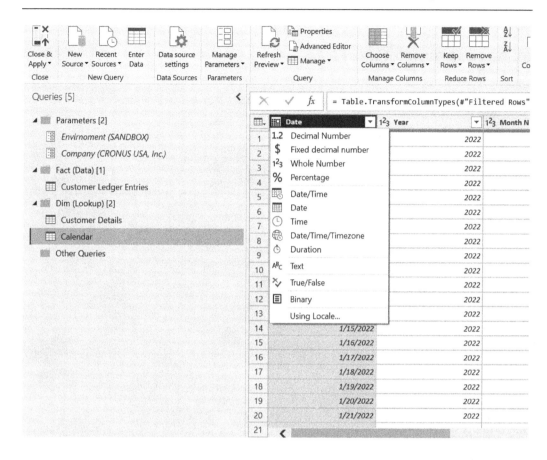

Figure 9.16 – Date only

Creating parameters

It is beneficial to include parameters in all my reports. This practice offers convenience when moving them from one environment to another or transitioning from a sandbox environment to a production environment:

1. To create a new parameter, select **Manage Parameters** on the **Home** ribbon and select **New Parameters**. You need one for the environment and one for the company. See the following screenshot for the settings that I used to set up **Manage Parameters**:

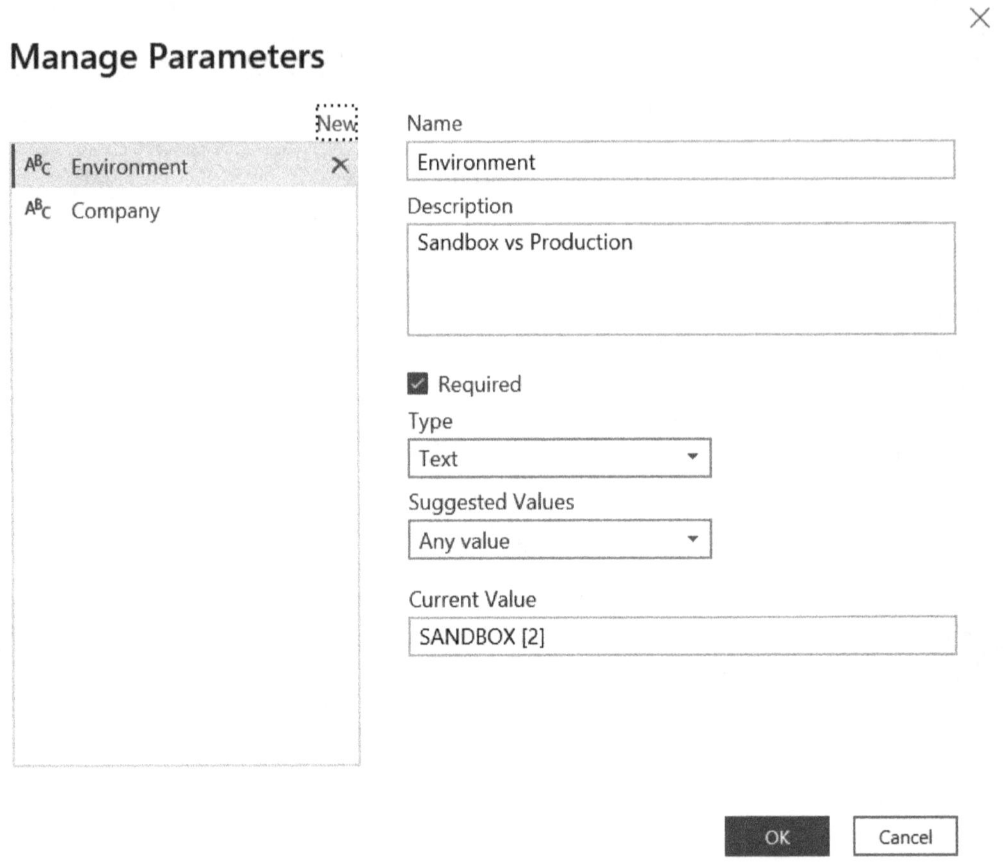

Manage Parameters

New

ᴬᴮc Environment   ✕

ᴬᴮc Company

Name

Environment

Description

Sandbox vs Production

☑ Required

Type

Text

Suggested Values

Any value

Current Value

SANDBOX [2]

OK   Cancel

Figure 9.17 – Environment parameters

Tip

This is a big tip, and I have gotten burned by this a few times. The environment and company are case-sensitive and *ALWAYS* in caps; I repeat, *ALWAYS* in caps. Another tip is that just because you go to the company information card or see the company name on the home screen in Business Central, this doesn't always mean it is the company's name. This is a good tip for troubleshooting as well.

I always create one for **Environment** and one for **Company** and name them so that the users know what information to enter:

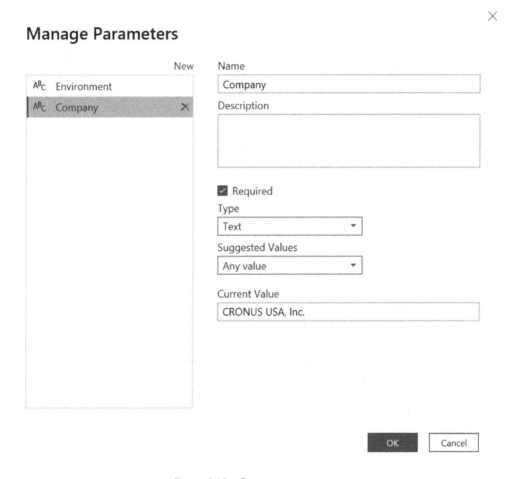

Figure 9.18 – Company parameters

The last thing we will talk about before we close and apply is **Star Schema**. There are many books and articles on this topic; I recommend that you do further research if you plan to do more Power BI report designs. First, Star Schema is a data modeling technique used in data warehousing. It helps organize data into central fact and dimension tables. I like to organize my tables by parameters, facts, and dimensions; this keeps me organized and helps me when I'm data modeling and linking the tables. I have added a screenshot in *Figure 9.13* of how I organized the modeling we have been doing in this section:

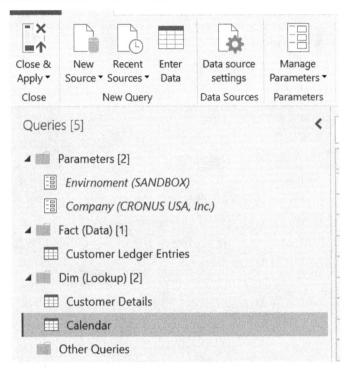

Figure 9.19 – Power Query

2. Once you have completed the modeling, select **Close & Apply** on the **Home** ribbon; also, take the opportunity to save the report if you haven't already saved it. Note that the application could take a few minutes, depending on your data, with the one we just created using the Cronus database, but it might take a few minutes in a production environment. I don't want you to be surprised when you do this for the first time in a larger dataset.

    This is an excellent time to discuss the **Ledger Entry** table, especially the Item Ledger Entry. As many of you know, this table can become a beast if you have worked with Business Central for a while. Therefore, I caution you when you use it. If the report needs to be refreshed on demand and depending on what you are using the report for, you should take the opportunity to add some filters and understand the business requirement because you could have frustrated users if they are waiting on the refresh. It could take hours to refresh the data. This might also be an excellent time to create a custom API, work with Postman, or review other tables that can be used to get the data other than the Item Ledger Entry. Keep in mind it is always best to do as much as you can upstream closer to the data source than downstream later in Power BI (Power Query). We refer to this as **Roche's Maxim of Data Transformation**: "*Data should be transformed as far upstream as possible and as far downstream as necessary.*" In using this theory, the approach promotes efficient data processing, data consistency, and data governance and performs downstream only as necessary, based on business requirements and user cases to make it user-friendly.

That covers the data modeling section. I want to recap a few things we discussed:

- Rename your API table; choose **Columns** once, and if you missed or need to add a column, go back to **APPLIED STEPS** and select the gear icon to make adjustments.

- Embrace the space and rename the columns to something that will make sense to the user and look nice on a report.

- Change your data type and make sure it's correct.

- Add parameters in. Remember that they are case-sensitive.

- You can rename **APPLIED STEPS**, especially if you are adding filter steps. I am sure there are many more, but that at least gets you started.

With that, we have covered transforming data using the Business Central API. Next, we need to review the **data modeling** function in Power BI. Some Power BI developers like to lay out the data modeling view in a Star Schema if you follow Star Schema. This chapter will connect the tables and discuss a few key points.

Setting up and managing the relationships between the tables is an important process. In the preceding example, we have three tables: **Calendar**, **Customer Details**, and **Customer Ledger Entries**. The following relationships should be set in the **Modeling** section. **Date** in the **Calendar** table relates to **Posting Date** in **Customer Ledger**. **Customer Number** in the **Customer Details** table relates to **Customer Number** in **Customer Ledger Entries**.

3. Select **Manage relationships** to set a relationship between the tables:

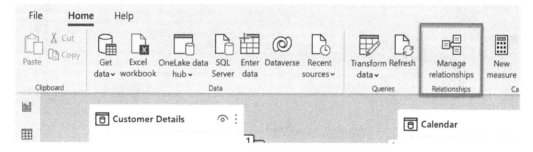

Figure 9.20 – Manage relationships

4. Select **Customer Details** and highlight **Customer Ledger Entries**. Set it to **Customer Number**. Then, set **Cardinality** to One to many (1:*) and **Cross filter direction** to Single:

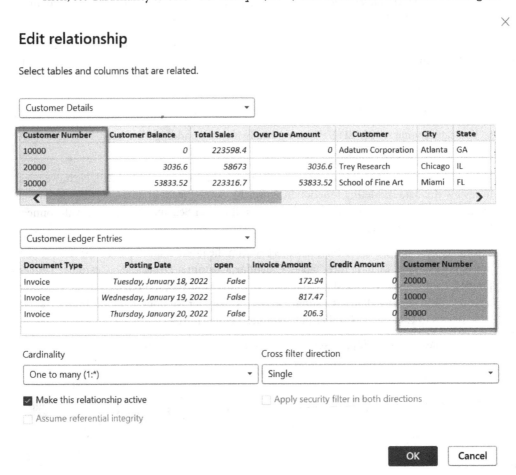

Figure 9.21 – Setting Customer Details to Customer Ledger Entries

5. Select **Calendar** and highlight **Date**. Set **Customer Ledger Entries** to **Posting Date**, **Cardinality** to One to many (!:*), and **Cross filter direction** to Single:

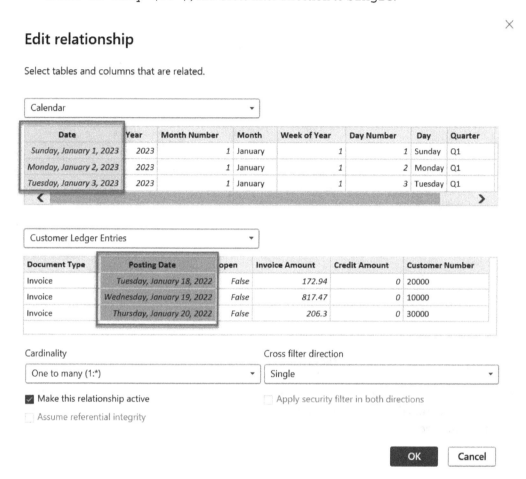

Figure 9.22 – Setting Calendar to Date, then Customer Ledger Entry to Posting Date

Here is the screenshot for the relationship settings:

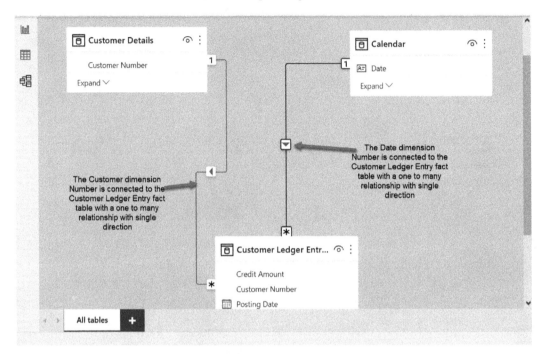

Figure 9.23 – Relationship

6. You also want to hide the fields in the **Customer Ledger Entries** transactions table. This allows the user only has the option to select the field in one table, and it makes it cleaner for filtering and slicing the data:

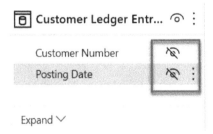

Figure 9.24 – Hiding Customer Number and Posting Date

7. You will want to mark the **Calendar** table:

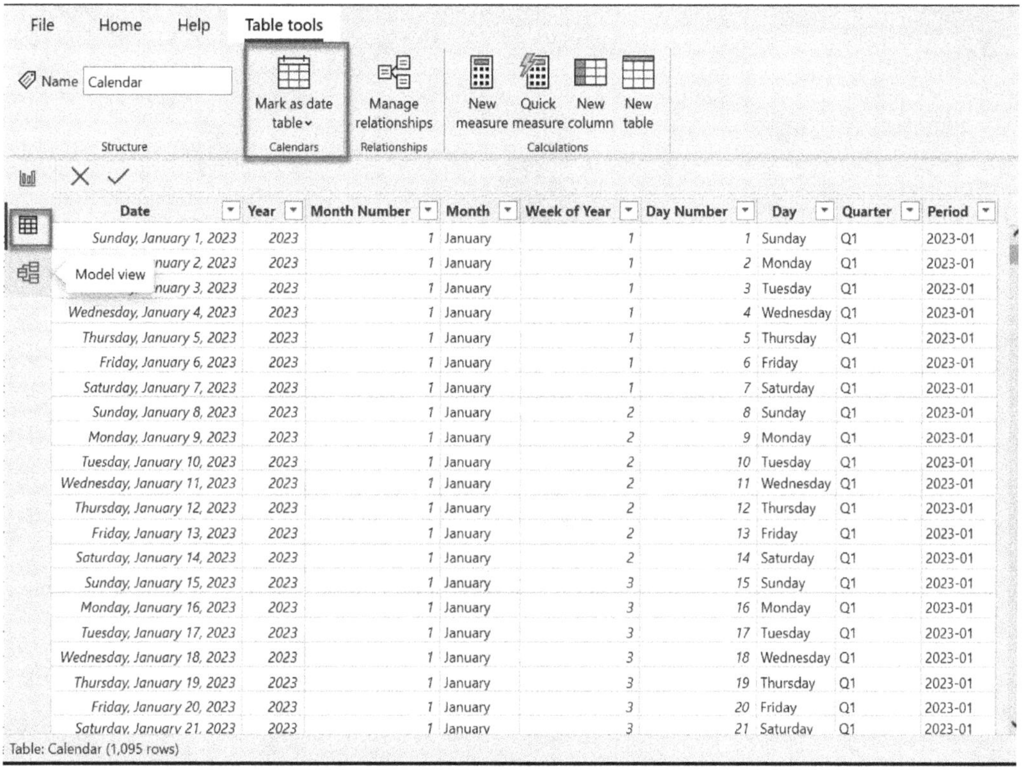

Figure 9.25 – Marking the Calendar table

8. After you select the **Mark as date table** option, you'll see this window; select **Date** and then **OK**:

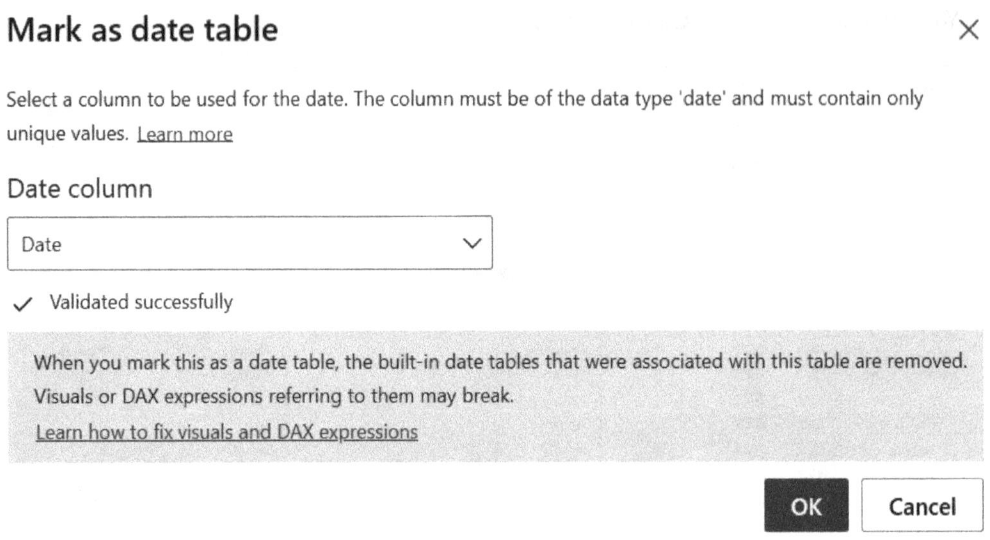

Mark as date table   ✕

Select a column to be used for the date. The column must be of the data type 'date' and must contain only unique values. Learn more

Date column

Date   ⌄

✓   Validated successfully

When you mark this as a date table, the built-in date tables that were associated with this table are removed. Visuals or DAX expressions referring to them may break.
Learn how to fix visuals and DAX expressions

OK   Cancel

Figure 9.26 – Selecting the Date column

Check out *Mastering Dynamics 365 Business Central, 2nd Edition* for further reading and learn how to create custom APIs and how to optimize performances.

With that, we have covered data modeling and the relationships between the tables; next, we will work on visuals and building out the reports.

Reviewing different visuals and publishing reports

When creating Power BI reports, you'll want to consider a few key things. First, is the data in the report accurate and up to date? In the previous section, we covered connecting to data and data modeling; in this section, we will review the report layout and different visualizations. It is just as crucial as data modeling when you are designing your report that you tell the story and know what story you are telling. If the user opens the report and must spend lots of time figuring out what the visuals are saying, or if it isn't clear, the user will not use it. We will dive into user adoption later in this book but always keep the user in mind when building your visuals. As you probably already know, I like to use color, but I am cautious with the color I use in my dashboard reports. Still, have fun with this section; even if you are not that creative, you can use many different sites to get inspiration, and I will add a few in *Further reading*. When all else fails, you can always go to Pinterest; I am sure some of you reading this book just said *no way*!

Power BI visuals

First, I would like to review some of the typical visuals that come with Power BI. You can always get more visuals and import them for multiple sites; there are probably hundreds of varieties. I recommend downloading the proper visual reference from Marco and Alberto.

Download the right visual reference from SQLBI: `https://www.sqlbi.com/ref/power-bi-visuals-reference/`.

Here are some common visuals:

- **Bar chart**: This is a comparison visual that's used to compare data across categories.

- **Line chart**: This is used to show trends over time and changes over time.

- **Pie chart**: This is used to show the proportions or percentage of a measure. The wedges are broken down into pieces that represent different categories, and the total wedge always adds up to 100%. Note that when you're using this visual, if you have too many categories or when the differences between the categories are minor, this chart will become challenging to read.

- **Ribbon chart**: This helps visualize changes in rank or position over time. It is used to compare different categories and data points and identify trends in patterns in the data.

- **Doughnut chart**: This is like a pie chart, but the center of the chart is blank. If you're comparing three to five categories, this chart can be helpful. However, if you have more than five categories, this visual can be challenging to read and interpret.

- **Gauge**: This is a comparison visual. Always start with zero when you use a gauge visual since they are often used when showing progress toward a goal or target. Gauges are best suited for displaying a single value.

- **Funnel**: This is a flow visual and is used to represent the stages in a process or progression of data to another category or stage. They can help identify bottlenecks or areas of improvement.

- **Scatter**: This has two value axes to show one set of numerical data along a horizontal axis. An example I like to use is if you want to see sales for a particular salesperson over time and see the trend. This can also show outliers.

- **Decomposition tree**: I like this visual and use it when I have multiple dimensions; it is nice to have when looking at different sales order types or customer groups; it allows you to drill down into your dimension to see further information. You can also use it to explore or conduct root cause analysis.

- **Map**: A map visual helps display measures and data across a mapped area and is commonly used to show sales numbers or shipping areas across a mapped area. You can use this to see whether a site is more concentrated than another area.

- **Table**: This is common because it is more like Excel, with data in rows and columns like in spreadsheets. It is used to display detailed data, and you can use conditional formatting on the values and add additional formatting.

- **Matrix**: This is like a table visual but it allows for more grouping and summarization of rows.

- **Cards**: This is a single visual that's used to represent one number.

- **Q&A**: This visual allows the users to ask questions about the data.

Let's add a few visuals to the Power BI report we worked on in this chapter.

Power BI report editor

The report editor is where you will design and add visuals and a matrix to your report or dashboard. The Power BI editor is divided into several sections: **Ribbon**, **Report Canvas**, **Filters**, **Visualizations**, and **Data**. It is essential to become familiar with each of the areas:

- **Ribbon**: The ribbon is standard with all Microsoft products, so you are probably familiar with this section

- **Report Canvas**: This is where you build your report/dashboard

You have three panes, **Filters**, **Visualizations**, and **Data**. Each of these sections has properties that relate to the filter, visual, and data:

- **Filter**: This pane displays any filters you have that link to the page or all pages.

- **Visualizations**: This pane shows all the available visuals. For each, you have visual, build, and format. This is where you manage all the properties for your visuals.

- **Data**: Finally, this pane displays all the tables, data, and measures you have available for your report/dashboard:

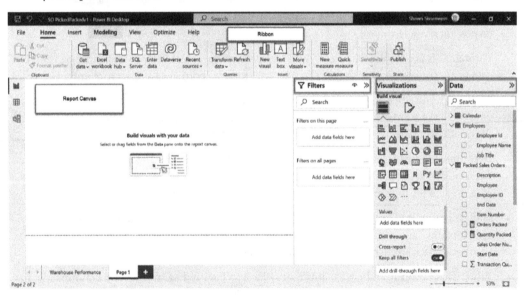

Figure 9.27 – Power BI navigation terminology

Overall, the report editor in Power BI has everything you need to design and create reports with a wide range of visual options, modeling tools, and formatting styles.

Start with a blank canvas; the first thing I like to do is add a light background color to the canvas. I usually always use a light gray:

1. Select the **paintbrush** tool in the **Visualizations** pane and go to **Wallpaper**; under **Color**, select one of the light grays or any light color you would like to use. You will notice that the canvas area will be your chosen new color:

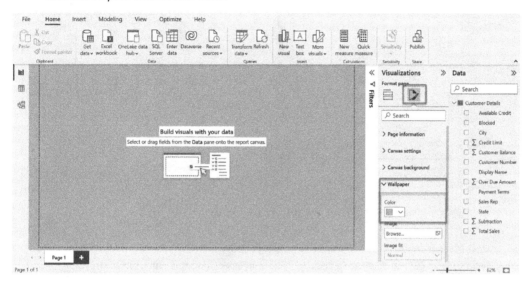

Figure 9.28 – Report Wallpaper

2. Our report needs a few measures to display the customer credit limit and available credit. These measures provide us with the flexibility to perform calculations on-the-fly and dynamically adjust them based on user interactions or filters applied to the data. They can calculate totals, averages, counts, minimums, maximums, and other statistical functions. A measure can become very complicated, but we will start with just a few in this report. Select **Measure tools** and **New measure** and in **fx code** enter Credit Amount = SUM('Customer Details' [Credit Limit]). Then, select **Format Decimal Number**:

> **Tip**
> As you start typing in the formula bar, it is always best to select the data from the drop-down list; this will help you remember the formula and pick the proper function and datasets. You will notice this when you start typing after =; Power BI Intellisense will begin to guess what you want to enter in the bar.

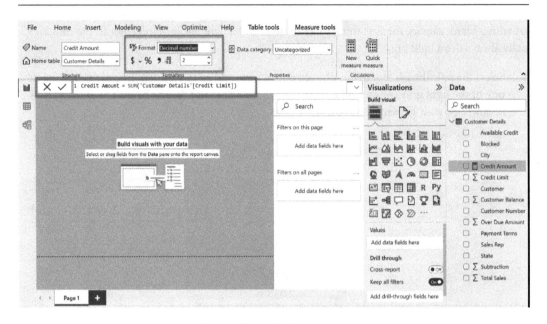

Figure 9.29 – Credit Amount

3. Select **Measure tools** and **New measure** and in **fx code**, enter Balance = SUM('Customer Details' [Customer Balance]). Then, select **Format Decimal Number**:

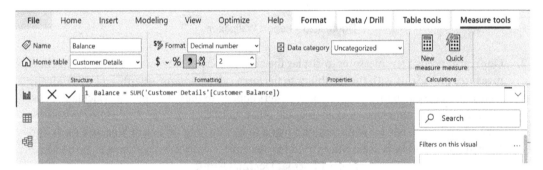

Figure 9.30 – Balance

4. Select **Measure tools** and **New measure** and in **fx code**, enter Available % Credit = DIVIDE([Credit Available]), [Credit Amount],0). Then, select **Format Percentage**:

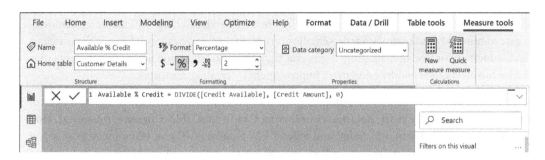

Figure 9.31 – Available % Credit

5. The next measure is **Available Credit**; in this measure, we'll add a couple of variables. The benefit of these variables is that we can use them in future measures. It is best practice to put each variable on a separate line, making it easier to read and understand. Format the value to a decimal number and add a comma:

```
1 Credit Available =
2 VAR _Balance = SUM('Customer Details'[Customer Balance])
3 VAR _Credit = SUM('Customer Details'[Credit Limit])
4 VAR _Avail = _Credit - _Balance
5 RETURN
6 _Avail
```

Figure 9.32 – Credit Available

6. Follow the previous steps to create measures for **Payments, Sales, Sales YTD, Document Amount**, and **Document year to date**:

A. `Payments = SUM('Customer Ledger Entries'[Credit Amount])`

B. `Sales = SUM('Customer Ledger Entries'[Invoice Amount])`

C. `Sales YTD = TOTALYTD([Sales], 'Calendar'[Date])`

D. `Doc Amount = VAR _Inv = SUM('Customer Ledger Entries'[amount])`

`VAR _Pmt = _Inv * -1`

`VAR _Result = IF(SELECTEDVALUE('Customer Ledger Entries'[Document Type]) = "Invoice", _Inv, _Pmt)`

`RETURN`

`_Result`

E. `Document Amount YTD =`

`TOTALYTD([Document Amount], 'Calendar'[Date])`

We have now covered all the necessary measures for creating the visuals. Power BI measures empower the user to move beyond basic data representation, enabling data analysis, complex calculations, and valuable metrics for decision-making. Users can transform raw data into actionable insights that enhance business understanding and drive improvement by creating measures.

In this section, we have established a foundation with various basic measures. Let's recap the measures we created: **Available % Credit**, **Balance**, **Credit Amt**, **Credit Available**, **Document Amount**, **Doc Amt**, **Doc Amt YTD**, **Payments**, **Sales**, and **Sales YTD**. Finally, I will give you a sneak peek at the visuals we will be building in the next section. We will leave a space on the right for the Power Apps app that we will build together in *Chapter 10*:

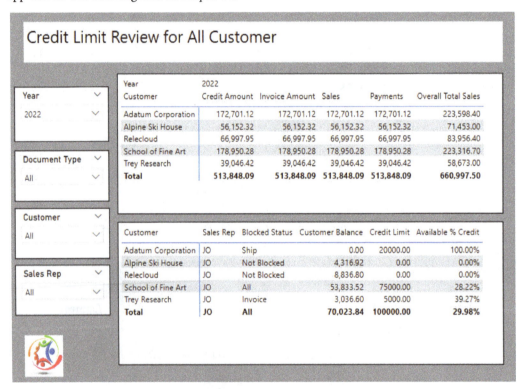

Figure 9.33 – Credit Limit Review for All Customer

We will start by adding four slicers from the **Visualizations** pane:

1. For the first filter, select the slicer visual and drop it onto the canvas area; once you have the slicer on the canvas and have it selected, select the **Data** pane and tick the **Year** checkbox. You can either drag it onto the visual or, in the **Visualizations** pane, drop it into the **Fields** section:

Figure 9.34 – Year slicer

2. Once you have one slicer, you can select it and copy and paste it three more times on the canvas. This will give you a total of four slicers. Once you have these slicers, replace the fields with **Document Type**, **Customer**, and **Sales Rep**. Your canvas should look like mine, with four slicers:

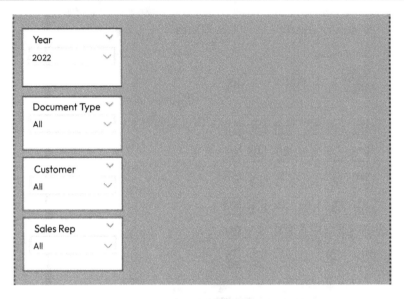

Figure 9.35 – The four slicers

3. We want to add a border around all four slicers so that they stand out. Select the **Visualizations** pane and highlight the **paintbrush** icon. Then, under **General**, select **Visual border** and set the button to **On**:

Figure 9.36 – Visual border

4. Repeat *Step 3* for all the visuals.

5. We have two more visuals to display. Here, we will use a **Matrix** visual. Select anywhere on the canvas in a blank area toward the bottom and select the **Visualizations** pane, then the **Matrix** icon. It will always drop the visual in the top-left corner:

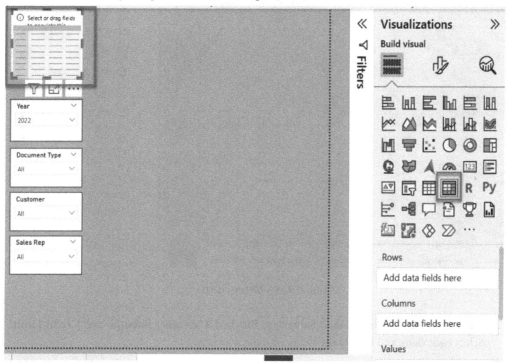

Figure 9.37 – Matrix Visual

6. Drag it toward the bottom and space it, as shown in the preceding figure. Now, in the **Visualizations** pane, add **Customers** as the row. The values we want to display in this visual are **Sales Rep**, **Blocked, Balance**, **Credit Amount**, and **Available % Credit**:

> **Tip**
> Make sure you have the visual selected before you add these fields.

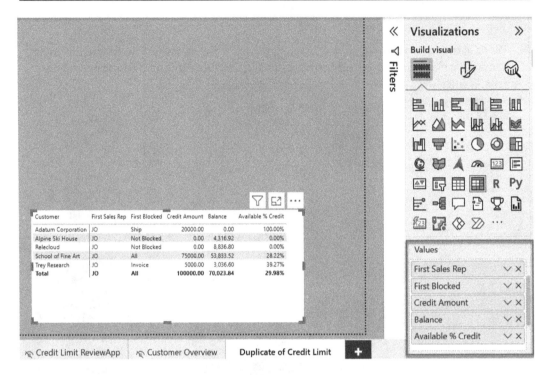

Figure 9.38 – Matrix visual

7. We want to rename these values **Sales Rep**, **Blocked**, **Customer Balance**, and **Credit Limit**. Select each value and update the fields with the new label.

8. Add a border around the visual by selecting **Paintbrush | General |Effects| Visual border**, just like we did in *Step 3*.

9. For the last visual, follow *Steps 5* to *6* and add **Customers** to **Rows** and **Year** to **Columns**. For the values, add **Credit Amount**, **Invoice Amount, Sales**, **Payments**, and **Overall Total Sales**.

10. To keep everything consistent with the rest of the visuals, turn on the **Visual** border.

11. The report needs a title. Go to **Home** and insert a text box by choosing **Text box**:

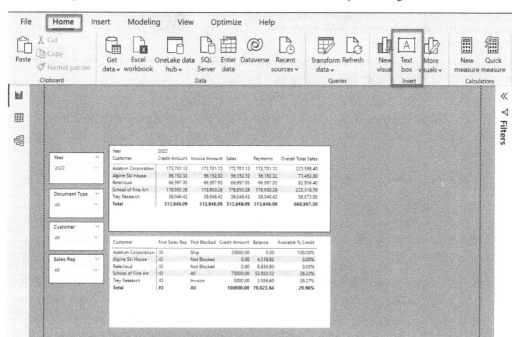

Figure 9.39 – Inserting a text label

12. Align the label at the top of the report and enter `Credit Limit Review for All Customers`. All the formatting options will be available to you. For example, you can select different fonts, sizes, bold, and italic:

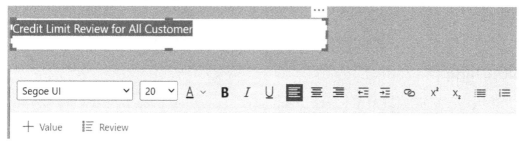

Figure 9.40 – Formatting the report header

> **Note**
>
> Power BI can add dynamic information that can update alongside your selected data. An example would be to add a customer name, which would allow the label to update with **Customer Name** if the customer is filtered in the report; another use would be date ranges or date filters. I encourage you to use this in future reports you build, especially if you want to show a date or specific data in the header based on dynamic information.

13. If you want to add a logo to the bottom of the report, select **Insert**, then **Image**, and navigate to your logo or image. Many customers like to use their specific logo and incorporate a company color theme.

14. Save the report as `CustomerCreditLimitReview`.

In this report, we have not implemented any conditional formatting or added icons. However, I highly encourage you to explore the various formatting options available. These options include background colors, font colors, and icons, which can effectively highlight and communicate your data, allowing it to tell a story more quickly.

For instance, if a customer exceeds their credit limit, you can change the color of their data to reflect this, perhaps transitioning from green to a lighter shade of red as they approach the credit limit. You can also utilize icons such as up and down arrows to indicate value increases or decreases. Additionally, you can apply different colors to values associated with different states or sales representatives, providing further differentiation and visual cues.

It's important to note that you have limitless data formatting options. However, it's crucial to exercise caution and ensure that the formatting choices serve a purpose and contribute to the report's narrative. Avoid overwhelming the report with excessive formatting as it may create noise and distract from the overall message. Remember, the formatting should enhance the story the data tells rather than overshadow it.

In the upcoming section, we will explore the process of publishing the report to a **Workspace**.

Publishing the report

Publishing a report in Power BI is straightforward, allowing you to share your reports with others in your organization. This also allows you to add your report to the Business Central home page. You want to have a workspace other than My Workspace to publish your report; this will enable you to share it with other users. You don't want to publish to My Workspace since that workspace is designed for only you.

Let's walk through creating a workspace for the development client you have used in this book:

1. Open your web browser, go to `apps.powerbi.com`, and log in:

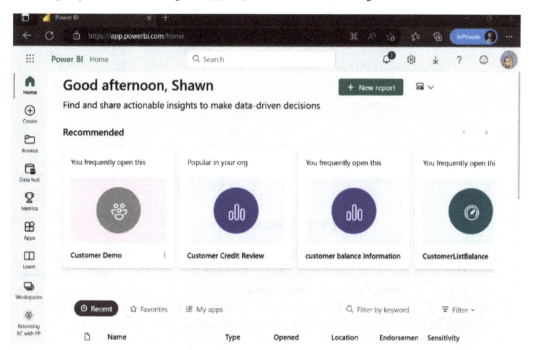

Figure 9.41 – The Power BI service home screen

2. Select **Workspace** and **+ New workspace**; the name I used was **Extending BC with PP**. Then, save it. Now that you have created this workspace, it will be available so that you can publish your reports to it.

3. Open the Power BI report you created in the previous section and on the ribbon, under **Home**, select **Publish** and select a destination. This destination will be the workspace you want the report to be saved. In this case, we want it to be saved under **Extending BC with PP**:

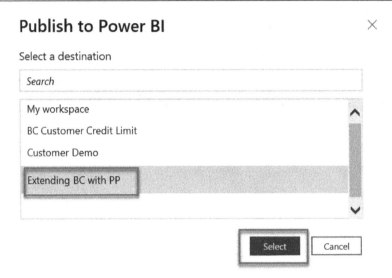

Figure 9.42 – Available workspaces

When you publish to the Power BI service in the cloud, you get two files: the report and the dataset you created when you did the modeling in the report. Once the report has been published, you can go to the Power BI service to view and interact with it. In the service, you have many additional options; you can run the report and share the report with your team members, as well as set up automatic data refreshes and customize the report's settings.

4.   Go back to the Power BI service; you will see your report and dataset:

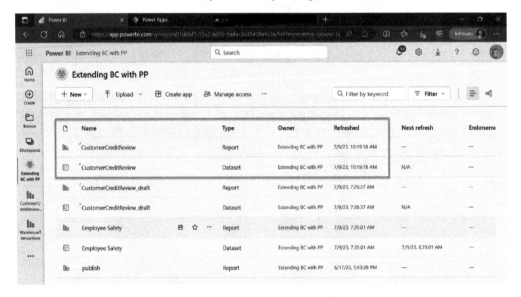

Figure 9.43 – Available report and dataset

In the next section, we will explore the topic of dashboards and visuals. Dashboards are highly effective tools that enable businesses to gain deep insights from their data and make informed, data-driven decisions.

Dashboard

Understanding dashboards and a few rules is essential when creating them. A **dashboard** is a collection of visualizations that provide a high-level overview of critical performance and other essential metrics. Dashboards are typically designed to be easy to understand and allow users to identify trends and outliers in their data quickly. A key benefit of using them is enabling users to monitor and analyze data in real time to help them make decisions. They can also be used as collaboration tools.

> **Tips on creating dashboards**
>
> Utilize **KISS**; define goals for the dashboard and design with the target audience in mind and be consistent and clear; choose the right colors and keep the background light; highlight the most relevant information; and pick the right charts.

Exercise – creating a dashboard from a customer report

1. Open the **CustomerCreditReview** report and select **Edit**; you will notice that the screen looks like the Power BI desktop screen. Select a new page; this will give you a blank canvas to work with. Rename the bottom tab to **Customer Dashboard** so that you can keep it separate from the other report pages:

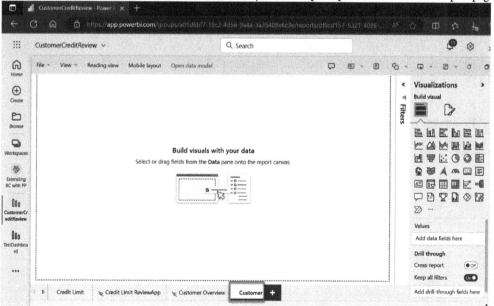

Figure 9.44 – Customer dashboard

2. Change the wallpaper to light gray by selecting **Visualization | Paintbrush | Wallpaper**. This is the same step we did in the *Power BI report editor* section.

3. We are going to add three cards for **Customer Payments, Customer Sales**, and **Customer Balance**. Start by selecting the **Card** icon on the **Visualizations** pane. In the first one, add the customer:

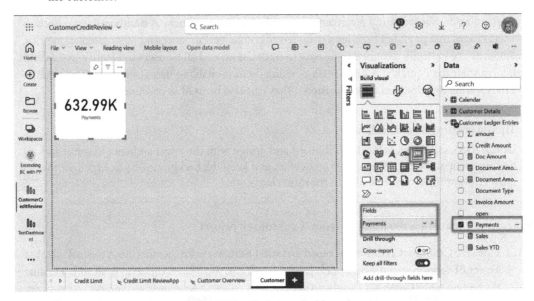

Figure 9.45 – Customer dashboard

4. For the next two cards, copy **Payments** and paste it twice. Replace one of the **Payments** fields with **Sales** and the other with **Balance**. Line them up and shrink them a little bit so that they fit next to each other.

5. Rename the cards by selecting the field's value and typing over the name of each field. Change **Payments** to `Customer Payments`, **Sales** to `Customer Sales`, and **Balance** to `Customer Balances`:

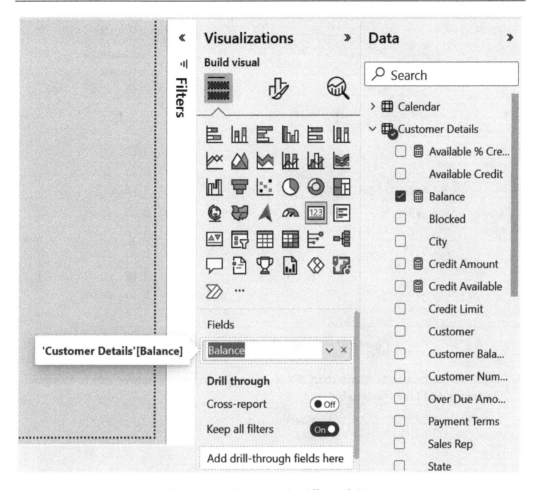

Figure 9.46 – Renaming the different fields

6.   Change the color of the cards by selecting the card. Then, go to the **Visualizations** pane and select **Paintbrush | General | Effects | Color | More Options | Enter Hex #**:

   A.   Set **Customer Payments** to Hex #ACD290

   B.   Set **Customer Balance** to Hex #A0D1FF

   C.   Set **Customer Sales** to Hex #C7BBE7

7.   Q&A is a nice way to give users the ability to ask different questions about the data. Select the **Q&A** icon on the **Visualization** pane.

8.   Now, I want to tie in the Q&A colors so that they match the blue on the customer balance. Do this by selecting the **Q&A** visual, then **Paintbrush**. In the **Visual** tab, under **Suggestions | Cards**, change the font to black and the card's color the light blue by using Hex #A0D1FF:

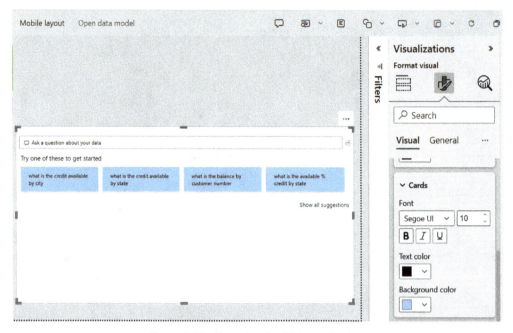

Figure 9.47 – Changing the Q&A card's colors

9. Add a line and stacked column chart. Set **X-axis** to **Customer**, **Column y-axis** to **Sales** and **Payments**, and **Line y-axis** to **Balance**:

Figure 9.48 – Line and stacked chart visualizations

10. Add a line chart visual. Set **X-axis** to **Customer** and **Y-axis** to **Balance**:

Figure 9.49 – Line and chart visualizations

11. Create a new dashboard to pin the visual to by selecting the **Pin** icon at the top right of the screen:

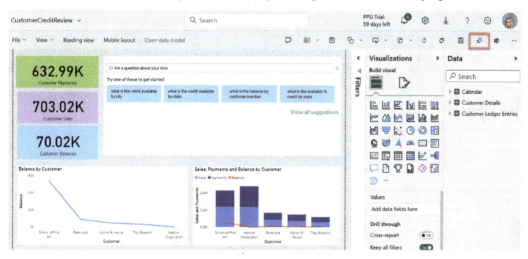

Figure 9.50 – Pin to dashboard

12. In this step, you will be prompted to pin to **Existing dashboard** or **New dashboard**. Select **New dashboard** and name it `Customer Analysis`:

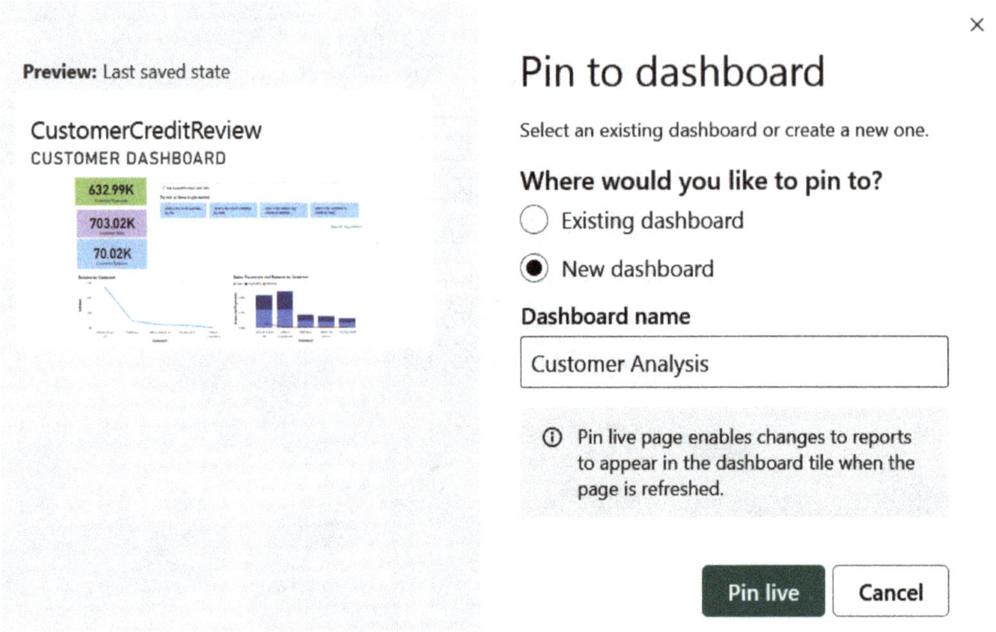

Figure 9.51 – New dashboard

This dashboard showcases many visual elements and demonstrates the versatility of creating different visuals. It highlights the ability to save these visuals to multiple dashboards, allowing you to efficiently organize and present data across various contexts. One thing to consider is setting up alerts to send the sales manager or account staff an alert when the customer balances are a certain dollar amount. Another common alert is showing the bank balance and, when it drops under a dollar amount, sending it to the accounting manager or CFO. How often do we go to a client and they ask, "*I want to see my bank balance?*"

Summary

In summary, this chapter was packed with all things Power BI, including enabling Power BI reports in Business Central, connecting to the Business Central API and Excel files, best practices for data modeling, reviewing different visuals, and publishing reports in Power BI services. I hope that if you haven't already started working in Power BI, this chapter has given you some inspiration to create a few reports and design a dashboard. If you have already started creating Power BI reports, we hope this chapter gave you some tips and tricks.

In the next chapter, we will combine all the functionality and Power Platform tools we have covered in the book. You will learn how Business Central and Power Platform are better together.

Further reading

To learn more about the topics that were covered in this chapter, take a look at the following resources:

- *Workspaces in Power BI*: https://learn.microsoft.com/en-us/power-bi/ collaborate-share/service-new-workspaces

- *Visualization types in Power BI*: https://learn.microsoft.com/en-us/power-bi/ visuals/power-bi-visualization-types-for-reports-and-q-and-a

- *Introduction to dashboards for Power BI designers*: https://learn.microsoft.com/ en-us/power-bi/create-reports/service-dashboards#Dashboard%20 basics

- *Create and manage relationships in Power BI Desktop*: https://learn.microsoft. com/en-us/power-bi/transform-model/desktop-create-and-manage-relationships

- I use this website to check colors that I am using to see how they will look if the person is color blind: https://colorkit.org/color-blindness#:~:text=How%20 to%20use%20Color%20Blindness%20tool%201%201.,of%20the%20HEX%20 Codes%20of%20the%20generated%20colors

10

Extending Functionality by Using Several Power Platform Solutions

In previous chapters, we focused on the individual pieces of Power Platform, and now in this chapter, we will look at how we can use all of them to create more robust solutions. We are not going to lie – this is the chapter we have looked forward to writing the most out of the whole book. We've had many conversations about what to include in this chapter, and along the way, we came up with quite a few examples that we kept saying we need to build when we have time. In this advanced exploration, we will dive into the integration of Power Apps within a Power BI report and the incorporation of Power Automate.

We will explore the following in this chapter:

- Best practices to extend functionality in **Business Central** (**BC**) using several Power Platform solutions

- A business case to review credit limits for customers in Power BI, either blocking the customer or raising their credit limit

- A business case for a new item setup

By the end of the chapter, you will be equipped with valuable and practical insights and knowledge to harness the power of these integrated solutions, enabling you to supercharge your organization's productivity and drive meaningful outcomes.

Extending functionality in Business Central using several Power Platform solutions

When we start thinking about extending functionality for Business Central and using several Power Platform solutions, things become more complicated. Any time we talk about multiple tools, we run the risk of over-engineering something or inventing our own spaghetti code. There are times when I think about a solution, and in the back of my head, I always check for spaghetti code.

In today's data-driven world, businesses rely on powerful tools such as Power BI to analyze and visualize data, gaining valuable insights to make informed decisions. However, as data becomes more complex and diverse, efficient data entry and interaction with data become increasingly vital. This is where Power Apps comes into play. We'll explore the seamless integration of Power Apps with Power BI, allowing users to enhance their data analysis experience through a custom-built application. We'll dive deep into the process of creating Power Apps app that streamlines data input, empowers users to interact with visualizations, and enhances collaboration across teams.

So, let's begin our journey into creating a Power Apps app for Power BI and discover the possibilities ahead!

Case study – creating a Power Apps app from Power BI Desktop

In this case study, we will explore the practical application of a Power BI report for a company aiming to enhance its customer balance review process and streamline credit limit management. The goal is to empower decision-makers with real-time insights, enabling them to make well-informed choices promptly. By leveraging the capabilities of Power BI, decision-makers will have access to up-to-date information, allowing them to efficiently address customer blocks and adjust credit limits as needed. This implementation not only improves the overall efficiency of the process but also enables decision-makers to make data-driven decisions that align with the company's objectives and financial goals.

The objectives for the project were the following:

- Develop a Power BI report that integrates with Business Central to provide real-time customer balances

- Enable decision-makers to review customers' balances and make informed judgments about blocking the customers or adjusting credit limits

- Automate blocking or raise credit limits directly from the Power BI report

During the solution design phase, we realized that we had already developed a valuable asset – a Power BI report that seamlessly connected to Business Central Customer data, providing real-time insights into customer balances. We knew we could leverage that and then embed a Power Apps app inside the Power BI report to block a customer or raise their credit limit in Business Central.

The solution will then use the following tools:

- **Power BI report**: This will be used for data analysis and visualization

- **Power Apps**: This will be used for creating custom applications and enhancing users', interaction with Business Central data

- **Business Central**: This will be used to connect to Business Central data in the Power BI report and Power Apps

Creation of the Power Apps app from inside the Power BI report

To create this solution, we will use the Power BI report we created in *Chapter 9* as the starting point, and then we will create the Power Apps app inside the Power BI report. The following steps are required to build the complete solution:

1. Open Power BI and the Customer Credit Review report we created in *Chapter 9*. The benefit of creating the Power Apps app inside Power BI is that when we select the fields, the system will automatically create the link to them.

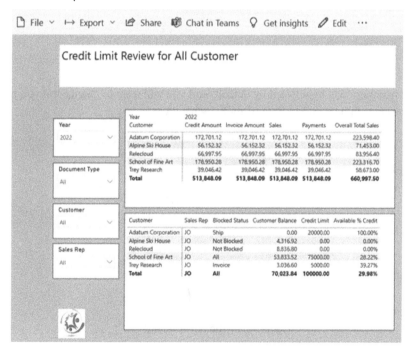

Figure 10.1– The Credit Limit Review for All Customer report

2. Create the customer app in the Power BI report; select the **Power Apps** icon on the visualization pane.

Figure 10.2 – The Power Apps icon

3. The environment will be selected by default, and you will want to change it if you have more than one environment. Select **Extending BC with PA**.

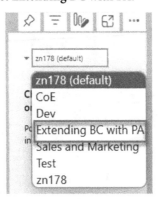

Figure 10.3 – The environment

4. Place the Power Apps visual to the right of the report visuals. Now, we want to add a link from the report visuals to the Power Apps app using the customer number. In the **Visualization** pane, add the customer number. This will allow the app to show the correct customer when the user highlights a customer in report visuals.

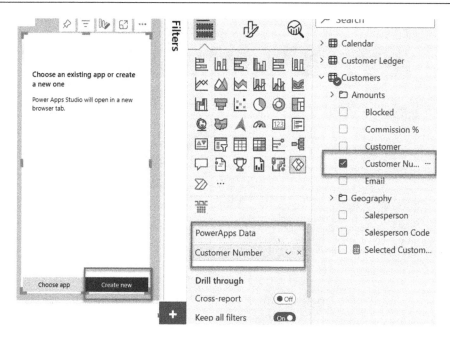

Figure 10.4 – Adding the customer number and creating the app

5. The next thing we will want to do is make some cosmetic changes to the app and add a few fields to the screens.

6. Update the gallery by removing the >.

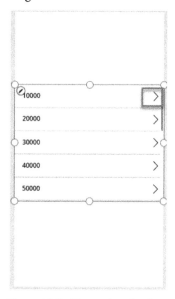

Figure 10.5 – The updated gallery

7.   To create a button to change the credit limit, select **Insert | Button**.

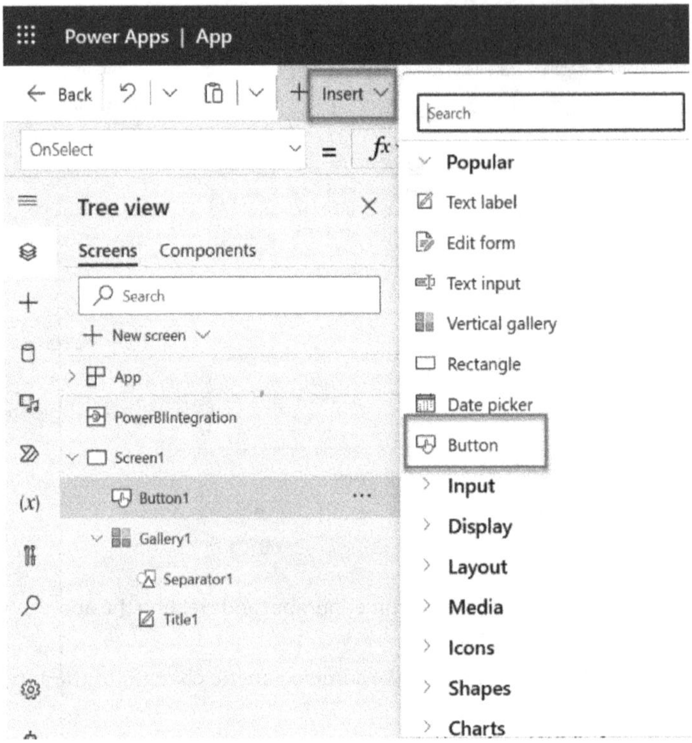

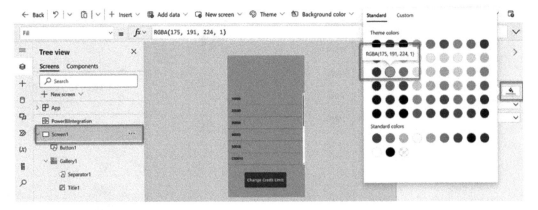

Figure 10.6 – Insert | Button

8.   To change the screen background, select **Screen1** in the tree view, and in the right-hand properties, select the **Fill** property and light blue.

Figure 10.7 – The screen background color

9. To change the gallery to white, select **Gallery1** in the tree view, and in the right-hand properties, select white.

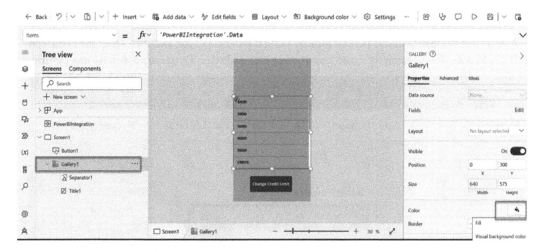

Figure 10.8 – Changing the line to white

> **Note**
>
> The **Fill** property can be selected, and if you know the RGBA numbers, you can change it in the **fx** bar.
>
>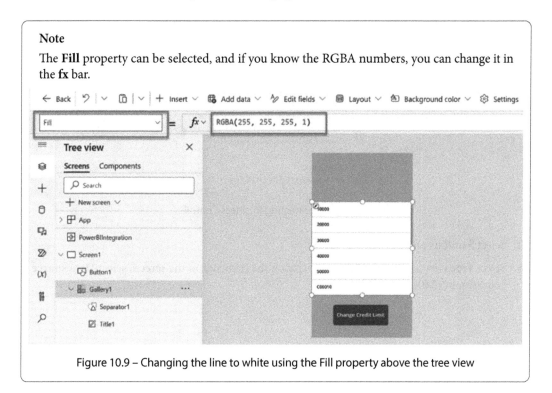
>
> Figure 10.9 – Changing the line to white using the Fill property above the tree view

10. Close **Screen1** before the next step.

11. Insert a new screen by selecting + **New screen**, located in the tree view, and select **Blank Layout**.

12. Insert an edit form by selecting **Insert | Edit Form**.

13. Connect to the data in Business Central by using the same API 2.0, and then select the **Data** icon | **Add data**. Then, search for business central and select **Dynamics 365 Business Central**.

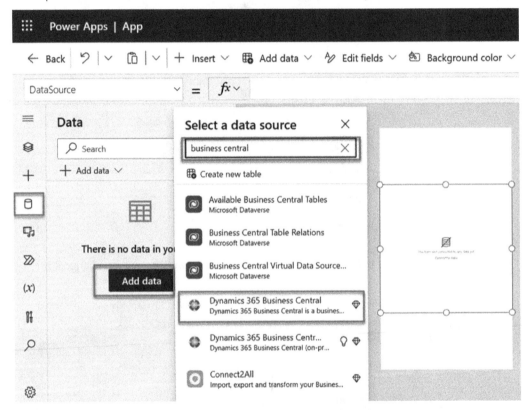

Figure 10.10 – Connecting Business Central

14. Select **Sandbox** and **customers (v2.0)**.

15. Select **Tree view**, and on the form property on the right side of the screen, select **Data source | customer (v2.0)**.

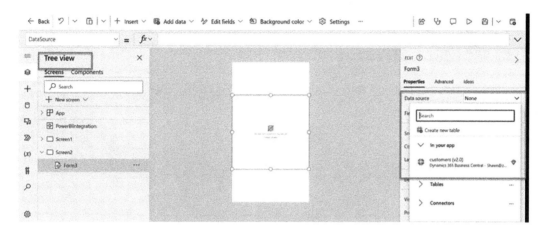

Figure 10.11 – Connecting customer (v2.0)

16. On the form, we want to remove the fields we don't need and add **Credit Limit** and **Blocked** by selecting **Edit fields** on the right **Properties** pane.

Figure 10.12 – Edit fields on the form

17. Now is a good time to rename all the screens and controls. When we created the app, the system created generic names for each screen and control. Rename **Screen1** and **Screen2** by highlighting the screen and selecting the ellipsis **…**; change **Screen1** to Home Screen and **Screen2** to Edit Customer.

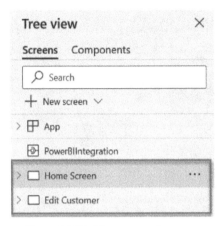

Figure 10.13 – The renamed screens

18. Rename the gallery, using the conversion naming chart featured in *Figure 5.13* in *Chapter 5*, to galCustomer; this will help identify the galley that is connected to the Customer table.

19. Rename the form frmEditCustomer.

Figure 10.14 – Renaming the form

20. The **No.** and **Display Name** fields will need to be viewed only; the user should not be able to change the fields. Select the **No.** field and unlock it by selecting the advanced property in the property section on the right-hand side of the screen. We don't want the user to be able to change the **No.** field, just view it. Select **DisplayMode** in the left property dropdown and update **fx** to Parent.DisplayMode.View.

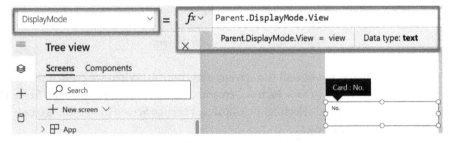

Figure 10.15 – Change No. to view only

21. Repeat the previous step for **Display Name**.

22. Add a border around the data fields by selecting **BorderThickness** in the left-hand pane's properties and changing it from **0** to 5 in the **fx** field.

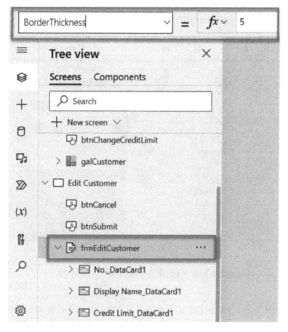

Figure 10.16 – Adding a border around the fields

23. Change the background from white to the same light blue color in *step 7*. I sometimes cheat if I know the color numbers, or I go back and copy the RGBA from the previous screen – in this case, it was RGBA(175,191,224,1). You can copy it in the **Fill** property.

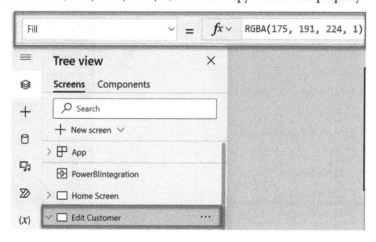

Figure 10.17 – The color fill

24. When the user of the report selects a customer, we want the form to link to that customer number. To do this, have **frmEditCustomer** selected and go to the **Item** property. In **fx**, using a **LookUp** command, look up the customer using the **No.** field, and when that is selected, use the number field to link to Business Central data – LookUp('customers (v2.0)', 'No.'= galCustomer.Selected. 'Customer Number').

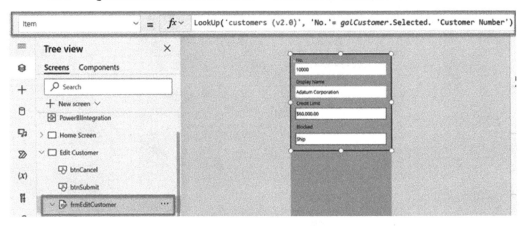

Figure 10.18 – Looking up the customer

25. For the **Credit Limit** field, we want to format it to show dollar amounts. We can do this by changing the value to text, selecting the **Credit Limit** field and the **Default** property, and in the **fx** field, typing Text(Parent.Default, "$#,###.00").

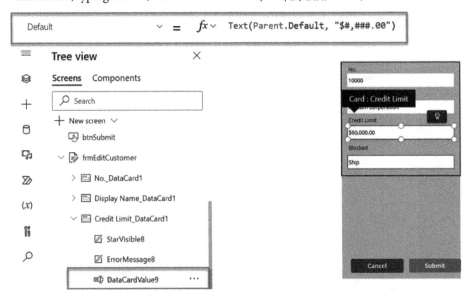

Figure 10.19 – Formatting the credit limit

26. Insert a button, rename it `Submit`, and change the color to green.

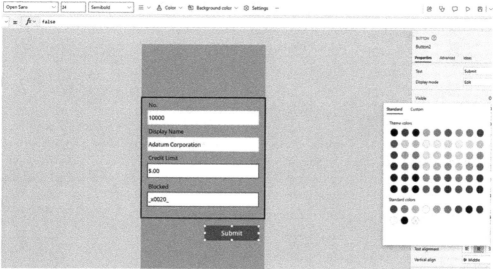

Figure 10.20 – Changing the Submit button color

27. Insert a button, rename it `Cancel`, and change the color to red.

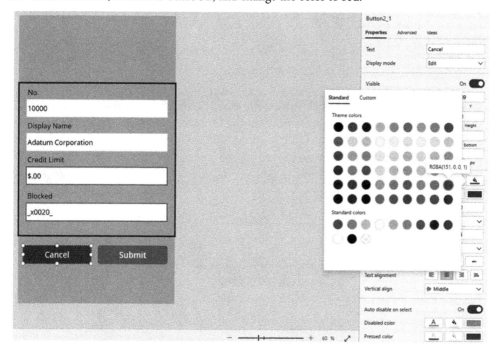

Figure 10.21 – Changing the Cancel button color

28. Rename the buttons `btnCancel` and `btnSubmit`, respectively.

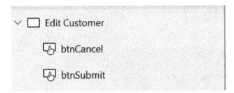

Figure 10.22 – Renaming the buttons

29. To add the code to the **Submit** button, we want the form to submit and navigate back to **Screen1**. To do this, select the **Submit** button and the **OnSelect** Property in the **fx** code, enter `SubmitForm(frmEditCustomer);`, press *Shift + Enter* to go to the second line, and then type `Navigate('Home Screen')`.

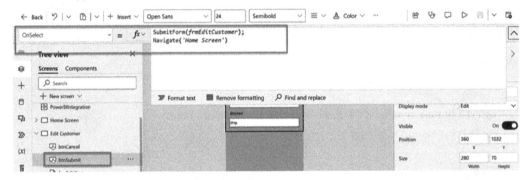

Figure 10.23 – Adding code to Submit

30. To add the code to the **Cancel** button, we want the form to go back to **Screen1**. To do this, select the **Cancel** button and then the **Onselect** property in the **fx** code, type `ResetForm(frmEditCustomer);`, press *Shift + Enter* to got to the second line, and enter `Navigate('Home Screen')`.

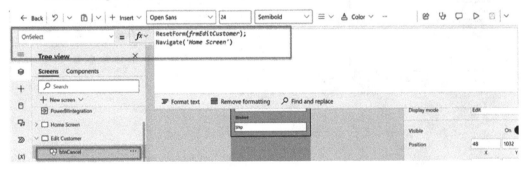

Figure 10.24 – Adding code to Cancel

31. The **Blocked** field in Business Central has four options, and the blank value you see in BC displays in the Customer AP as **_X0020_**, and we need to make some adjustments that will allow the user to select **Blank**, **Ship**, **Invoice**, or **All**. To accomplish this task, we'll first add a drop-down field, select + **Insert** and the search dropdown, and add the drop-down box under the **Blocked** field by dragging and dropping to align it.

32. In the **Items** property in the **fx** field, enter `["Not Blocked", "Ship", "Invoice", "All"]`. This will update the value of the user interface.

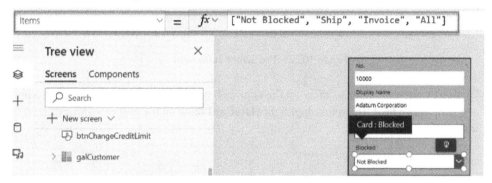

Figure 10.25 – The drop-down code update

33. Highlight the **DataCardValue11** value, shrink it, and move it toward the end of the screen, as shown in *Figure 10.26*.

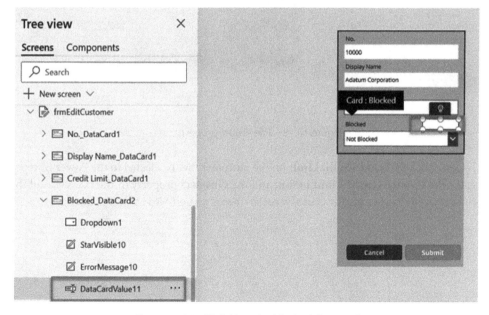

Figure 10.26 – Shrinking the blocked data card

34. The next thing we need to do is add a `Switch` statement, which is like an `if` statement. Copy this code into **fx** – `Switch(Dropdown1.SelectedText.Value,"All",3,"Invoice",2,"Ship",1,"Not Blocked",Blank())`.

Figure 10.27 – The Switch statement

35. We don't want both fields to show on the app; we'll need to hide the data field and keep the new drop-down field. To do this, highlight **DataCardValue** on the property and turn off the **Visible** flag.

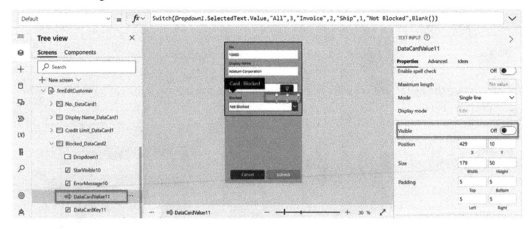

Figure 10.28 – The Visible property

36. To add code to **Change Credit Limit** on the customer that is selected in the Power BI report, select the **Change Credit Limit** button and the **Onselect** property in the **fx** code, and then enter `EditForm(frmEditCustomer); Navigate('Edit Customer')`.

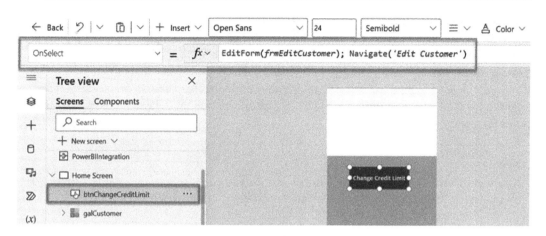

Figure 10.29 – Adding code to Change Credit Limit

37. To update the selected line to a different color other than white, select **galCustomer** and the **TemplateFill** property, and in the **fx** code, enter If(ThisItem.IsSelected, LightGray, GhostWhite). When the user selects the line on the app, it will be light gray; otherwise, the line will be white. This will allow the user to know which customer record they have selected.

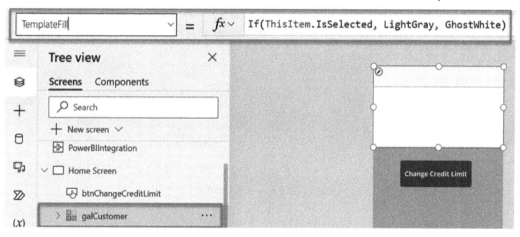

Figure 10.30 – Adding code to change the color of the selected line

Now that we've thoroughly covered creating the Power Apps app, it's time to take the next step and introduce Power Automate to refresh the data in our Power BI report automatically. This powerful integration will automate the data update, ensuring our insights are always current and reliable. The seamless collaboration between Power Apps and Power Automate promises to elevate our data management and analysis to a new level.

Creating Power Automate to refresh the dataset when a customer is updated

In this step, we'll walk through adding a Power Automate flow that will update the credit limit on the report. In the previous exercise, when the user changed the credit limit, we had to wait for the next data refresh. Ideally, we want the report to update as soon as the user submits the change. Linking the flow to the Power Apps **Submit** action will automatically refresh the dataset, providing real-time updates for a seamless user experience.

> **Note**
>
> Note that this will count toward the number of flows you run if you are on a pay-as-you-go plan or have a limited number of Power Automate runs:

1. Create a Power Automate flow from the Power Apps screen and select the **Power Automate** icon.

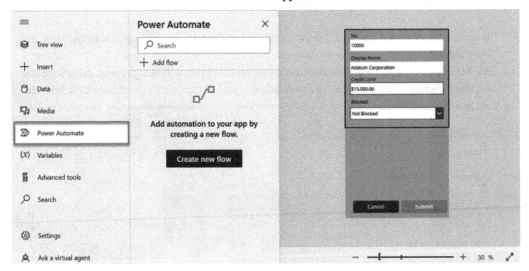

Figure 10.31 – Power Automate

2. Select **Create new flow** | **+ Create from blank** | **+ New Step** in this trigger operation; add Power BI by searching for Power BI.

Create your flow

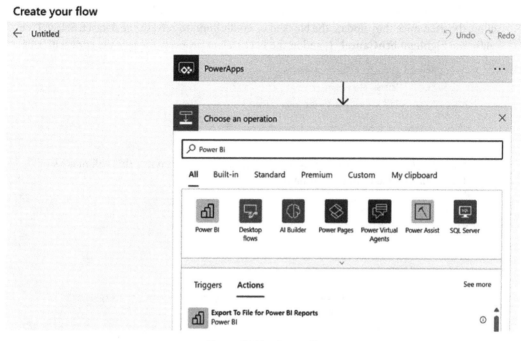

Figure 10.32 – Power BI

3. The action will be **Refresh a dataset**. Select **Workspace** and **Dataset**.

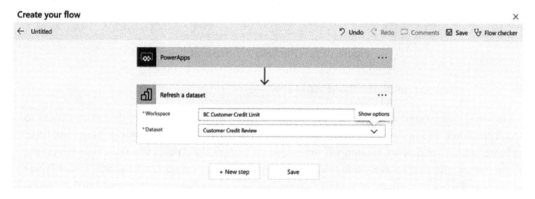

Figure 10.33 – Select Workspace and Dataset

4.   Select **Save**; once it is available in your app, we'll add it to the **Submit** button, and this will allow the user, once they update the blocked or credit limit, to refresh the dataset. Select **Tree view** and highlight **btnCancel_1**, and in the **fx Onselect** property, replace the code with this:

```
SubmitForm(frmEditCustomer);
Navigate ('Home Screen');
'PowerApp->Refreshadataset-2'.Run()
```

> **Note**
> As you type in the **fx** bar, always select the code from the drop-down list; this will make sure you select the right information or command.

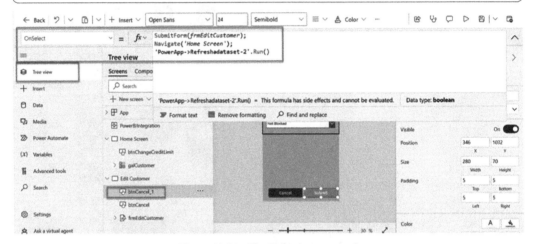

Figure 10.34 – The Refresh command

5.   Lastly, save and publish the Power Apps app.

In summary, you created a Power Apps app embedded in a Power BI report that allows users to select a customer, and update either the credit limit or change the blocked status in BC in real time. The Power Automate flow we created will automatically refresh the dataset when the user selects the **Submit** button, allowing for real-time information on the Power BI report. A final note is that Power Automate will use a flow count, so if you are watching how many flows you run and doing a pay-as-you-go, this will count.

Stepping into the next section, we will leverage the comprehensive capabilities of Power Platform, utilizing Dataverse, Power Apps, BC, and Power Automate to effectively automate and streamline the new record creation process, elevate data accuracy, and facilitate seamless collaboration among teams.

Case study – a new item setup

The case study that we will look at next is a case study for a new item setup. We have several clients that struggle with their process for new item setup. Several clients start a new item setup by filling out a spreadsheet and then passing it around to different departments to do the setup. Sometimes, it sits in someone's inbox for days and does not move to the next department until later. With Power Platform, users now have more and better options for this to be accomplished.

In this case study, we will look at *Company XYZ*. This company operates in the retail industry and constantly introduces new products to meet changing customer demands. The traditional manual process of setting up new items was time-consuming and prone to errors, leading to delays in product launches and inefficiencies in managing an inventory. To address these challenges, Company XYZ decided to leverage Microsoft Power Apps, Dataverse, and BC to create an automated and centralized system for a new item setup.

The objectives of this project were the following:

- Automate and streamline the new item setup process
- Improve data accuracy and integrity by centralizing item information
- Enable seamless collaboration between teams involved in item setup
- Enhance visibility and tracking of item setup progress

The solution involved the following tools:

- Dataverse – to store the item information before it was pushed into Business Central
- Power Apps – to capture the information related to the new item
- BC – where the item ultimately needs to be set up
- Power Automate – notifications for the workflow and process

Creating a solution

Let's look at how the solution was built. The first thing we need to do is create a solution:

1. To do this, log in to Power Apps, select + **Create**, and then select + **New solution**.

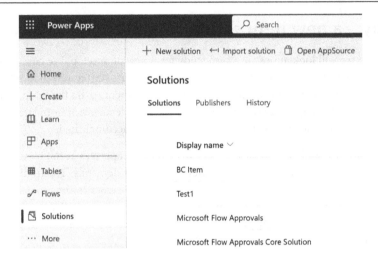

Figure 10.35 – Creating a new solution

2. Fill in the name of the solution, select the publisher, fill in a description for the solution, and then select **Create**.

Figure 10.36 – Creating a new solution

The next thing we will need to do is create a table in Dataverse to store information.

Creating a table in Dataverse

Here are the steps that we need to follow to create a table in Dataverse:

1. Log in to Power Apps and select **Solutions** from the menu. Then, select **Tables**.

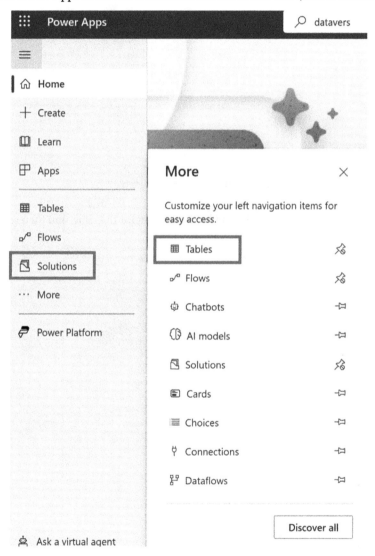

Figure 10.37 – Selecting Solutions and then Tables from the Power Apps menu

2. From the table screen, select **+ New table** to create a new table.

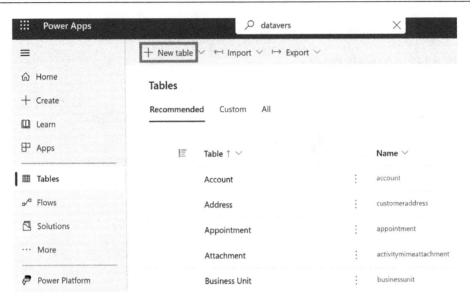

Figure 10.38 – Creating a new table

3.   Enter Item as the name of the table, add a description for the table, and then select **Save**.

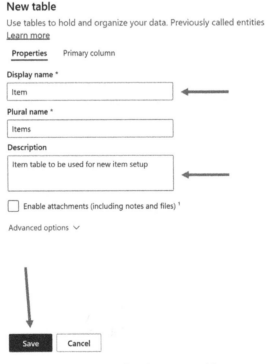

Figure 10.39 – Creating a new table

4. When the new table is created, select **+ New column** to add columns to capture data. For this exercise, we will keep it short.

Figure 10.40 – Creating a new column in the new table

5. For the first column, let's add the **No** field that will be used for the **No** field in BC. Enter the display name and the description, leave everything else as default, and then select **Save**.

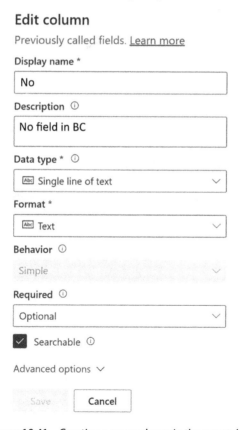

Figure 10.41 – Creating a new column in the new table

6.   Repeat *steps 4* and *5* and create a **Description** column.

Figure 10.42 – Creating a new column in the new table

7.   Select + **New row** and enter some data for the items. Enter a couple of records by entering information in the **Description** and **No** fields.

Figure 10.43 – Entering data in the table

Now that we have our Dataverse table and some data entered, we can begin building our Power Apps app.

Creating a Power Apps app

To create the Power Apps app, we will have to do the following steps:

1. From the **Power Apps** home screen, select **+ Create** and then **Dataverse** from the **Start from** area.

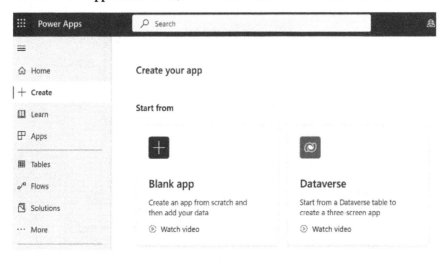

Figure 10.44 – Creating a Power Apps app from the Dataverse

2. Select the Dataverse and then **Items** on the **Connections** screen.

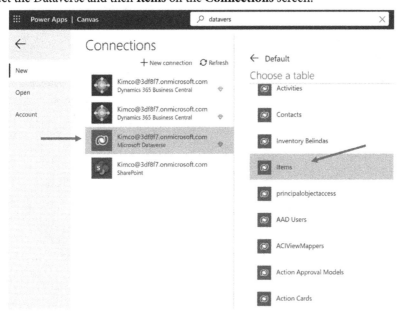

Figure 10.45 – Selecting the Dataverse connection and Items table

3.   The app will open, and you'll see an app screen with items on it.

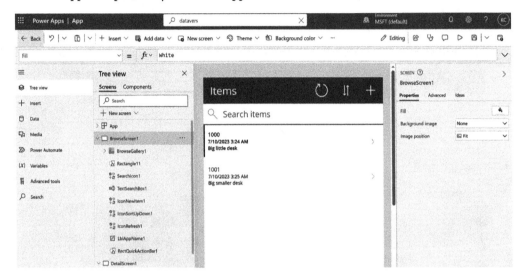

Figure 10.46 – The app will open when it is finished being created

4.   Select > next to **BrowseScreen1** to close it and note the other three forms that were created.

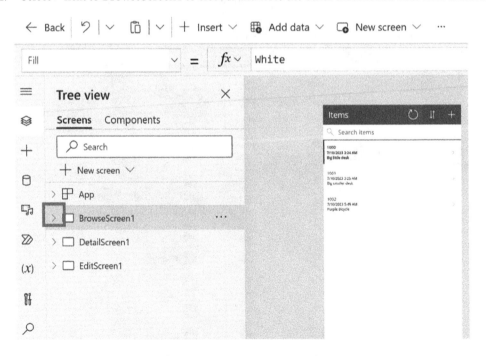

Figure 10.47 – Closing the app screens on the tree view

5. Select the word **Items** on the top menu and change it to `New Items`.

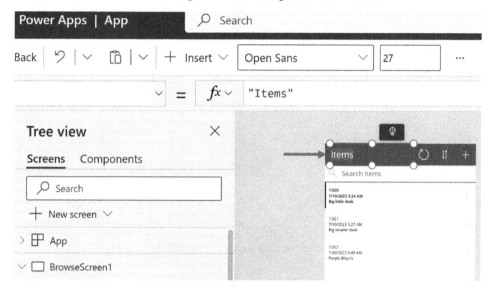

Figure 10.48 – Rename the screen New Items

6. Select **EditScreen1**, and then the ellipsis on **Tree view**. Then, select **Duplicate screen**.

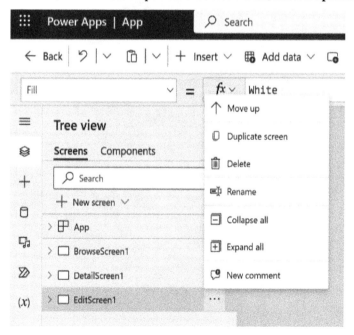

Figure 10.49 – Duplicate the EditScreen1 form

7. **EditScreen1_1** will be created. Select **EditForm1_1** and then **Data source**.

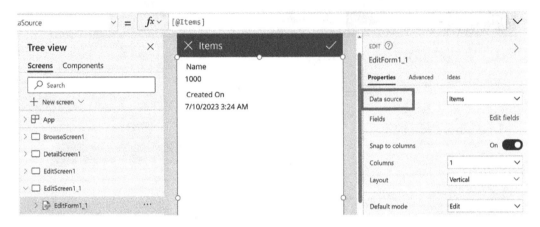

Figure 10.50 – Editing the data source from EditScreen1 Form

8. The **Data source** window will open. Select **Connectors** to create the connection to BC.

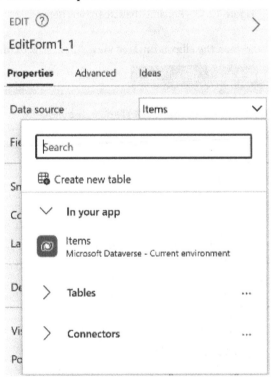

Figure 10.51 – Choosing the connectors

9. Select the **Dynamics 365 Business Central** connector.

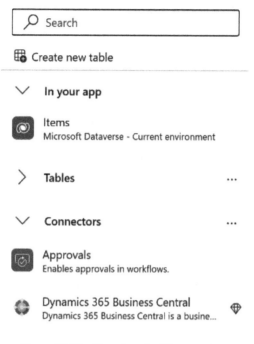

Figure 10.52 – Choosing the BC connector

10. Choose a dataset to connect to:

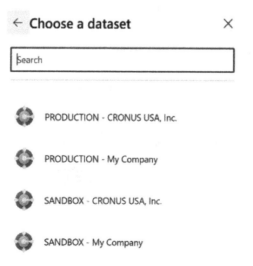

Figure 10.53 – Choosing the dataset for the BC connection

11. Select the **items (v2.0)** table from the list of tables and select **Connect**.

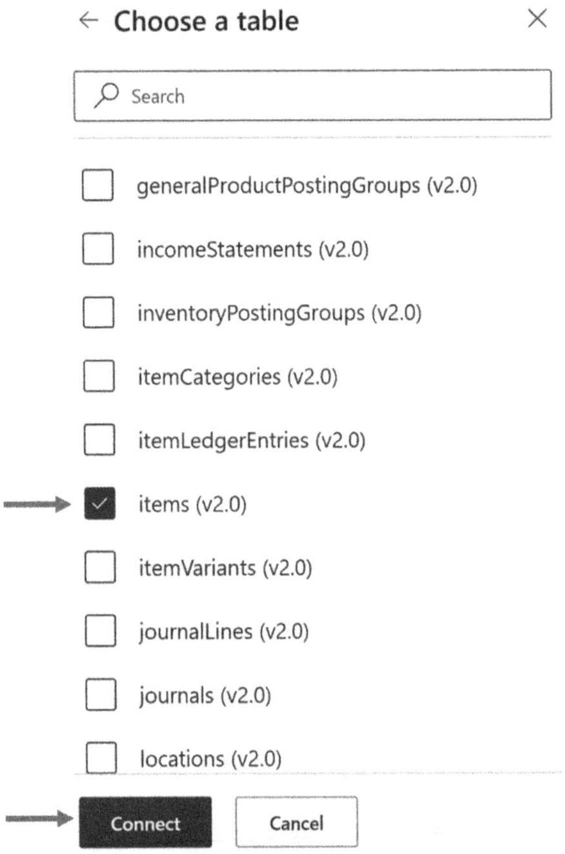

← **Choose a table**   ✕

🔍 Search

☐   generalProductPostingGroups (v2.0)

☐   incomeStatements (v2.0)

☐   inventoryPostingGroups (v2.0)

☐   itemCategories (v2.0)

☐   itemLedgerEntries (v2.0)

→ ☑   items (v2.0)

☐   itemVariants (v2.0)

☐   journalLines (v2.0)

☐   journals (v2.0)

☐   locations (v2.0)

→ **Connect**   Cancel

Figure 10.54 – Choosing the table from BC to connect to

12. The following message will be shown. Select **Replace my data cards**.

Would you like to replace the data cards?

This will replace all the cards on this form with new ones, based on your data.

→   **Replace my data cards**   No thanks

Figure 10.55 – A message asking about replacing the data

13. A screen with the new item fields will be shown. Select **Edit fields** to remove some of the fields from the form.

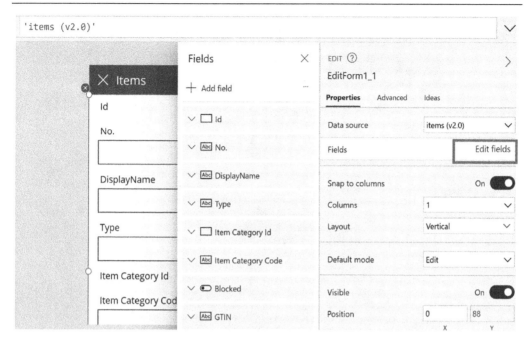

Figure 10.56 – Editing the fields for the form

14. To delete fields, select the ellipsis on the field you would like to remove, and then select **Remove**. Repeat this for all fields except **No.**, **DisplayName**, **Type**, and **Blocked**.

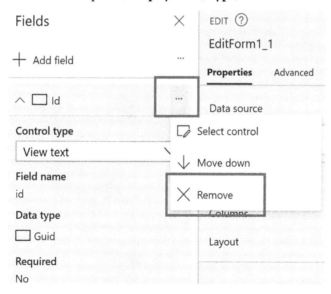

Figure 10.57 – Removing fields from the form

15. The form should look like the following screenshot when you are done.

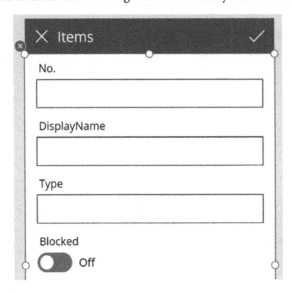

Figure 10.58 – The Items form after removing fields

16. Rename **EditScreen1_1** by selecting the ellipsis, then **Rename**, and entering Add to BC.

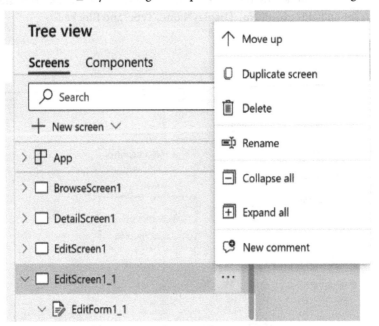

Figure 10.59 – Renaming the screen

17. Rename the title of the form by changing the word **Items** to BC Items.

Figure 10.60 – Renaming the form from Items to BC Items

18. Click on the bottom of the form to highlight it, select **Advanced**, scroll down to find **DefaultMode**, and then change the value from **FormMode.Edit** to FormMode.New. Delete the value for **BrowseGallery1.Selected** under **Item**.

Figure 10.61 – Setting the default mode on the form

19. Double-click on the first field on the page, select **Advanced** from the menu, and then click on **Unlock to change properties**.

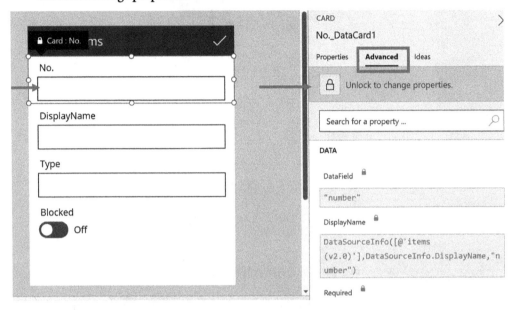

Figure 10.62 – Editing the properties on the form

20. Scroll to find the **DATA** section, and then update the value in the **Default** field to BrowseGallery1.Selected.No.

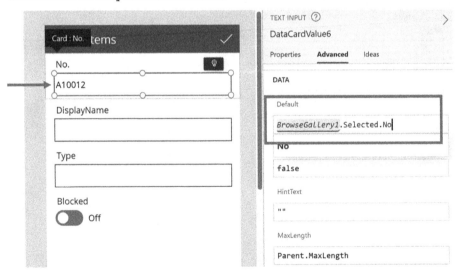

Figure 10.63 – Editing the properties on the form

21. Double-click in the **DisplayName** field, and then update the value in the **Default** field to BrowseGallery1.Selected.Description.

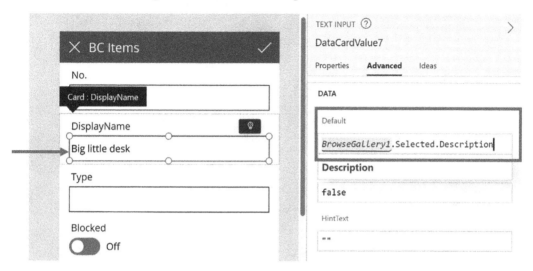

Figure 10.64 – Editing the properties on the form

22. Double-click on **Type** and then enter the word Inventory.

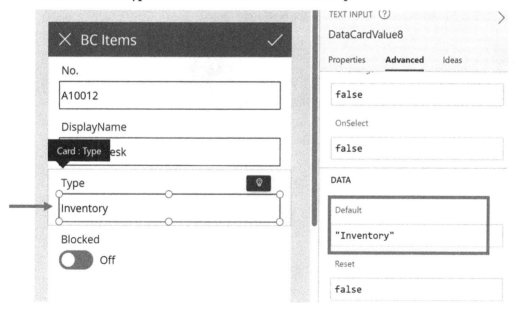

Figure 10.65 – Editing the properties on the form

23. Select **Blocked** and set **Default** to true.

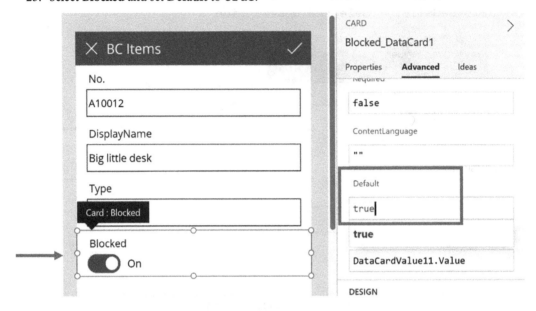

Figure 10.66 – Editing the properties on the Form

24. Select **BrowseScreen1** to change to the **New Item** screen.

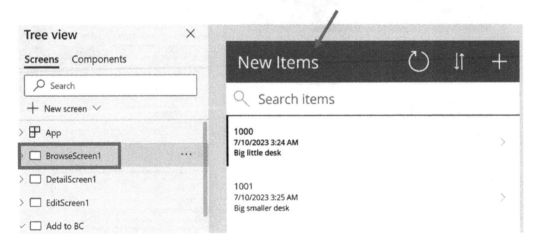

Figure 10.67 – Switching to BrowseScreen1

25. Select the form and then update **OnSelect** with the `Navigate('Add to BC',` `ScreenTransition.None)` value.

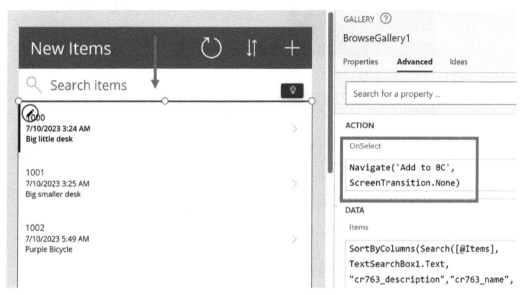

Figure 10.68 – Switching to the BrowseScreen1

26. Select **Properties** and then **Edit**.

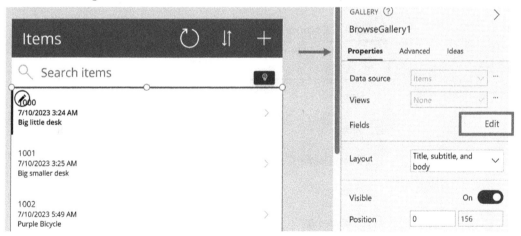

Figure 10.69 – Switching to BrowseScreen1

27. Under the field named **Title1**, select **No**.

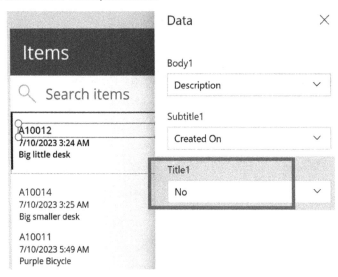

Figure 10.70 – Editing the fields on the form to use the No field

28. Select **EditScreen1**; this will allow us to edit the fields just on this screen.

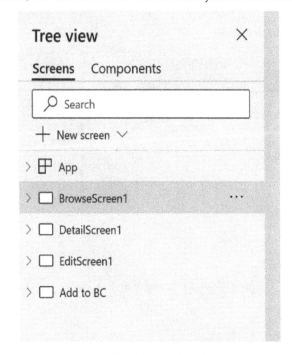

Figure 10.71 – Selecting EditScreen1

29. Select **Edit fields**.

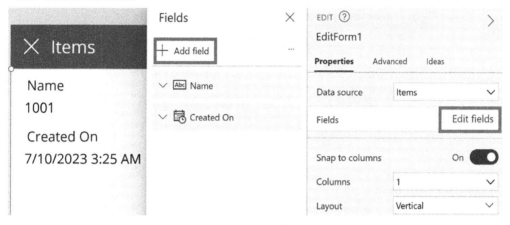

Figure 10.72 – Selecting Edit fields and Add a Field

30. Select **No** and **Description**, and then select **Add**.

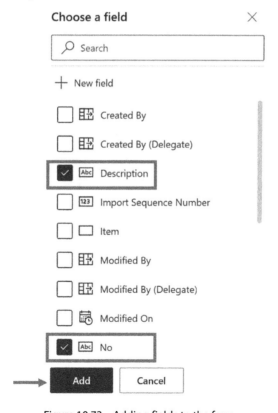

Figure 10.73 – Adding fields to the form

31. The **Items** screen should look like the following screen.

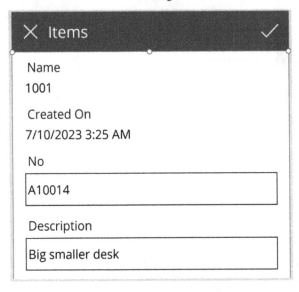

Figure 10.74 – The Items screen with new fields added

32. Select **Save** on the menu to save the app.

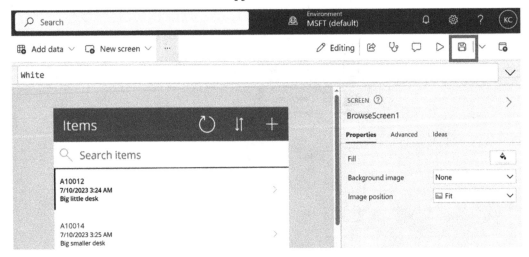

Figure 10.75 – Saving your app

33. Select the play button to test the solution.

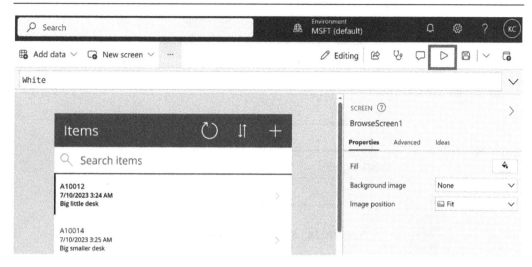

Figure 10.76 – Testing the app

34. The app will open, and you can test it. Select the + icon to add a new item.

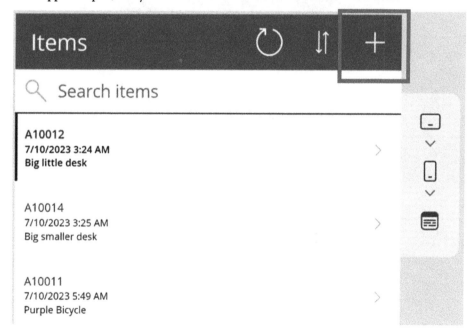

Figure 10.77 – Select the + icon to add a new item

35. Enter an item number and description, and then select the check mark.

Figure 10.78 – Select the check mark

36. The main screen will open. Select the item you entered.

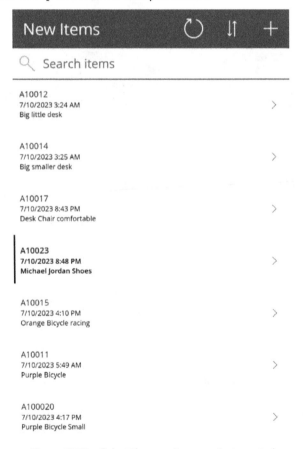

Figure 10.79 – Select the new item you just created

37. The **BC Items** screen will open. Select the check mark.

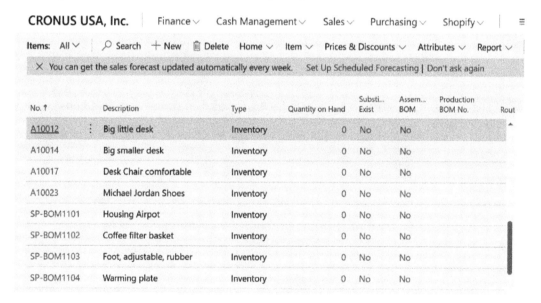

Figure 10.80 – The BC Items screen

38. Open BC and then the item screen to verify that your item was created in BC.

No. ↑	Description	Type	Quantity on Hand	Substi... Exist	Assem... BOM	Production BOM No.	Rout
A10012	Big little desk	Inventory	0	No	No		
A10014	Big smaller desk	Inventory	0	No	No		
A10017	Desk Chair comfortable	Inventory	0	No	No		
A10023	Michael Jordan Shoes	Inventory	0	No	No		
SP-BOM1101	Housing Airpot	Inventory	0	No	No		
SP-BOM1102	Coffee filter basket	Inventory	0	No	No		
SP-BOM1103	Foot, adjustable, rubber	Inventory	0	No	No		
SP-BOM1104	Warming plate	Inventory	0	No	No		

Figure 10.81 – Verifying that the new items are in BC

After we verify that the Power Apps app is created and working, we can work on the notification in Power Automate to inform the team when a new item is created in BC, and the workflow can then start in it.

Creating a Power Automate flow

To create a Power Automate flow, follow the following steps:

1. Open Power Automate, select **+ Create**, and then select **Automated cloud flow**.

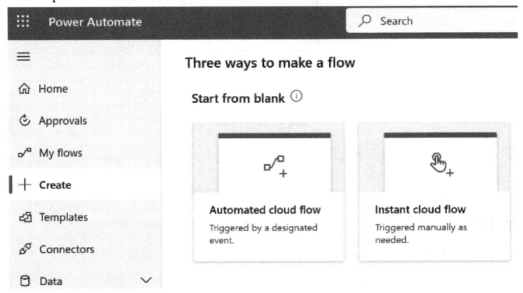

Figure 10.82 – Creating a new instant cloud flow

2. Enter a name in **Flow name** and search for Business central under **Choose your flow's trigger**.

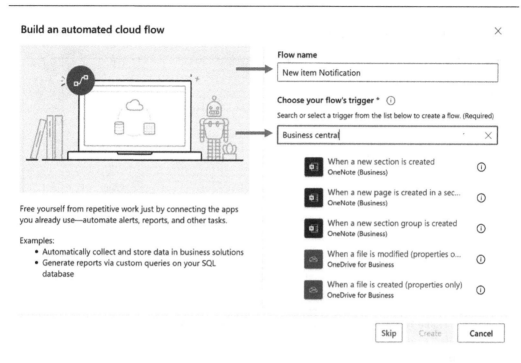

Figure 10.83 – Creating a new instant cloud flow

3.   Select **When a record is created (V2)** and then **Create**.

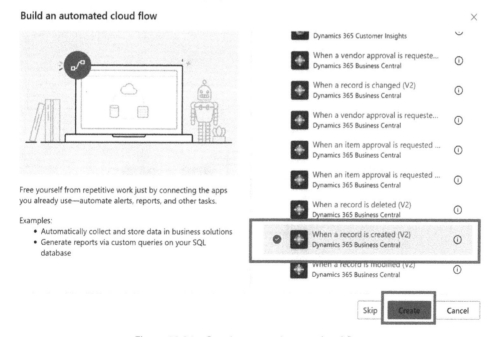

Figure 10.84 – Creating a new instant cloud flow

4.   Enter the **Environment**, **Company name**, and **Table name** details, and then select **+ New step**.

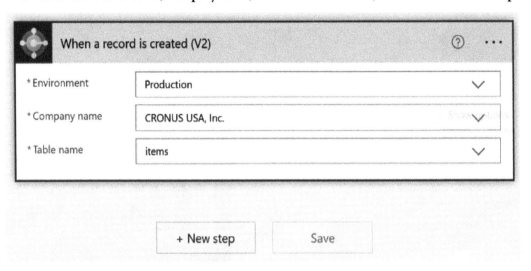

Figure 10.85 – Entering the information for When a record is created (V2)

5.   Search for Business Central and select **Dynamics 365 Business Central**.

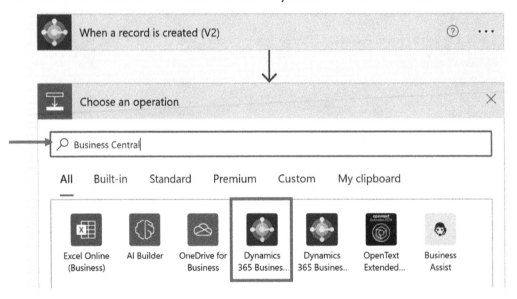

Figure 10.86 – Searching for BC actions

6. Select the **Get record (V3)** under **Actions**.

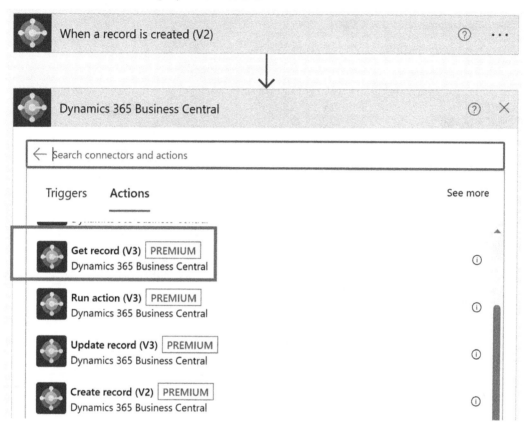

Figure 10.87 – Selecting the Get record (V3) action

7. Enter this information in the respective fields and then select **+ Next step**:

- **Environment**: PRODUCTION

- **Company**: CRONUS USA, Inc.

- **API category**: v2.0

- **Table name**: items

- **Row id**: Row Id

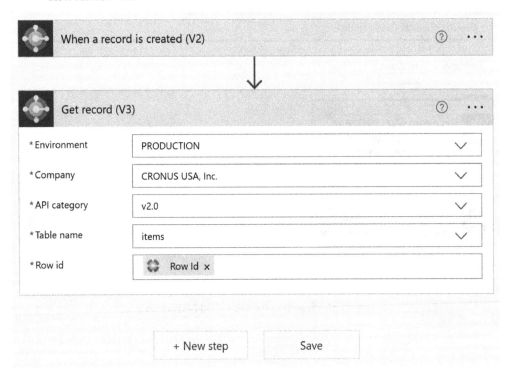

Figure 10.88 – Entering the information in the Get record (V3) action

8. Search for Teams and select **Post message in a chat or channel**.

Figure 10.89 – Selecting the Post message in a chat or channel action

9. Enter the information in the respective fields:

- **Post as**: Flow bot
- **Post in**: Channel
- **Team**: Item Setup
- **Channel**: General

- **Message: New Item** No. **is created** | **Item Description** –DisplayName | **Item type** – Type

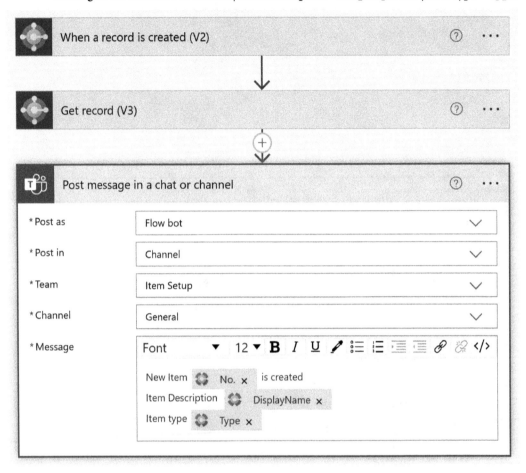

Figure 10.90 – Entering the information for the Post message action

10. Select **Save** to save the flow, and then select **Test**.

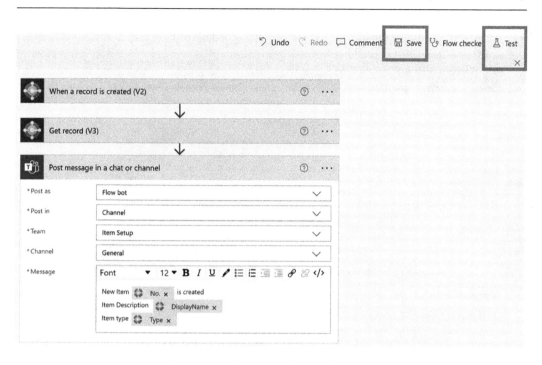

Figure 10.91 – Saving the flow and testing it

11. Select **Manually** and select **Test**.

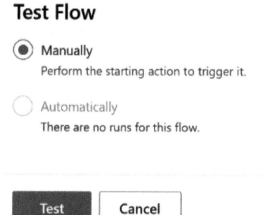

Figure 10.92 – Testing the flow

12. Once you have started the test, log in to Power Apps and test the Power Apps app. Then, verify in BC and Teams that everything worked.

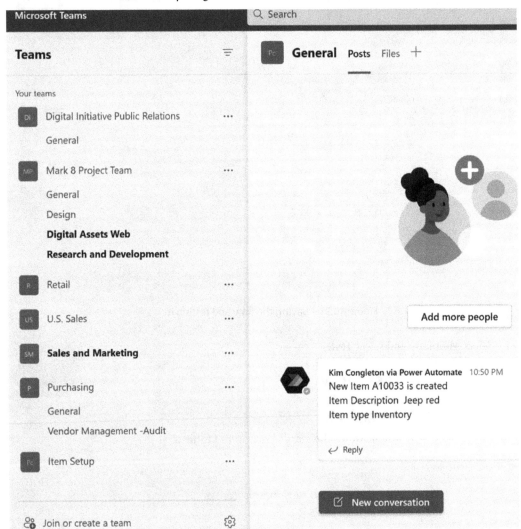

Figure 10.93 - Verifying the testing flow

In summary, our exploration of Power Apps and Power Automate has led us to successfully automate the creation of new items in BC, resulting in improved data management and increased efficiency. In the next section, we will focus on the best practices to extend functionality in BC.

Best practices to extend functionality in BC using several Power Platform solutions

Here is a list of the best practices we follow when extending functionality and building any solution, whether it is in BC, Power BI, Power Apps, or Power Automate:

- Don't reinvent the wheel. Make sure you check to see whether a solution already exists that meets your needs.

- Make sure you have a good set of requirements. We can't stress this enough. If the requirements are not good, then the solution will not meet them.

- Take the time to do a design document. Don't just start building. As much as I joke about these tools being like a certain type of building block, it is way too easy to start building and then realize you are not heading in the right direction. Think about what you're building and then start doing it.

- Use a tool such as Visio or something similar where you can use a swim lane or similar document to show which tool owns which part of the solution.

- Make sure your solution is broken down into smaller, modular components; this way, it is easier to develop, test, and troubleshoot.

- Use connectors and APIs provided by Power Platform to integrate with other systems. Know when to build an API and when not to.

- Don't forget about security, especially when multiple systems are involved.

- Test, test, test, test, and then test some more.

- Don't forget to think about the future; make sure you understand and plan for how scalable the solution must be.

- Document the solution, and make sure the next person after you will be able to support the solution or troubleshoot it if needed.

- Never stop learning about the new features of Power Platform. Things change so quickly now; you must stay up to date on when new features are introduced.

In this section, we discussed the essential best practices to extend BC using Power Platform. By adhering to these best practices, businesses can confidently leverage Power Platform to extend the capabilities of BC.

Summary

In this chapter, we covered a lot of different solutions and ways to combine multiple tools together to provide complete solutions to real-world problems. We also covered some best practices that we should follow when extending BC with Power Platform. In the two case studies, we reviewed and saw how to create solutions to combine multiple tools from Power Platform. These solutions can be used as a starting point to build your own solutions.

Armed with this knowledge, you will be empowered to unlock Power Platform's full potential and extend BC's capabilities, facilitating smooth workflows, enhanced data management, and streamlined processes. With the ability to build upon the existing solutions presented in this chapter, you can embark on exciting endeavors to create customized and tailored solutions that cater to your unique business needs. Ultimately, this newfound expertise will enable you to drive productivity, efficiency, and transformative growth within your organizations.

In the next chapter, we will dive into user adoption and Microsoft's mapping guide. The foundation of any successful technology implementation rests on user adoption and the process of engaging, educating, and empowering users to embrace new tools, software, or systems in their daily workflow. Also, making sure you have the appropriate license to run all the solutions you need is just as important.

Part 4 –
Tips and Tricks
for Common Issues

In this part, we will delve into essential strategies to drive user adoption, navigate licensing considerations, and establish a successful Center of Excellence to support your organization's growth and success. Implementing new technologies or practices within a company can present its fair share of challenges. Still, with the right approach and a solid understanding of the potential pitfalls, you can maximize your chances of a smooth and successful transition. By incorporating these tips and tricks into your organization's strategy, you'll be better equipped to drive transformative change and achieve long-term success. Let's navigate these challenges together and unlock the full potential of your organization's initiatives.

This part contains the following chapters:

- *Chapter 11, User Adoption and Licensing Mapping Guide*
- *Chapter 12, Understanding the Center of Excellence and Why It Is a Valuable Tool*

11
User Adoption and Licensing Mapping Guide

In this chapter, we will focus on user adoption and explore the valuable tools provided by Microsoft to facilitate a seamless adoption process. To kickstart your user adoption journey, we will guide you through the process of leveraging the three main areas of user adoption planning, including communication, training, and support. By focusing on these areas, you can foster a culture of adoption and ensure that users will embrace the new technology. At the heart of user adoption lies the user's experience. In this chapter, we will emphasize the importance of user-centric design and highlight best practices for building and rolling out solutions that cater to business requirements.

In addition to user adoption, understanding Microsoft licensing is crucial for effectively utilizing the available tools in Power Platform. Lastly, we will review Microsoft 365 E3 plans, Business Central, and the different types of Power Platform licensing.

In this chapter, we're going to cover the following main topics:

- User adoption
- Microsoft 365 plans, Business Central, and Power Platform licensing

User adoption

In this chapter, I want to specify the highlights of user adoption. **User adoption** refers to how users within an organization or business effectively use and derive value from a new technology or system, such as Business Central or Power Platform. It is a critical factor in the success of any implementation as it directly impacts the business and the end users. User adoption, or keeping the end user in mind, has always been number one for me – I started in Navision years ago as the end user. With many years of experience, both painful and rewarding, the one thing I took away was to keep the person who is using the system in mind because if you take a simple process and complicate it, the user suffers. User adoption is so significant that Microsoft has built a whole training module around user adoption.

Microsoft Power Platform Adoption Planning consists of three main areas: **Envision**, **Onboarding**, and **Scale**.

Envision

Envision includes assembling your team, defining a business strategy, and determining readiness, but what does all that mean? Let's break down the steps:

1.   The first step is to determine who your team members are, and you need someone in each of the following categories: Executive Sponsors, Success Owners, Early Adopters, and Champions:

Role	Responsibilities	Department
Executive Sponsor	Communicate a high-level vision. Plays an important role in championing transformations throughout the organization.	Executive Leadership
Success Owner	Ensure the business goals are realized. Plays an essential role in championing collaboration service strategy throughout the organization.	Any Department
Program Manager	Oversee the entire launch and rollout, from pre-launch project planning and assignments to execution and success assessments.	IT
Champions	Help evangelize and manage objection handling. Builds awareness, understanding, and engagement across the organization.	Multiple Departments
Training Leaders	Manage and communicate training content. Establishes a thorough understanding of the software and its intended use among the end users.	IT or Other Departments
Department Leads	Identify how specific departments will use software and encourage engagement.	Any Department-Management
IT Specialists	Oversee all technical aspects of the rollout.	IT
Communication Leader	Oversee company-wide communication.	Corporation Communication or IT

Figure 11.1 – Adoption team member role details

2.   Define your business strategy and requirements. Most of you are probably familiar with gathering business requirements. Here are some common questions you can ask to drive the conversation: what are some pain points? What would you like to improve? If it was Christmas and you could ask for anything, what would it be? What is the process? Why do you do that the way you do it?

3.   Identify scenarios, schedule a workshop, and use this workshop to create unit cases and process testing or a process flow; I usually use these workshops to ensure we have gathered all the requirements and use them as a base for testing down the road. During these workshops, prioritizing business scenarios can be crucial. This will help gauge the impact and difficulty of each of the requirements.

4.   Define success criteria and identify KPIs. Use **Specific, Measurable, Achievable, Realistic, Time-Related (SMART)** goals to define KPIs. This will help you measure improved business cases and help show leadership.

You can find examples of this adoption planning workbook at `https://learn.microsoft.com/en-us/dynamics365/adoption/adoption-workbook-overview`.

5. Determine your readiness acceptance plan. This plan will help determine whether you are ready for the rollout and remember that change is hard.

That wraps up the Envision phase; remember to identify the team, requirements, scenarios, and acceptance criteria. In the next section, we will review the Onboarding phase.

Onboarding

This phase includes preparing your environment, building an adoption plan, launching early adopters, adjusting your project, and training your users.

In this phase, one of the critical components in user adoption is supporting your champion user group. Microsoft has a champion community. This is a great spot to help you build, grow, and collaborate with other champions in other organizations. Supporting and training the champions in your organization is a great asset to the success of your projects. Some companies will put together rewards and recognition; this is a great way to have fun with any project. Some theme ideas include Champion of the Week, Solution of the Week, Most Creative Idea, and Most Active; these are just a few. Another fun thing to do when you start the project is to have a contest to create a name for your project.

Communication is another critical component; having a clearly defined communication process will help with awareness. No one likes to get blindsided, and communication and awareness are the best ways to prevent it. You also want to build excitement with the team and organization. Some ideas that have helped us are show and tell and Lunch and Learn. Lunch and Learn is a great way to show some key features and start your training in short sessions. I love show and tell; this is good for the whole organization to get engaged and help people be excited to show off what they have learned, built, or come across in the process.

A good training plan will be helpful for the training phase, but it helps with communication, and the users will be better prepared for what is to come. Training can be delivered through various methods, depending on the organization and how the teams are structured. Sometimes, if you have a department that needs to be available to answer phones and it would be hard to close that department down for a few days or even a few hours, you can split the teams, allowing phone coverage all day. Breaking up the session into no more than 4-hour sessions is helpful. If you try more than 4 or 5 hours, the students tend to absorb only some of the content. I like to include many hands-on exercises; people learn better if they can touch a keyboard and walk through the steps. Drop-in sessions are another great way to help your users, especially after you have conducted formal training and want the user to go in and practice. I like to set up an hour-long Teams meeting where users can join with a question or even use this time to test while I am online for questions that come up; if you have a group of users join, they can also learn from each other, and it can be an excellent collaborative working session.

Data migration is one area that needs to be considered. If you are dealing with data migration in your project, start early and add additional time to your timeline. Have the critical user involved early on and ensure you have a sound testing plan.

Microsoft has a lot of templates and tools for you to use, especially if this is your first project and your organization doesn't already have a framework. The key areas are communication, training, and getting your users involved early in the project. Remember to have a little fun – projects are challenging and stressful, and everyone deals with this differently. Try and ensure teamwork and collaboration and have a little fun with it.

Scale

One of the main components in the Scale phase is the **Center of Excellence (CoE)**. I will briefly talk about the CoE since we have devoted the last and final chapter in this book to it; I don't want to spoil anything before you get the chance to read through that chapter. The context of user adoption and the process of Scale refers to the ability to expand or grow user adoption. Some key aspects of scaling in the user adoption process are increasing the user base, change management, and additional training.

Many organizations use SharePoint or Teams sites to share resources and best practices and provide additional learning. Having an excellent issue-tracking system is essential as well. Keeping track of the issues and how long it takes to resolve them will keep users confident in the system and the support team. This information can be used to build a knowledge base and troubleshoot guidance.

Team touchpoints, engagement topics, and activities can be managed on a team's calendar. Microsoft has some sample calendars in its Power Platform Adoption Planning PowerPoint. It is also recommended to use a crawl, walk, then run approach; just like anything, I think it is best to start small with a few meetings, and you can increase the time as needed. In some organizations, just a few touchpoint meetings work; in others, a more frequent meeting frequency works best. This also depends on your phase and your organization's goals. It is nice to have at least one lunch and learn or Tips and Tricks session each month; planning them out a few sessions at a time gives everyone a chance to add things to the agenda and opportunities for the teams to ask for topics they are interested in learning more about or need help.

Ask an expert is another excellent session; having it once a week is sometimes too much. However, you might find that at the beginning of a new project or after the go-live of a new system, app, or significant process change, once a week might be the excellent frequency for a while until everyone is comfortable with the new solution.

Technology is changing so much, and it seems like every week or so, something new is coming out. Having a user group within your area or organization is another way to stay informed. Remember to reach out to the community for speakers and community leaders – it is nice to bring on guest speakers, and everyone in the community is always willing to join for 30-60 minute sessions to talk about new things, share experiences, and learn from each other. Most user groups now have an online option, making it easy for users to join other user groups. You could also put together a new letter within your team or cross departments to let other departments know what your team is learning or has learned to share with others. These are all excellent ways to technically strengthen your and your team's abilities and provide opportunities for citizen developers to communicate and collaborate.

Adoption best practices

A key objective is creating a technical and culturally speaking environment where your users can thrive. Microsoft Power Platform best practices are a collection of documentation, guidance, and best practices proven to accelerate your journey. Since Microsoft has a whole section on this in Learn Microsoft, which I will provide a link to at the end of this chapter, I will not copy it; instead, I will give you a few highlights. Microsoft has aligned it into four buckets: **Strategy and Vision**, **Admin and Governance**, **Nurture and Educate**, and **Support**:

- **Strategy and Vision**:

  - **Define clear objectives**: Ensure the objectives align with the overall organizational strategy and desired outcome. Establish measurable targets.

  - **Align with the business strategy**: Ensure the user adoption strategy aligns with the broader business strategy and goals.

  - **Create a clear vision**: Develop a vision that outlines the future state and benefits of the technology adoption.

  - **Stakeholder engagement**: Engage key stakeholders early in the adoption process. Seek their input, address their concerns, and involve them in decision-making.

  - **Develop a roadmap**: Create a roadmap that outlines the key milestones, timelines, and activities for the user adoption initiative.

  - **Change management**: Develop a change management plan, anticipate potential challenges and resistance, and proactively address them through communication, training, and support. Remember, change is hard, and almost everyone has a hard time with it, so be patient with those who might need a little bit more time to adjust; open communication is also beneficial. This leads us to the next topic: having a communication plan.

  - **Communication plan**: Communicate the vision, objectives, progress, and benefits. Having a good communication plan is critical.

  - **Training and support**: Provide comprehensive training and ongoing support. Offer a range of training formats and be flexible with the department's existing commitments.

  - **Continuous improvement**: Foster a culture of continuous improvement and learning.

- **Admin and Governance**:

  - **Establish governance**: Outline policies, procedures, roles, and responsibilities and define clear guidance for user access, security, data privacy, and compliance.

- **Define users' roles and permissions**: Establish appropriate access levels and privileges.

- **Implement change control**: Establish change control processes to manage updates, upgrades, and version control.

- **Communicate and educate**: Communicate the admin and governance policies.

- **Monitoring and audit**: Regularly monitor and audit the usage and access reports. We will discuss this in the next chapter in detail.

- **Documentation**: Maintain the documentation of admin and governance processes and policies.

- **Collaboration and community engagement**: Foster collaboration among team members and users in the communities and user groups. Encourage knowledge sharing, best practices, and support.

- **Nurture and Educate**:

  - **Comprehensive training plan**: Offer a mix of training formats, such as instructor lead, learning, and hands-on training and workshops. Be flexible, and don't plan long training sessions.

  - **Encourage peer-to-peer mentorship**: Encourage mentorship programs, establish user communities or discussion forums, and learn from each other and the community.

- **Support**:

  - **Dedicated support system**: Set up a dedicated support system that includes helpdesk support, a ticketing system, or a designated support team.

  - **Create a knowledge base**: Develop a comprehensive knowledge base and organize the information in a user-friendly searchable format.

  - **Conduct supportive training sessions and offer training and learning resources**: Provide ongoing training and learning resources to support users learning. Create a safe and supportive environment where users feel comfortable seeking clarification and guidance. This is another critical component that I feel is very important.

By following these best practices for user adoption, organizations can effectively drive adoption, maximize the benefits of technology, ensure a smoother implementation process, and have a little fun and team collaboration. In the next section, we will discuss the Power Platform Maturity Model before moving on to one of my favorite topics: licensing.

Power Platform Maturity Model

The **Power Platform Maturity Model** is a framework that can be used to assess your level or organization's adoption and maturity level. This framework has five levels: **Level 100** is Initial, **Level 200** is Repeatable, **Level 300** is Defined, **Level 400** is Capable, and **Level 500** is Efficient. Let's explore the goals and opportunities associated with each level:

- **Level 100, Initial**: At this level, the goal is to introduce Power Platform and build awareness. Here, the organization might have individual department Power Apps apps or automate simple workflows. There is no overall strategy or governance approach. Opportunities to explore low-hanging fruit use cases with Power Platform can provide some quick wins. Identify and address any initial barriers or resistance to adoption. Start to build excitement around Power Platform.

- **Level 200, Repeatable**: The goal is to expand the usage and adoption of Power Platform. Develop complex apps, automate business processes, and generate reports and dashboards. Start to put structure around the deployment of Power Platform. The Center of Excellence Starter Kit is deployed in this phase. Establish **data loss prevention (DLP)** policies and mitigate the risk of breaking apps and flows by performing a DLP impact analysis. Encourage citizen developers to build and share apps and provide training and support to users to enhance their skills.

- **Level 300, Defined**: The goal is to achieve a high level of proficiency and integration of Power Platform solutions. Develop advanced applications and integrate them with other systems. You should have dedicated Power Platform product owners and a defined understanding of Power Platform in your organization.

- **Level 400, Capable**: This level aims to provide a fully mature and integrated Power Platform ecosystem. Power Platform solutions are embedded in business processes, and a culture of continuous improvement exists. Establish a support team.

- **Level 500, Efficient**: This level aims to establish a dedicated CoE for Power Platform. The CoE provides governance, expertise, and support for Power Platform adoption throughout the organization. We'll do a deeper dive into the CoE in *Chapter 12*.

By understanding the definitions and goals associated with each level of the Power Platform Maturity Model, you can set clear objectives, identify areas of improvement, and maximize the value and impact of Power Platform within your environment.

In the next section, we will review license plans and pay-as-you-go.

Microsoft 365 plans and licensing

I would generally say I stay far away from the topic of licensing, and I am pretty sure you need a master's degree to figure it out. The number one question in almost every session I am in or presenting is about licensing. With that said, I felt it was important enough to include it in this book. I've included the latest information available at the time of writing the book. If you have been around for a bit, you'll know that the licensing models change, so I will try and lay this out as best I can and hope it doesn't change.

The Microsoft 365 admin center

Microsoft 365 E3 includes the following programs: Word, Excel, PowerPoint, Outlook, OneNote, SharePoint, OneDrive, Microsoft Teams, and Windows applications.

The Microsoft 365 admin center console is the best place to manage all your admin needs. In this section, we will spend a little time reviewing the **Billing** section. I like having this admin section in one spot since it is an easy way to see billing and your products, licenses, and billing information:

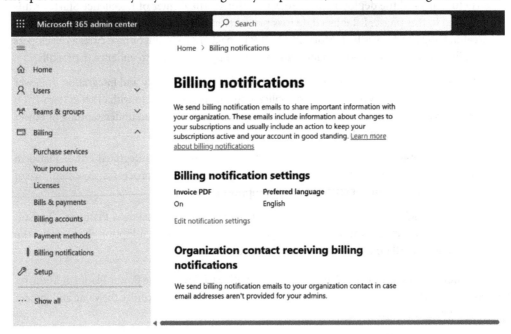

Figure 11.2 – The Microsoft 365 admin center

A few key sections to point out are **Purchase service**, **Your products**, **Licenses**, **Bills & payments**, and **Billing notifications**:

- **Purchase service**: Here, you can find available products and services. You can view them by category and see their pricing. If your company qualifies for special pricing, this option will be available before you check out if you are choosing to purchase new software.

- **Your products**: These are products owned by your organization.

- **License**: On this screen, you can see available licenses, the assigned number of licenses, and assign a license to users.

- **Bills & payments**: In this section, you can see invoices, payment methods, and billing profiles.

- **Billing notifications**: This is where you can set up the preferred language; billing notifications are sent to your billing admin and global admin.

Business Central license

Business Central has two categories of licenses for the application, and it primarily depends on if the organization needs access to Manufacturing or Service Management. If you do not need these two granules or functionalities, you can use Business Central Essentials; however, if you need Manufacturing or Service Management, you must have the **Premium** license.

Business Central has a **Team** license, which can be used if the user needs to be able to read and access certain data in Business Central.

Business Central also has a **Device** license, which provides limited access to a subset of Business Central capabilities.

Included in your Business Central license, you receive a Microsoft Power Automate license that can be used to create and connect to your data from internal and external sources through Business Central. Inside Business Central, you can create and run a Power Automation flow. There are three flow types: **Automated**, **Scheduled**, and **Instant**.

Microsoft has made the Business Central license easy to follow, and most companies, if they don't have a manufacturing process or want to use Service Management, can use Essentials.

The *Further reading* section contains a link to the Microsoft article on how to use Power Automate flows in Business Central.

Power Platform license

Power Platform offers several licensing models and has a range of plans that can cater to your organization's needs. A few of the models are subscription plans that range from per-user plans, per-app plans, capacity add-ons, Power Apps and Power Automate standalone, and Power Apps Portals.

Pay-as-you-go is a way to pay for Power Apps and Power Automate using Azure subscriptions. This lets you start building and sharing apps without a huge upfront commitment. You can review license consumption in your environment by going to **License and Billing**.

If additional capacity is required, you can use the Capacity add-ons, which allow you to allocate additional capacity to support Power Platform's data storage and usage needs. This is used at a tenant level, not an individual user level.

You will also need to watch out for connectors that require a premium license and, when building apps and flows, what connectors will be needed to connect your data.

The best advice I can give you is to understand what you already have as far as licenses and what you will need to purchase before you start working on a solution. The best way to do this is to use the Microsoft 365 admin center and download the latest and greatest licensing document from Microsoft. Alternatively, you can reach out to your Business Central partner if you have one so that they can help you determine what will be needed. Lastly, test, test, test, and have the end users test all the processes. This will ensure you have the correct license and that the users have the correct permissions to run everything in the solution.

Summary

In summary, user adoption is important, and Microsoft and the Microsoft community have great resources to help you with any new project, big or small. In this chapter, we discussed the importance of this and focused on maximizing the value of your Microsoft investment in people and software. By prioritizing user adoption and implementing licensing strategies, you can enhance productivity, achieve compliance, and optimize your investments.

In the next and final chapter of this book, we will dive into the CoE program, uncover the primary purpose of the CoE, learn why it was established, and see how it can be used to drive innovation and provide guidance and support to individuals and teams within your organization.

Further reading

- *Microsoft Power Platform Adoption*: `https://adoption.microsoft.com/en-us/powerplatform/`

- *Introduction: Planning a Power Apps project*: `https://learn.microsoft.com/en-us/power-apps/guidance/planning/introduction`

- *Support Microsoft Power Platform champions in your organization*: `https://learn.microsoft.com/en-us/power-platform/guidance/adoption/champions`

- If you're interested in getting certified, check out `https://learn.microsoft.com/en-us/training/powerplatform/`

- Power Platform user community: `https://powerusers.microsoft.com/`

- Power Platform documentation: `https://powerusers.microsoft.com/`

- *Power Platform adoption maturity model: Detailed capabilities*: `https://learn.microsoft.com/en-us/power-platform/guidance/adoption/maturity-model-details`

- Licensing overview for Microsoft: `https://learn.microsoft.com/en-us/power-platform/admin/pricing-billing-skus#power-apps-and-power-automate-for-dynamics-365`

- *Use Power Automate Flows in Business Central*: `https://learn.microsoft.com/en-us/dynamics365/business-central/across-how-use-financials-data-source-flow#Power%20Automate%20features`

12

Understanding the Center of Excellence and Why It Is a Valuable Tool

In this chapter, we will focus on the **Center of Excellence** (**CoE**) and its significance within an organization. We will utilize the CoE kit and the array of tools available from Microsoft and the community. You will learn how to initiate your journey with the CoE and how it serves as a flexible framework and methodology that can be tailored to your organization's specific needs. Furthermore, we will explore importing the CoE solution into the environment, granting access to valuable tools and Power BI dashboards for securing, monitoring, and optimizing Power Platform solutions.

Lastly, we will address the importance of governance and audit compliance, providing insights into how the provided tools can assist in these critical areas.

So, in this chapter, we're going to cover the following main topics:

- Center of Excellence
- Additional admin tools and monitoring Power BI dashboards
- Governance and audit compliance processes

Technical requirements

Download the Creator Kit – this will be required before you can import any of the CoE solutions: `https://learn.microsoft.com/en-us/power-platform/guidance/creator-kit/setup`.

The CoE examples and downloads can be found on GitHub: `https://github.com/microsoft/coe-starter-kit`.

The following is a list of prerequisites before you get started. However, you can always review this information online at Microsoft; they keep the list updated with all the features (`https://learn.microsoft.com/en-us/power-platform/guidance/coe/setup#download-the-solution`):

- The user installing the CoE kit needs to have the appropriate privileges; you need to be a service admin or global tenant admin
- Power Apps user license
- Power Automate user license
- Email must be enabled since the CoE sends emails, and they are sent from the email you use to install the kit
- If you want to collect audit information, you must access the Microsoft 365 audit log; this feature will allow you to see information such as app launches and the user per app
- A Power BI Pro license is required if you want to share Power BI reports; if only the admin is viewing them, you don't need a Pro license
- The roles and licenses must be available permanently and not temporarily

Center of Excellence

A CoE is a team, a shared facility, or an entity that provides leadership, best practices, research, support, or training for a focus area. You can have a CoE in any place of your business. The CoE concept in technology is often associated with a new software tool, technology, or business concept. The CoE can be complex or straightforward, depending on the organization's goals. This chapter will focus on four responsibilities of the CoE: **Secure**, **Monitor**, **Alert and Action**, and **Nurture**.

As I started researching the topic and consulted with colleagues and customers, it became evident that the perception of the CoE varies among individuals. Some had negative experiences, while others appreciated the availability of office hours, ongoing training, and an emphasis on governance.

Before we dive into each category, the chapter discusses defining a CoE and where to begin. The first step is establishing a clearly defined strategy with written goals and expected outcomes. Consideration must be given to people, processes, and systems. Microsoft launched the CoE to assist companies in fostering organic growth while maintaining governance and control. This makes me think about when I went onsite with one of my long-time customers, and we started documenting the current and to-be processes as they began a reimplementation project. The IT director asked me to interview all the department managers, and each department had its Access database, which was used mainly for reporting. At one time, they had one person in accounting who was an Access guru, so when anyone needed reports or information, this accounting Access guru created an Access database for them.

The reason I am sharing this story is that without digging in and speaking with each department head, IT might not always know what the departments are implementing and whom you have as Champions in your organization. While it is ideal for all departments to adhere to company policies and involve IT in requirements, this is not always the case, especially in tools such as the Power Platform that empower users to create applications. The chapter discusses the balance between fostering collaboration and enforcing controls through a CoE. It highlights the role of the CoE in nurturing and supporting team members, establishing policies and procedures, and creating a secure environment. It also encourages organizations to embrace technology and leverage the CoE to maintain governance, manage their environment, and foster knowledge sharing and growth among team members with shared business goals.

> **Important note**
>
> A clearly defined CoE can bring several significant benefits to your organization, including administration, governance, nurturing, support, and operations. Having a clear strategy and understanding where you are in the adoption journey, why you are setting up a CoE, and what you aim to accomplish are some essential considerations as you start the journey. Treating it like any other implementation will be critical to your success. This is also not something created once and done; you must maintain it and adjust some of your components as technology changes and your business needs change. You will also want to treat the CoE as a framework/methodology and use the pieces and templates that make sense for your organization.

As you start to define what the CoE looks like for you, here are some typical areas to keep in mind:

- **Strategy**: The purpose of the CoE – what is the reason for establishing it? This will help as you move forward. What is the goal, and what are you trying to achieve? Remember that the vision of the CoE should always align with your business strategy and goals.

- **Best practices**: Provide support and direction on technology change management, standard approaches, processes, tools, and methodologies.

- **Support**: Deliver shared training, templates, communication, user guides, and a knowledge base of known issues or error messages.

- **Training**: Provide skills assessments, e-learning, and certification programs. For example, I have one customer who is starting to do more in Power BI, so one of the requirements for team members who want to develop Power BI reports is that they must go through an online training program and take and pass the PL300 Power BI Microsoft Certification.

- **Governance**: Provide an overview of access, usage, performance, and data management.

Figure 12.1 shows a nice flow diagram that helps explain some of the steps in the CoE journey (**Secure**, **Monitor**, **Alert and Action**, and **Nurture**) and you can see how you might not have all of them in place today. However, it might be something you strive to have in place in the future. This gives you some guidelines and ideas.

Figure 12.1 – CoE journey

Hence, a CoE can be applied to any topic or function in your organization. As you can see, it can mean different things to different organizations, and you must find the right pieces and solutions that meet your needs, keeping in mind the reason and goals of why you are establishing your CoE. Microsoft has a set of tools to help assist you with the CoE. Let's walk through some of the setup steps together in the following few sections so you can get hands-on with the tools.

Creating a dedicated environment to run a CoE and import a CoE solution

Microsoft recommends having a dedicated environment with Dataverse to run a CoE. In this exercise, we will walk through setting up a new environment. I am going to set up a Trial-type environment; when you run this in your work environment, you will want to have the type of environment as **Production** and not **Trial**. By the end of this book, you will be an expert in creating environment:.

1. Log in to your Power Platform development environment and select **Power Platform Admin Center**, and in the **Environments** section, select **+New**.

2. Choose a name. In *Figure 12.2*, I am naming it CoE. In **Region**, select **United States**, which is the default. The environment's **Type** is going to be **Trial** for the exercise. As mentioned previously, you will want the type to be **Production** when doing this in your organization environment. Select to add Dataverse; the CoE requires a Dataverse running in the environment. When creating your **Production** environment, you can select a pay-as-you-go subscription. When choosing the **Trial** type, this option is grayed out.

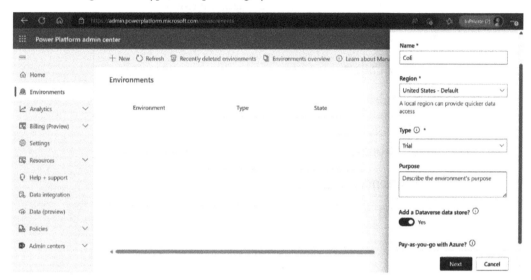

Figure 12.2 – New CoE environment

3. In the last step, don't set the security groups in this environment; select the option to opt for open access. See *Figure 12.3*.

> **Important note**
>
> Leaving the environment access open is an essential step because the CoE uses several processes, and if you restrict access, users will be unable to interact with the approval tasks.

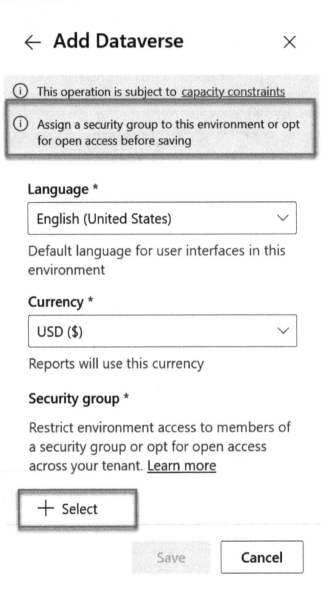

Figure 12.3 – Security group

4.   Once you select the **+ Select** button under **Security group**, the following screen will be available
     for you to opt out (**Open access**).

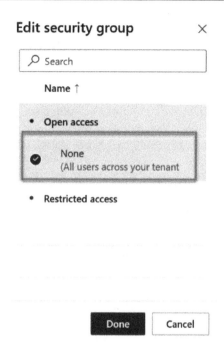

Figure 12.4 – Edit security group: Open access screen

5.   Once you select **Open access**, select **Done** and **Save**. Creating a new environment can take a few minutes. This is an excellent time to get a coffee or tea or take a break before moving on to the next section on importing in Creator Kit and CoE solutions.

Before you jump in and install the CoE kit, you will want to gather environment variables and identify how you want to communicate with your admins, makers, and users. Once you have determined the users and the groups, you will want to set up a security group for each. For example, set up three groups: Admin, Makers, and Users. During the import process, filling in all the variables is not required, and you can leave some empty until you need the connections. Here are the ones you want to gather before moving on to the next step. I usually open Notepad and copy the links; that way, you have them available during the setup process. *Figure 12.5* is a sample notepad to use as a guide.

```
Mandatory Environment Variables, Other Variable you can set later.

Admin email- Shawn@admin.onmicrosoft.com
Company Name- Shawn Company
Individual Admin- c1ee2cd9-49f0-4f6d-a206-fa91652429a0
Power Platform Maker Microsoft 365 Group- 2a48f968-cad5-40ab-ab33-929763362515
Power Platform User Microsoft 365 Group- 7577064d-9731-4a24-86f3-f22b3cfa3af3
Graph URL Environment Variable-  https://graph.microsoft.com/
Power Automate Environment Variable- https://make.powerautomate.com/environments/110316ae-daca-e053-b442-5b5504870a0e/home
Power App Maker Environment Variable- https://make.powerapps.com/environments/110316ae-daca-e053-b442-5b5504870a0e/home
Power Player Environment Variable- https://make.powerapps.com/environments/110316ae-daca-e053-b442-5b5504870a0e/home
Tenant ID  af7525aa-3218-43bd-afd5-b35db1665379
```

Figure 12.5 – Sample notepad

This is the link to the documentation on the Microsoft website: `https://learn.microsoft.com/en-us/power-platform/guidance/coe/setup`.

Importing the Creator Kit and CoE solution

The CoE is built using solutions, and you can import a solution once you have downloaded it from GitHub. Save the zipped file and extract it. This will allow you to import the managed solution into the new environment you created in the last exercise. To import each solution, you can follow these steps:

1. Select **Power Apps** in the CoE environment and go to **Solutions** and **Import Solutions**, then browse to the Creator Kit file; if you didn't download the Creator Kit at the beginning of the chapter, you need to download it and save it on your computer. The Creator Kit is a required solution to import before moving to the next step. See *Figure 12.6.*

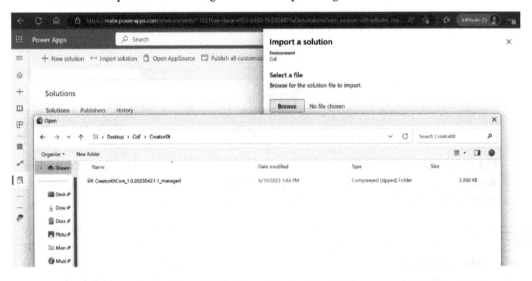

Figure 12.6 – Importing the Creator Kit

When the Creator Kit has completed the import, you will see the import successful screen message, and the Creator Kit will be available in the **Solutions** list.

Figure 12.7 – Creator Kit successfully imported

2. The next step is to import the CoE solution. Select **Import solution**, and browse for the CoEStarterKit file. The link to the file on GitHub is at the beginning of the chapter if you didn't download it at the beginning. You have several options in CoEStarterKit; we will install the CoE core components in this exercise. I have provided a link to a page with the details of each component in the Further reading section at the end of the chapter.

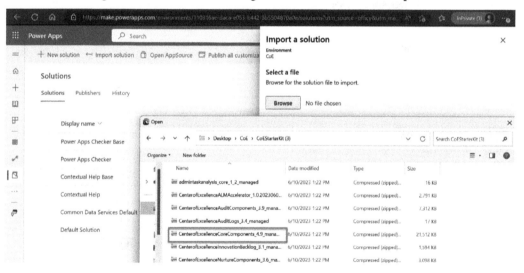

Figure 12.8 – Importing CoE solutions

3. You will need to establish a connection to each component, all 22 connections, and select them one at a time, but this can be done quickly. You can set up the connection before you install this component, but it is just as easy to set it up at this step. *Figure 12.9* will show you what the first screen looks like.

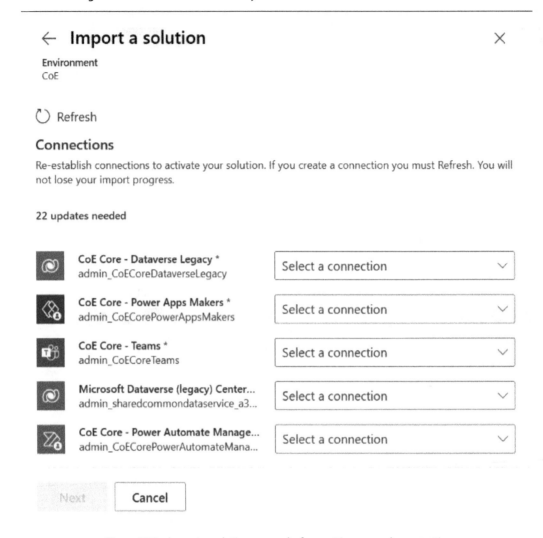

Figure 12.9 – Import a solution screen before setting up each connection

Figure 12.10 will show you what the screen looks like when all the connections are selected.

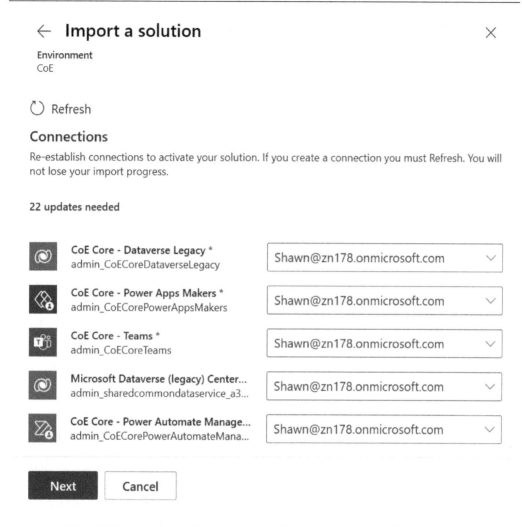

← **Import a solution**   ✕

Environment
CoE

◌ Refresh

Connections

Re-establish connections to activate your solution. If you create a connection you must Refresh. You will
not lose your import progress.

22 updates needed

	CoE Core - Dataverse Legacy * admin_CoECoreDataverseLegacy	Shawn@zn178.onmicrosoft.com ⌄
	CoE Core - Power Apps Makers * admin_CoECorePowerAppsMakers	Shawn@zn178.onmicrosoft.com ⌄
	CoE Core - Teams * admin_CoECoreTeams	Shawn@zn178.onmicrosoft.com ⌄
	Microsoft Dataverse (legacy) Center... admin_sharedcommondataservice_a3...	Shawn@zn178.onmicrosoft.com ⌄
	CoE Core - Power Automate Manage... admin_CoECorePowerAutomateMana...	Shawn@zn178.onmicrosoft.com ⌄

[**Next**]   [Cancel]

Figure 12.10 – Import a solution screen after all components' connections are set u4

1. Next, you need to set up your environment variables. Step through each field, and each
    variable will give you a description and let you know whether it is required. Alternatively,
    you can skip this step during this setup and return later as you decide what tools you plan to
    use going forward in your environment. You must also have completed all the prerequisites
    and have your information ready. Use the notepad that we created in *Figure 12.5* with all the
    required information.

Suppose you don't set up your environment connections during the installation or you have skipped some
of them when you went into Power Apps – in that case, you will receive a message with a count of how
many you need to set up before you can run each of the tools, and you can follow the link to get back to
the setup page. This makes it easy to go back and set up, and if you decide later you want to use one of
the tools, you can set up one at a time instead of setting them up all at once during the import process.

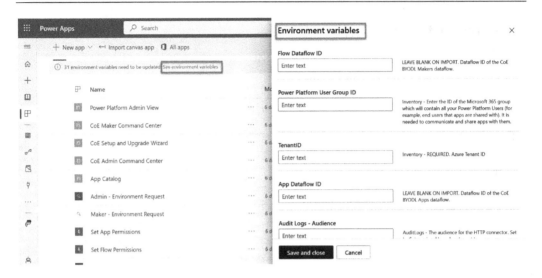

Figure 12.11 – Environment variables

Now you have imported the solution for the components in the CoE kit. You can use your **Trial** environment, become familiar with each component, and determine which ones make sense for your organization.

Inventory component

Using the inventory component will allow you to understand what you have running in your environment. The benefit of understanding all your solutions is that you can effectively manage all activities, enabling better collaboration, knowledge sharing, and documentation. Here are the common components you can install and run against your environment: compliance process, inactivity process, app quarantine components, and Microsoft Team governance. For each one of the components, you can install and run *à la carte* based on your needs, check out `https://learn.microsoft.com/en-us/` `power-platform/guidance/coe/setup-core-components`.

An example of a standard core component is that you can change app ownership; you can use this if you have someone who has left the company or changed roles and no longer owns the app. This process uses a canvas app. The DLP Editor is another one that you can use to update your policies using a canvas app, and it shows the list of canvas apps and Power Automate apps that are impacted by the policy configuration.

We set up a dedicated environment in this section and imported the Creator Kit and CoE kit. We didn't touch upon the Creator Kit other than the fact it is a requirement to run the CoE. However, in *Chapter 5*, our Power Apps chapter, we walked through some of the core components. Further, it is a good idea to have them in your toolkit, especially if you have several App Makers and want a specific look and feel to match your organization's brand. In the next section, we will look at the Power BI dashboards and the Power App tools.

Additional admin tools and monitoring Power BI dashboards

The CoE kit provides additional admin tools and monitoring Power BI dashboards to aid in managing and overseeing your environment effectively. Each Power App is available in your solution and designed to help you manage and monitor your environment. Here are the Power Apps you can use: Dynamics 365 Custom, App Catalog, CoE Admin Command Center, CoE Maker Command Center, CoE Setup and Upgrade, Power Platform Admin View, and Solution Health Hub.

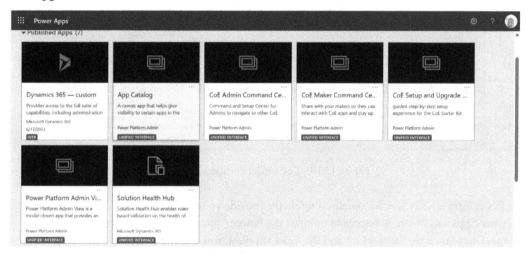

Figure 12.12 – List of CoE core components

- **Dynamics 365**: This Power App allows you to create a custom application using the Dynamics 365 platform.

- **App Catalog**: When you launch this app, it will search for apps available in your organization; you can leave feedback for makers and request access to the app.

- **CoE Admin Command Center**: This app is designed for admins and provides a centralized dashboard for managing and governing Power Apps and Power Automate.

- **CoE Maker Command Center**: This app is designed for App Makers to provide a set of tools and features to support app development and manage activities.

- **CoE Setup and Upgrade**: This app uses a wizard setup, and you can use this for the first time or during an upgrade process; this will also give you the status of your setup and walk you through the following steps. You will also see all the different components available to you and, if you are missing any, the setup for each.

- **Power Platform Admin View**: This section provides you with all your makers, the environment, and an area to see everything together; you save your view and tailor it to your needs.

- **Solution Health Hub**: This section can help you monitor the health and performance of your solutions.

Figure 12.13 displays a quick reference to each category, scenario, and the available toolkit components.

Step	Scenario	Toolkit Components
Secure	DLP Editor	Canvas App
Monitor	Power Automate Templates to collect data and Power BI Dashboard	Power Automate Power Apps Power BI Dashboards Connector for Office 365 Audit Log
Alert & Action	Maker and Admin notification via Power Automate templates and Model Driven Apps	Canvas App & Model Driven Power Automate
Nurture	App Catalog, Welcome Email, Internal Community and Channel Links	Canvas App- Catalog App Power Automate- Welcome Email

Figure 12.13 – CoE toolkit components

The Power Apps and Power Automate components provide you with a core to start using CoE. You get Power Apps and Power Automate to monitor the Power Apps and automation your makers create and use. Once you have them set up and the flows running, you can use several Power BI reports to help secure, monitor, govern, and nurture. Now, let's explore Power BI.

Power BI dashboards

In the CoE kit that you downloaded from GitHub, there will be several Power BI dashboards. These dashboards provide visualizations and analytics to track your Power Platform environment's key metrics, performance, and usage patterns. To use the Power BI dashboards, you must at least have the CoE core component solutions imported into your environment and have the audit log solution imported. Before you run the reports, you will need to get your environment URL.

Go to **Power Platform admin center** and select **Environments**; once you have the environment you want to monitor selected, copy the organization URL and have it handy and ready to paste into the URL when you open the Power BI reports. You must also ensure you have Power BI Desktop installed and must be logged in to your Office 365 account.

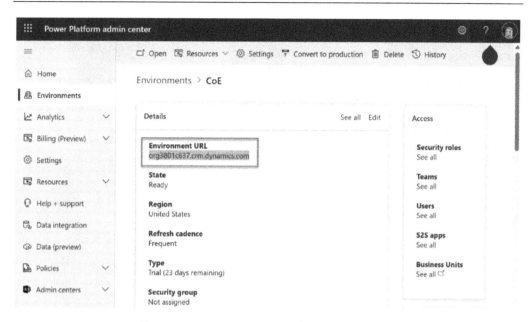

Figure 12.14 – Environment URL for Power BI reports

Next, let's learn about the production CoE dashboard.

Production CoE dashboard

Use the Power BI dashboard reports to gain insight into your tenant. The production CoE dashboard has 48 pages, packed with detailed information. I recommend starting with the **Introduction** page; this page is broken up into **MONITOR**, **GOVERN**, and **NURTURE sections**. You can begin to see a theme with the CoE.

From the downloaded CoE files, you can open the Power BI report (`.pbit`) file in Power BI Desktop. Use the URL you copied in the last section, and once you have it opened and refreshed, go ahead and publish it into your Power BI workspace. This will allow you to also share the dashboard with other users and use the report to help guide you.

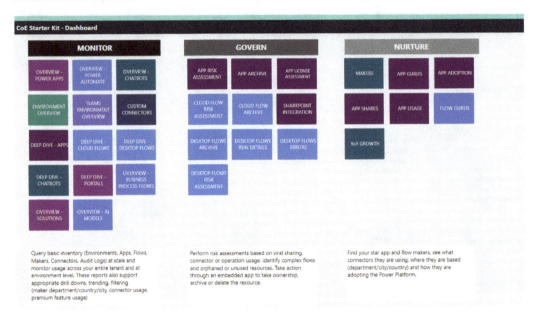

Figure 12.15 – CoE Starter Kit dashboard, Introduction section

> **Important note**
>
> If you want to change the Power BI dashboard, you can adjust the Power BI report to fit your requirements.

By utilizing these Power Apps and Power BI monitoring tools, you can effectively administer, monitor, and enhance your Power Platform within the CoE framework. In the next section of the chapter, we will discuss governance and audit compliance.

Governance and audit compliance processes

Governance and audit compliance play a pivotal role in the efficient functioning of the CoE and in ensuring alignment with regulatory and organizational mandates. The CoE encompasses a dedicated section focused on these aspects, and it is imperative to establish a robust framework by connecting and configuring the audit log while also installing the necessary governance components.

One essential step is to develop comprehensive policies and procedures that govern the operations of the CoE. These policies should encompass various areas such as solution development, change management, security measures, data privacy, and compliance with relevant regulations or standards. Documenting these policies clearly and concisely is crucial to establish a baseline for CoE operations.

Equally important is effectively communicating these policies to all team members involved in the CoE. This ensures that everyone knows the established guidelines and procedures and understands their responsibilities in adhering to them. Regular communication and updates regarding governance and compliance measures help foster a culture of accountability and ensure ongoing adherence to the defined policies.

By implementing strong governance practices and maintaining audit compliance within the CoE, organizations can effectively manage risks, safeguard sensitive data, and meet regulatory requirements. These measures contribute to the overall success of the CoE and enable it to operate securely and competently while driving innovation and achieving organizational goals.

In the final section of the chapter, we will discuss CoEs with Business Central and Power Platform.

Business Central plus Power Platform

Implementing a CoE for a **Business Central** (**BC**) and Power Platform project can bring significant benefits to organizations. A CoE represents a dedicated team that provides guidance, best practices, and support for successfully adopting and utilizing technology within an organization. By establishing a CoE specifically for your BC and Power Platform project, you ensure that these powerful platforms are utilized to their fullest potential. The CoE becomes a strategic enabler, fostering a culture of innovation and continuous improvement throughout the organization. With its expertise and resources, the CoE empowers employees to effectively use the platforms, unlocking new functionalities, enhancing their skills, and driving successful BC and Power Platform implementations.

Implementing a CoE also ensures the implementation of standardized processes. The CoE team collaborates closely with stakeholders to define and document best practices, workflows, and guidelines for utilizing BC and Power Platform solutions. This standardization enhances efficiency, reduces redundancies, and improves collaboration among teams and departments. By implementing standardized processes, organizations can streamline operations, ensure consistency in task execution, and minimize errors and inefficiencies. Moreover, standardized processes enable scalability and adaptability, enabling organizations to swiftly respond to evolving business requirements and market dynamics.

Reliable data serves as a crucial foundation for effective decision-making and strategic planning. Through the implementation of a CoE, organizations can establish robust data governance policies and quality standards for their BC and Power Platform projects. The CoE team ensures the proper management, integration, and validation of data, resulting in reliable and accurate information. This empowers decision-makers to make well-informed choices based on trustworthy data insights. With reliable data at their disposal, organizations can monitor key performance indicators, track business metrics, and identify trends and patterns that drive informed decision-making. The CoE plays a pivotal role in maintaining data integrity, improving data quality, and fostering a data-driven culture within the organization.

In addition to optimizing platform utilization, standardizing processes, and ensuring reliable data, implementing a CoE for BC and Power Platform projects offers a significant **return on investment** (**ROI**). The CoE becomes a catalyst for increased productivity, improved operational efficiency, and enhanced collaboration. By leveraging the expertise and support provided by the CoE, organizations can overcome implementation challenges, maximize the potential of their technology investments, and achieve better outcomes. The CoE also promotes continuous learning and innovation, driving the development of new solutions and enabling organizations to stay ahead in a competitive market. Ultimately, the CoE's focus on effective technology utilization, standardized processes, reliable data, and ROI ensures long-term success for BC and Power Platform projects within the organization.

Summary

In summary, using the CoE can help organizations maximize the value derived from Power Platform. It provides expertise, guidance, standardization, and collaboration, enabling teams to work more efficiently, innovate effectively, and align with strategic goals. Having the tools helps not only to administer and monitor but also provides the ability to audit compliance and nurture team members. Further, it is important to keep in mind that there is no one-size-fits-all when it comes to Power Platform administration and governance. The CoE Starter Kit aims to provide a starting point. The kit offers different templates to use as you embark on your journey. Remember that you don't necessarily have to reinvent the wheel; many resources are available. Remember: crawl, walk, run!

Further reading

- How Microsoft established a Center of Excellence: `https://learn.microsoft.com/en-us/power-bi/guidance/center-of-excellence-establish`

- CoE Starter Kit: `https://learn.microsoft.com/en-us/power-platform/guidance/coe/setup`

- Center of Excellence overview: `https://learn.microsoft.com/en-us/power-platform/guidance/coe/overview`

- Collect audit logs using an HTTP Action: `https://learn.microsoft.com/en-us/power-platform/guidance/coe/setup-auditlog-http`

- Governance components: `https://learn.microsoft.com/en-us/power-platform/guidance/coe/before-setup-gov`

Index

A

advanced Power Automate setups 232
conditions 232
error handling 233, 234
exception management 233, 234
expressions 233
iterative processes 233
loops 233
**Allow Action Automate ID 9630
system permission 276**
ALM lifecycle 240
build & test stage 240
deploy stage 240
develop stage 240, 241
monitor & learn stage 241
operate stage 240
plan & track stage 240
APIs
used, for connecting data in
Power BI 295-302
App Catalog 417
**Application Lifecycle Management
(ALM) 239**
for admin 239
for citizen 239

for pro developers 239
lifecycle 241
Apply to Each loop 233
approvals 264
common troubleshooting tips 286, 287
environment, configuring for 264-267
process, configuring in BC 270-274
artificial intelligence (AI) 15
Azure Active Directory (AAD) 46, 250
configuring, for using Postman and
Business Central 46-54
secret 51

B

bar chart 313
Business Central (BC) 337
approval process, configuring 270-274
best practices, to extend functionality
with Power Platform solutions 389
Power BI report, enabling 291-293
Power Platform integration, for
performance improvement 4, 5
Power Platform solutions, used for
extending functionality 336
record, inserting with Power
Automate 222-231

use case 13, 14

users, importing into 268, 269

Business Central and Power Platform ecosystem 14

Business Central APIs 39, 40

AAD, configuring for using Postman 46-54

Advanced APIs 42

advanced APIs, versus standard APIs 42

API permissions, adding 55-59

calling, Postman used 66, 67

connecting 44-46

GET request, creating in Postman 60-66

limitations 68, 69

performance, improving 69

tips and tricks 69

viewing 40-43

Business Central by user(s)

Power Automate, enabling 275

Power Automate permission, enabling 276, 277

Business Central home screen

Power BI report, adding to 294

Business Central in cloud

connecting to 83-91

key differences in connection, with BC on premises 71, 72

Power Automate flow, building 92-107

Business Central license 401

Business Central on-premises

connecting to 73-83

Business Central plus Power Platform 421

Business Central vendor virtual table

requisition request form exercise 127-136

business events

using, in Power Automate flow 212-222

business process flows 181

documenting 182

business unit development environments 242

C

Canvas apps 23, 152

creating 161-167

descriptions, customizing 168-178

fields, customizing 168-178

labels, customizing 168-178

cards 313

CASE 233

Center of Excellence (CoE) 396, 405-407

admin tools 417

best practices 407

Creator Kit, importing 412

dedicated environment, creating 408-412

governance 408

inventory component, using 416

journey 408

Power BI dashboards 418

Production CoE dashboard 419

solutions, importing 413-416

strategy 407

support 407

toolkit components 418

training 408

citizen developer

versus pro developers 151

CoE Admin Command Center app 417

CoE Maker Command Center app 417

CoE Setup and Upgrade app 417

Common Data Service (CDS) 17, 245

components

importing 158-161

connector reference overview

reference link 154

Contact canvas app
  creating 150
**continuous integration/continuous
    delivery (CI/CD) 258**
Creator Kit
  Reference app 155-157
  reference link 150, 156
CRONUS database 12
customer report
  dashboard, creating from 327-332

D

D365 BUS FULL ACCESS 59
dashboard 327
  creating 327
  creating, from customer report 327-332
data
  connecting, in Power BI with APIs 295-302
**data loss prevention (DLP)
    policies 235, 243, 399**
  reference link 235
data modeling 307
data sources 154, 155
  types 155
Dataverse 17, 112
  Business Central integration 117-122
  table, creating in , 116, 117, 357
decomposition tree 313
development environment
  setting up 5-12
develop stage, ALM lifecycle
  Azure DevOps 241
  pipelines 241
  solutions 241
  source control 241
Device license 401
DevOps 259

doughnut chart 313
Do Until loop 233
Dynamics 365 417

E

Environment Admin 243
Environment Maker 243
environments
  default 242
  developer 242
  Microsoft Dataverse for Teams 242
  overview 241,-243
  production 242
  reference link 242
  sandbox 242
  trial 242
error notifications 234

F

flow, for new vendor
  creating 185-199
Fluent Theme Designer 157, 158
funnel 313

G

gauges 313
governance and audit compliance 420, 421
Graph Explorer
  reference link 85

H

HTTP status code 68

I

IF/ELSE logic 232
iterative processes 233

K

KISS principle 327

L

line chart 313
logical operators
   AND 233
   NOT 233
   OR 233
LookUp command 346
loops 233
   Apply to Each loop 233
   Do Until loop 233
   reference link 233

M

managed solutions 244
   versus unmanaged solutions 244
map 313
matrix 313
Microsoft 365
   licensing 400
   plans 400
Microsoft 365 admin center 400
Microsoft Common Data Service (CDS) 112
Microsoft Fabric 72
   reference link 73
Microsoft Graph API 84
   URL 84

Microsoft OneLake 72
model-driven app 23, 152
   creating 137-145
My Workspace 293

N

new item setup case study 355

O

on-premises data gateway 73, 74
   considerations 76
   utilizing 75, 76
on-premises version, BC
   connecting to 73-83

P

parameters
   creating 303-312
PBIX extension 293
pie chart 313
pipelines 258
   setting up, for Power Platform 259
PL-100 Microsoft Power Platform
      App Maker certification 151
portals 23, 153
portal templates
   reference link 154
Postman 44
   account, creating 45
   download link 44
   GET request, creating 60-66
   installing 44
   reference link 85
   used, for calling Business Central API 66, 67
   welcome screen 46

Power Apps 14, 22, 24, 417

AI models 23

App Catalog 417

Canvas apps 23

CoE Admin Command Center 417

CoE Maker Command Center 417

CoE Setup and Upgrade 417

creating 24

creating, inside Power BI report 337-351

decision flowchart 154

Dynamics 365 417

model-driven apps 23

portals 23

Power Platform Admin View 418

Solution Health Hub 418

templates 24

Power Apps app

creating 361-379

creating, from Power BI Desktop 336, 337

Power Automate 14, 20-22

Actions 184

advanced setups 232

creating 380-388

creating, to refresh dataset on
    customer update 352-354

enabling, in Business Central by user 275

integration, setting up 274

options, for creating flows 183

permission, enabling in Business
    Central by user(s) 276, 277

template, used for setting up
    purchase approvals 277-286

Triggers 184, 185

used, for inserting record into BC 222-231

Power Automate flow

building 92-107

building, from scratch 200-212

business events, using 212-222

creating, for new vendor 185-199

Power Automate flow, best practices 234

debugging 236

scalability and performance 234, 235

security considerations and
    data privacy 235, 236

testing 236

version control and flow management 237

Power BI 16

dashboards 418, 419

dashboard, creating 290, 291

data, connecting with APIs 295-302

report, publishing 324-327

Power BI report 337

adding, to Business Central
    home screen 294

creating 290, 291

enabling, within Business Central 291-293

Power BI report editor 314-324

Power BI visuals

bar chart 313

cards 313

decomposition tree 313

doughnut chart 313

funnel 313

gauges 313

line chart 313

map 313

matrix 313

pie chart 313

Q&A 313

reference link 312

reviewing 312

ribbon chart 313

scatter 313

table 313

Power Pages 16, 153

Power Platform Admin View section 418

Power Platform environment 241

setting up 113-115

Power Platform license 401, 402

Power Platform Maturity Model 399

Level 100, Initial 399

Level 200, Repeatable 399

Level 300, Defined 399

Level 400, Capable 399

Level 500, Efficient 399

Power Platform solutions

best practices, for extending functionality
in Business Central 389

used, for extending functionality
in Business Central 336

Power Virtual Agents 15-17

actions 18, 19

considerations 19

entities 18

topics 17

Premium license 401

pro developers

versus citizen developer 151

Production CoE dashboard 419, 420

purchase approvals

setting up, with Power Automate
template 277-286

Q

Q&A visual 313

Quality Assurance (QA) 239

R

repeatable components 155

retry mechanisms 234

return on investment (ROI) 422

ribbon chart 313

Roche's Maxim of Data Transformation 306

S

Scale 396

scatter 313

Shared Workspace 293

Software-as-a-Service (SaaS) 16

solution 243

components 245

creating 245-253

existing components, adding 246-249

managed 244, 245

security and permissions, reviewing 254-258

unmanaged 244, 245

Solution Health Hub section 418

Specific, Measurable, Achievable, Realistic,
Time-Related (SMART) 394

Star Schema 305

SWITCH 233

T

table 155, 313

creating, in Dataverse 116, 117, 357

Tabular 155

Team license 401

Triggers 184

automated Triggers 184

instant/manual Triggers 184

scheduled Triggers 184

truck check-in app

creating 25-37

U

unmanaged solutions 244
  versus managed solutions 244
User Acceptance Testing (UAT) 242
user adoption 393
  best practices 397, 398
  Envision phase 394, 395
  Onboard phase 395, 396
  Scale phase 396, 397
users
  importing, into Business Central 268, 269

V

virtual tables 123
  benefits 123, 124
  limitations 124
  restrictions 124
  setting up 125, 126
Visio
  reference link 183

W

Workspace 293

Packtpub.com

Subscribe to our online digital library for full access to over 7,000 books and videos, as well as industry leading tools to help you plan your personal development and advance your career. For more information, please visit our website.

Why subscribe?

- Spend less time learning and more time coding with practical eBooks and Videos from over 4,000 industry professionals

- Improve your learning with Skill Plans built especially for you

- Get a free eBook or video every month

- Fully searchable for easy access to vital information

- Copy and paste, print, and bookmark content

Did you know that Packt offers eBook versions of every book published, with PDF and ePub files available? You can upgrade to the eBook version at packtpub.com and as a print book customer, you are entitled to a discount on the eBook copy. Get in touch with us at customercare@packtpub.com for more details.

At www.packtpub.com, you can also read a collection of free technical articles, sign up for a range of free newsletters, and receive exclusive discounts and offers on Packt books and eBooks.

Other Books You May Enjoy

If you enjoyed this book, you may be interested in these other books by Packt:

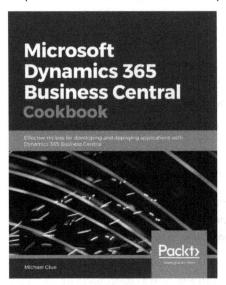

Microsoft Dynamics 365 Business Central Cookbook

Michael Glue

ISBN: 9781789958546

- Build and deploy Business Central applications
- Use the cloud or local sandbox for application development
- Customize and extend your base Business Central application
- Create external applications that connect to Business Central
- Create automated tests and debug your applications
- Connect to external web services from Business Central

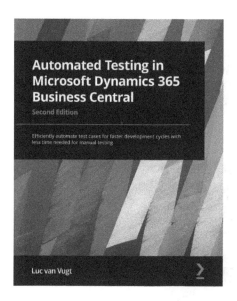

Automated Testing in Microsoft Dynamics 365 Business Central - Second Edition

Luc van Vugt

ISBN: 9781801816427

- Understand the why and when of automated testing
- Discover how test-driven development can help to improve automated testing
- Explore the six pillars of the Testability Framework of Business Central
- Design and write automated tests for Business Central
- Make use of standard automated tests and their helper libraries
- Understand the challenges in testing features that interact with the external world
- Integrate automated tests into your development practice

Mastering Microsoft Dynamics 365 Business Central

Stefano Demiliani, Duilio Tacconi

ISBN: 9781789951257

- Create a sandbox environment with Dynamics 365 Business Central
- Handle source control management when developing solutions
- Explore extension testing, debugging, and deployment
- Create real-world business processes using Business Central and different Azure services
- Integrate Business Central with external applications
- Apply DevOps and CI/CD to development projects
- Move existing solutions to the new extension-based architecture

Packt is searching for authors like you

If you're interested in becoming an author for Packt, please visit `authors.packtpub.com` and apply today. We have worked with thousands of developers and tech professionals, just like you, to help them share their insight with the global tech community. You can make a general application, apply for a specific hot topic that we are recruiting an author for, or submit your own idea.

Share Your Thoughts

Now you've finished *Extending Microsoft Business Central with Power Platform*, we'd love to hear your thoughts! Scan the QR code below to go straight to the Amazon review page for this book and share your feedback or leave a review on the site that you purchased it from.

`https://packt.link/r/1-803-24071-7`

Your review is important to us and the tech community and will help us make sure we're delivering excellent quality content.

Download a free PDF copy of this book

Thanks for purchasing this book!

Do you like to read on the go but are unable to carry your print books everywhere?

Is your eBook purchase not compatible with the device of your choice?

Don't worry, now with every Packt book you get a DRM-free PDF version of that book at no cost.

Read anywhere, any place, on any device. Search, copy, and paste code from your favorite technical books directly into your application.

The perks don't stop there, you can get exclusive access to discounts, newsletters, and great free content in your inbox daily

Follow these simple steps to get the benefits:

1. Scan the QR code or visit the link below

https://packt.link/free-ebook/9781803240718

2. Submit your proof of purchase

3. That's it! We'll send your free PDF and other benefits to your email directly

www.ingramcontent.com/pod-product-compliance
Lightning Source LLC
Chambersburg PA
CBHW060645060326
40690CB00020B/4521